also by marian burros

Eating Well Is the Best Revenge
20-Minute Menus
Keep It Simple: 30-Minute Meals from Scratch
The Best of De Gustibus
Pure and Simple
You've Got It Made

With Lois Levine
The Elegant but Easy Cookbook
Second Helpings
Freeze with Ease
Come for Cocktails, Stay for Supper
The Summertime Cookbook

also by lois levine

The Kids in the Kitchen
The Delicious Diet Cookbook
Vegetable Favorites

the new
elegant but easy
cookbook

Marian Burros
and Lois Levine

Simon & Schuster

SIMON & SCHUSTER
Rockefeller Center
1230 Avenue of the Americas
New York, NY 10020

Designed by Bonni Leon

Manufactured in the United States of America

5   7   9   10   8   6

Library of Congress Cataloging-in-Publication Data
Burros, Marian Fox.
The new elegant but easy cookbook / Marian Burros and Lois Levine.
p.   cm.
Includes index.
1. Entertaining.   2. Cookery.   I. Levine, Lois.   II. Title.
TX731.B83   1998
641'.5—dc21   97-46884
CIP
ISBN 0-684-83244-5

acknowledgments

Without Susan Simon this book would still be in the computer. Susan, who did the food styling for my tour appearances in New York, Connecticut, and Pennsylvania for my last book, *Eating Well Is the Best Revenge*, made everything look beautiful. When work on *The New Elegant but Easy* was far behind, she came to my rescue and tested dozens of recipes. She also contributed several of her own. And then she offered to proofread the manuscript, adding many more useful suggestions. Susan owns a catering and food styling company called SueChef in Hawthorne, New Jersey, and I am lucky to call her a friend.

Thanks go also to Roy Coleman, who has cheerfully eaten all the entries for the book. He often gave me ideas for making the good dishes better, but also was quite frank about those that did not make the grade.

Thanks to my son Michael, who decided he did not want to be a lawyer anymore and has moved to the part of the world that he loves the most, Santiago de Compostela in the northwest corner of Spain, and opened a restaurant, O Cabaliño do Demo (Dragonfly). He contributed several recipes and tested others for me.

And to the technical wizards at the *New York Times* and elsewhere who patiently and graciously helped me get the manuscript from the disks onto paper—I couldn't have managed alone.

And finally special thanks to my agent, Amanda Urban, and my editor, Sydny Weinberg Miner, for their patience and understanding.

M.B.
Bethesda, Maryland
March 1997

!!!! warning !!!!

Those who own older versions of *Elegant but Easy* should not discard them until they have looked for their favorite recipes in this new version.

Judging by recent conversations with owners of the earlier book, I believe some favorites may not be in this book.

contents

introduction

In 1995 I was on a countrywide tour with my new cookbook, *Eating Well Is the Best Revenge*. Often, while I was autographing the new book, copies of *Elegant but Easy*, dog-eared, food-stained, and occasionally in such bad shape that the pages were held together with a rubber band, would be handed to me to be autographed, too.

The conversation with the owner generally ran something like this:

> *Book owner:* I just love your *Elegant but Easy*. I cook from it all the time.
> *Me:* Do you still use it?
> *B.O.:* (sheepishly) Well . . . (and then brightening) I make some things but I've changed them a lot. We don't eat the way we used to.

Hardly anyone does. Cooking a single onion in ½ cup butter; flinging MSG around as if it were salt; using processed cheese food to make a dip and serving Jell-O molds for every dinner party—not likely.

My coauthor Lois Levine and I have wanted to revise *Elegant but Easy* for at least fifteen years, but it wasn't until *Elegant but Easy*'s publisher, Macmillan, was purchased by the publisher of my last three books, Simon & Schuster, that a revision became possible.

Lois and I cook so differently from the way we cooked when *Elegant but Easy* was originally published in 1960 that we often laugh nervously when someone mentions a recipe that contains mushroom soup mix or refrigerator biscuits or canned condensed tomato soup. In hindsight we think we should have known that these products of technological progress were not making food taste better, but, like almost everyone else, we were conned into believing that these timesavers would not compromise the taste or integrity of a dish and would give us more free time. Free time to do what? Work harder and longer hours at other jobs.

I have long since given up convenience foods, having found better-tasting ways to cook quickly while also controlling what goes into my food. But there's no point in making fun of what we did almost forty years ago. In *Stand Facing the Stove* (Henry Holt and Company, 1996), the delightful biography of Irma Rombauer and

Marion Becker, the mother and daughter who produced *Joy of Cooking* (my bible for years), Anne Mendelson writes: "It's ridiculous to be uppity about condensed milk, cherry Jell-O, canned vegetables, thick white sauce, processed cheese, condensed tomato soup, canned fruit cocktail, or spaghetti cooked to the consistency of baby cereal.

"Plastering retrospective snobberies over such foods because they are not chic today is purely silly. The fact is that all cultures form their own accommodation with the resources that their agriculture and technology make available to them. The attitude that some of our grandmothers or great-grandmothers held toward the products of American know-how precisely parallel the attitudes of modern gourmetdom toward 'boutique' olive oils or 'artisanal' cheeses."

Rereading an article I wrote for the *New York Times* in 1985 and reprinted with comments from readers in *The Best of De Gustibus* (Simon & Schuster, 1988), I was reminded why I should know better than to make fun of my old recipes.

Ellen Brown and Ann Brody, both food consultants, invited me to a black tie "Déjà Vu" dinner in Washington. They thought it would be interesting to see how people would react to a meal based on recipes from the 1950s and '60s.

I reported on the event in the *New York Times:* "While the fifty guests enjoyed much of the food, the tomato aspic was an unmitigated failure. 'It was universally decided,' Brown said, 'that our palates had progressed past the point at which we would tolerate tomato aspic.' Which probably explains why it has been at least twenty years since I made my version of tomato aspic, which contained raspberry gelatin as well as horseradish."

After I got through poking fun, the mail began to arrive and I stopped laughing. "Help," wrote a reader from Westchester County, New York. "I did not realize that recipes and food are dated. *Elegant but Easy* happens to be one of my favorite cookbooks. What should I replace it with so that my cooking can be 'now'?

"Your column in today's *Times* was really depressing. Are there any recipes in your book that can still be used without appearing gauche? Just three or four weeks ago I made Sweet and Sour Meatballs and all the guests thought they were wonderful. Does this mean we are all out of touch?

"All kidding aside, is there another cookbook that tells you where to stop when preparing a recipe in advance? I have used *Elegant but Easy* and *Freeze with Ease* for at least seventeen years; both books have been reliable; now I feel self-conscious when selecting a recipe."

Worse still was a note from an equally upset Connecticut reader: "I consider it needlessly unkind to ridicule the food preferences of other times, places, or people. Some of us like tomato aspic, though I never get to serve it because my family decided it was unpalatable (icky) in the 1940s, considerably ahead of the guests at the Déjà Vu party."

This is *not* the way for a cookbook author to get people to buy her books. For all the outdated recipes and ingredients in the original *Elegant but Easy*, including the aspic, there are still some dishes I never stopped making—Toasted Mushroom Rolls, Sherley's Parmesan Puffs, Frozen Grand Marnier Soufflé, Lemon Angel Trifle, and, of course, the Fruit Torte, which is now called Original Plum Torte and is the most requested recipe I have ever published in the *Times*. It was one of Lois's contributions to the book, and every fall the letters and calls come in asking me to reprint it because the one from the previous year has been lost.

There are about fifty recipes from the first edition in the new one. So why not start anew? Because the concept behind *Elegant but Easy* is as good today as it was in 1960: recipes that can be prepared in advance so that the cook can enjoy her (there were hardly any "his" then) party instead of slaving over the stove. The idea of stirring a risotto while everyone else is gossiping in the living room is (still) not my idea of fun.

While a few cookbooks today do suggest how much of a recipe can be prepared in advance, most don't, usually because the dish cannot be prepared ahead of time and maintain its texture and flavor. Much current cooking is *à la minute*, which is great for restaurants where the chef's staff preps it and cooks it and you eat it. Right away. That kind of cooking does not translate well to the home unless you have a kitchen staff, and if you do, you don't need this cookbook. The result is that fewer and fewer people give dinner parties or parties of any kind at which they serve their own food.

Fortunately there are still some who would really like to try, a fact that was brought home to me in December 1996, when I wrote a piece for the *New York Times* about giving a dinner party and spreading the work over a two-week period. It provided a game plan so that the cook could include strategies to get the food on the table without a meltdown of either the cook or the food. In a recent nationwide survey, 26 percent of Americans said the hardest part of entertaining is preparation, like cooking.

The menu for the article came from the new version of *Elegant but Easy*. What surprised me was the response from readers: the article was being clipped from

Washington, D.C., to Los Angeles because the recipes and the game plan had put entertaining at home within the reach of anyone who knows how to toast a cheese sandwich.

The *Easy* part of the original book title still holds. As in the original *Elegant but Easy*, there is a snowflake (❄) beside each recipe that can be frozen and a refrigerator sign with a number indicating how many days ahead a dish can be made and refrigerated: ⊟2 for two days.

Elegant? As Americans have become more sophisticated about food, it's unlikely that many think of black bean chili or chicken cacciatore as elegant, and while there are plenty of dishes that can be served at today's version of a formal dinner party, there are even more that are informal. This is a cookbook for those who still want to entertain, at least once in a while, with as little stress as possible, whether it's two for a Sunday night supper, company invited only that morning, or something more impressive like a sit-down dinner for twelve. In addition, many of the recipes in the book, which came from my "Plain and Simple" column in the *New York Times*, are so quick and so easy they would be perfect for a family supper.

Despite my reputation for featuring low-fat food with moderate calories, *The New Elegant but Easy* is about entertaining, not about day-in and day-out healthful eating. I don't think entertaining is the time to watch every fat gram and calorie. If you do that the rest of the week, some splurges are not only perfectly acceptable but absolutely necessary.

The keynotes here are taste and ease of preparation. Wherever less fat has no impact on the taste of the dish, I've cut back and suggested lower-fat alternatives such as light sour cream and nonfat yogurt. But there is plenty of heavy cream, butter, and cheese, even though the idea that I use them may come as a shock to those who think I never stray from the low-fat path.

M.B.

a look back

Culling recipes suitable for the late 1990s from books I wrote between 1960 and 1980, either alone or with Lois Levine, has turned into an amusing, and sometimes startling, exercise in culinary archaeology.

The books have always reflected contemporary themes: sometimes the results were good, sometimes they were simply fashionable, and sometimes they were perfectly horrid.

Lois and I both began cooking in the 1950s when: fat was good and no one had ever heard of cholesterol; garlic was exotic and cumin unheard of; women stayed home and spent hours preparing meals for their families and for entertaining; and Americans began to travel abroad in significant numbers.

So the first *Elegant but Easy*, written in 1960, was a mix of both homegrown and imported, seasoned with tubs of butter, quarts of cream, and lots of cheese, especially American, and a generous helping of convenience foods. But the book also had wonderful recipes for clam chowder made with fresh clams; my mother's noodle pudding; chocolate roll; and a fruit torte, the now-famous plum torte. In other words we were not complete Philistines.

To give you the flavor of the first book, here is a menu suggestion for a "formal" dinner party:

Toasted Mushroom Rolls
Tuna-Cheese Spread
Chicken Divan
Cornflaked Potatoes
Spinach Tarte
Orange Coconut Mold
Heat-and-Serve Rolls
Chocolate Roll
Coffee

I don't know whether to blush or howl. The menu was a combination of some of the worst of the 1950s and '60s and some of the best. The chocolate roll, an ethereal flourless creation, has barely been altered since the day I learned to make it from Cordon Bleu cooking teacher Dione Lucas. With some judicious alterations, toasted mushroom rolls and the spinach tarte are as good today as they were then (but I wouldn't serve a cream-based dish like Chicken Divan with a cream-based spinach tarte today).

Some of the dishes on the menu are culinary curiosities that tell us a lot about food and entertaining back then. Our idea of sophistication was rich and complex cooking, and chicken Divan, a creation of the chef at the Divan Parisien in New York, was a prime example. It was a restaurant dish calling for poached chicken, freshly cooked broccoli, hollandaise sauce, and béchamel sauce. Our recipe used frozen broccoli but everything else was fresh. We did not, however, use hollandaise.

Though we did not use instant mashed potatoes to make the cornflake potatoes (they always tasted like chemically treated sawdust to me), we did serve a tuna cheese spread that was made with processed Old English cheese, a can of tuna, mayonnaise, and Worcestershire sauce.

As for the Jell-O mold . . .

Poring over the recipes, I was struck by how limited good ingredients were forty years ago but, at the same time, how expansive the prepared food section had already become. Enamored in those early days of all the new convenience foods that were supposed to make our lives simpler, we threw away many of our recipes that called for making sauces and soups from scratch, trimming green beans and peeling carrots, and we uncritically reached for the prepared mix or box from the freezer section. It is comforting to find that in the cookbooks of some of the most respected food writers from that period—James Beard, Craig Claiborne—they, too, were willing on occasion to accept the manufactured in place of the fresh. But this acceptance was shrinking our choices instead of expanding them.

Elegant but Easy is filled with convenience foods: canned deviled ham; condensed tomato soup, mushroom soup, and green pea soup; canned mushrooms; vanilla pudding mix; some mix called Danish dessert; and, of course, Jell-O. In the original salad chapter more than half of the recipes are for gelatin molds.

When my editor at Simon & Schuster, Sydny Miner, and I discussed the revision, the first words out of my mouth were "The Jell-O molds will be the first to go." She laughed. People who serve them today usually relegate them to Thanksgiving and Christmas, when tradition demands that whatever was served to the previous two generations must still be served today. So our Fourth of July gelatin mold (red, white, and blue layers) has been excised from the book, along with eleven others. Don't get me wrong. I use gelatin, but not Jell-O.

With the exceptions of ingredients like canned tomatoes and tomato paste, frozen corn kernels and tiny peas, and frozen stocks, there are no convenience foods in *The New Elegant but Easy*. There haven't been in any of my books for almost twenty years.

Our style of flavoring has changed, too. It goes without saying there is no MSG: we stopped using that thirty years ago. Sugar and fat—butter, cream, cheese, well-marbled meats—used to play big roles in our recipes. Herbs and spices have replaced not only all of the MSG and some of the salt but much of the cheese. We continue to use butter and cream, but in smaller quantities, and we have reduced the amount of sugar in many recipes.

In the 1950s meat, preferably red, was the centerpiece of the meal and had to be served at least once a day. Steaks routinely arrived at the table in one-pound portions, or larger. We now use much leaner cuts of meat and have many more recipes for chicken and fish. In the original version of *Elegant but Easy* there were thirty-one recipes for red meat, twenty-five for poultry, nineteen for fish, and no vegetarian entrées at all. Today there are fewer for red meat than either fish or poultry.

Elegant but Easy paid homage to many other trends of the fifties and sixties: shish kebabs, foil-wrapped foods, and anything in a chafing dish.

I'm sure we eagerly embraced the use of foil because it was supposed to save cleanup time. Why else would we wrap things like garlic bread and baked potatoes in foil and steam them when they were supposed to be baked? Shish kebabs have been banished too, because they are a time-consuming pain in the neck. In the amount of time it takes to stick dozens of small chunks of something or other on dozens of skewers, you could make an entire dinner.

Many other recipes in the original book had to be discarded, not because of their ingredients but because they really cannot be made ahead and reheated.

This is how Armenian Vegetable Salad first appeared in *Elegant*. Nothing fresh in the entire salad except the scallions. Great if you live in the backwoods of Alaska and can't get to the store all winter long. See pages 183, 115, and 155 for the revised versions of these three recipes.

armenian vegetable salad

Mix together

2 nine-oz. packages frozen cut beans, slightly undercooked

1 seven-oz. can pitted black olives, drained and diced

1 four-oz. can pimento, drained and sliced

1 bunch scallions, white part only, sliced

1 eight-oz. can button mushrooms, drained

Well-Flavored French dressing

Marinate overnight in Well-Flavored French Dressing.

Serve without lettuce in large glass bowl, for this is beautiful as well as delicious. Let stand at room temperature for 15 minutes before serving.

yield: 8 servings

The original Boeuf Bourguignonne has a lot of strange ingredients, to say the least.

boeuf bourguignonne

Combine in large casserole

2 pounds cubed beef (chuck, round steak, etc.)

3–4 carrots, cut up

1 cup chopped celery

2 onions, sliced

2 cups canned tomatoes

1 cup tomato sauce

1 clove garlic

3 tablespoons quick-cooking tapioca

1 tablespoon sugar

½ cup red Burgundy

Cook at 250 degrees for 5 hours. During last hour add

1 cup sliced water chestnuts	1 one-lb. can small Irish potatoes
1 six-oz. can mushrooms	

After four hours of cooking, freeze, if desired. To serve, defrost and cook at 250 degrees for 1 hour, adding water chestnuts, mushrooms, and potatoes.

yield: 4–6 servings

eggplant parmigiana

Simmer uncovered for 30 minutes

1 one-lb. can tomatoes	2 tablespoons tomato paste
2 tablespoons olive oil	Pinch salt

Wash, dry, and cut into ½-inch slices

1 large eggplant, peeled

Fry for 3 minutes on each side in

Hot olive oil

Mix together

1 cup bread crumbs	1 clove garlic, crushed
½ cup Parmesan cheese, grated	Salt and pepper to taste
1 tablespoon parsley, chopped	

Put a layer of eggplant on bottom of casserole. Sprinkle with crumbs and pour tomato sauce over all. Alternate layers. Finish with eggplant. Cover with

1 eight-oz. package mozzarella
  cheese, sliced

When ready to serve, bake at 375 degrees for 20 to 30 minutes.

yield: 6 servings

The emphasis in *The New Elegant but Easy* on prepare-ahead food remains, but other things are different: our tastes have changed because of our exposure to so many superior ingredients, the amount of time we can spare for cooking, and our awareness that there is some connection between diet and health.

Increased sophistication and the availability of the best-quality raw ingredients did not happen all at once: there have been several phases from the days when American cooking meant hot dogs and hamburgers, through the heights of Julia Child's French cooking in the 1960s and '70s, into the less formal Italian phase in the 1980s, which was followed by a Pacific Rim period of the early nineties that has morphed into the current anything-goes period of fusion cooking. Mix a little Thai with some Jamaican and some Spanish, have it cooked by a Japanese chef, and before you know it you have fusion cooking, sometimes marvelous but sometimes a mess. Concurrently an appreciation of nostalgia cooking has been growing, a return to the simple foods of the forties and fifties, often lighter and always better seasoned. But I think the comeback of steak houses, cigar dinners, and outsized martinis is a defiant statement that you don't have to be perfect all the time, that there are special occasions when splurging is not only okay but good for you. I agree (but not about cigars).

For most people steaks, cigars, martinis, and maybe even Jell-O are special occasion treats, not everyday events.

By the time Lois and I were ready to write *Second Helpings*, our 1963 sequel to *Elegant but Easy*, we thought we had mastered a thing or two about fancy cooking. I had taken a few cooking classes and had learned how to bone a chicken and turn it inside out. (I have never since turned a chicken inside out but it seemed like a useful skill at the time.)

Second Helpings had pretensions of grandeur. There are fewer convenience foods; the number of Jell-O molds is down to eight. Quiche, pâté, crêpes, daube de boeuf provençale, duckling in wine and liqueur, poached salmon, crème brûlée, custard sabayon, quenelles de brochet—most recipes quite authentic—could be found among the pages of this sequel. We labored under the assumption that if a dish was difficult to prepare, surely it was gourmet.

In *Second Helpings*, in hot pursuit of the cuisine du jour, we began to introduce some of the ethnic food that was making its way to the United States, even if some of the versions no more resembled the authentic dishes than Tang resembles orange juice. We had recipes for Mexican eggplant, so-called, I suppose, because it had chili powder; Chinese beef because it had soy sauce; pastitsio, a Greek casserole of pasta and meat, topped with American cheese in our version; mattar paneer, an Indian dish of peas and cheese with large-curd cottage cheese substituted for the unavailable Indian cheese.

We followed other fads as well, and even took up the flambéing of America. Though we had the good sense not to flambé hot dogs as they did in the Pump Room in Chicago (it was bad enough putting them in a chafing dish), we flambéed steak Diane, cherries Jubilee, and crêpes Suzette.

In *Freeze with Ease*, published in 1965, we were still showing off. Like the other books, it is a mixture of the sublime and the ridiculous. Coulibiac is both. It is a fabulous five-part Russian dish in which 1½ pounds of lobster meat (it was cheap in those days!), sour cream, and hard-cooked eggs are wrapped in brioche dough and baked. I don't make it anymore but I wouldn't mind if someone wanted to serve it to me in a restaurant.

Along with stupefyingly time-consuming show-off dishes, *Freeze with Ease* had some wonderful recipes that are as good today as they were thirty years ago, and you will find them here: two hors d'oeuvres in particular—cheese cigarettes and cheese boereg, or cheese in phyllo. In 1965 the use of phyllo, the paper-thin pastry of Greece and Turkey, was not widespread, but as a food writer I had met a number of women of Greek descent who had taught me how to make these fabulous cheese-and-spinach-filled pastries. The hard part was buying the phyllo. First you had to find a Greek market. Today frozen phyllo is sold in supermarkets.

The health food phenomenon of the 1960s did not attract us, probably because at the time the people who were leading it were interested not in how food tasted but in whether it was what we would call today "politically correct." Tofu burgers did nothing for me then and don't now.

In 1970 Lois and I wrote *Come for Cocktails, Stay for Supper*, about a style of entertaining that is still with us—the cocktail buffet. We coauthored our last book, *The Summertime Cookbook*, in 1972. The book contained a fair sprinkling of dishes from places besides France: Greek salad made with feta cheese; moussaka; guacamole; a salad made with bulgur; red snapper with tomato sauce with the following headnote: "Called huachinango veracruzano in Mexico, it is served with boiled potatoes and chiles largos, if they can be found"; South African shish kebab (heaven knows what made it South African); gazpacho made with canned tomato soup, and an iced curry pea soup made with canned green pea soup; kataifi, the Greek dessert made with shreds of phyllo (in our version, made with shredded wheat). We did say it was an American adaptation. Pita turned up for the first time under the name Arabic or Syrian bread.

In *The Summertime Cookbook* we also paid homage to the best of our own country: roasted corn on the cob, potato salad, brownies, and devil's food cake. The recipe for Maryland crab cakes in the book is virtually the same as the one we have included in *The New Elegant but Easy*.

There were only three Jell-O molds in the salad chapter. Instead there were salad recipes calling for bulgur and chick-peas and there was a fairly authentic version of salad niçoise. Fresh herbs began to come into their own, and scattered throughout are recipes calling for fresh tarragon, fresh chives, fresh dill, fresh basil, even fresh cilantro. Things were looking up.

But before too much smugness sets in I must confess that this is also the book that contained the achingly sweet bar cookie called Hello Dollys, named for the Broadway show that became synonymous with Carol Channing. The headnote with our recipe says: "Somewhere in the dim, dark past is a story about a southern ladies' club naming these for Carol Channing when she came to town." They are made with butter, graham cracker crumbs, chocolate chips, flaked coconut, and pecans, all held together with a can of sweetened condensed milk.

Just the other day someone mentioned that Hello Dollys, which you may know as "Magic" or "7-Layer Bars," were still her son's favorite cookies, but he won't find them in this book.

In 1978 I struck out on my own and wrote *Pure and Simple*. I was fascinated with nouvelle cuisine, the French food revolution that changed the face of cooking forever, but preparing such food at home seemed terribly time-consuming, especially since I was, by that time, a full-time newspaper reporter. The part of nouvelle cuisine that interested me was the use of fresh seasonal ingredients. They were appealing because of their superior taste and because such ingredients were less likely to contain harmful chemicals. The subtitle of *Pure and Simple* was: "Delicious recipes for additive-free cooking," and in the book I confessed that in the 1950s and '60s, "like the vast majority of other Americans I couldn't wait to try the newest convenience product." But now convenience foods were gone and with them the last of the Jell-O molds.

Instead here was an entire chapter on how to make convenience foods from scratch: pudding and pie filling mix, biscuit mix, poultry seasoning, etc. If you wanted the speed of convenience foods, at least those made at home used good wholesome ingredients and did not contain unpronounceable additives. You could say I was weaning myself from convenience foods in stages. But I couldn't resist including one of the made-from-scratch convenience mixes from that book in *The New Elegant but Easy:* chocolate chip cookie mix. It's still good.

My awakening to the superiority of scratch cooking coincided with my exposure to some of the finest food in the world on trips abroad and increasingly to the incredible food that American chefs were producing in their kitchens. In the introduction I wrote: "by one of those strange twists of fate, just as I was beginning to question the taste of the highly processed foods, I began to get little hints that some of the things being put into them might not be safe either."

In a bit of wishful thinking I noted that people were turning away from factory-produced convenience. Attendance at cooking schools was high and men as well as women were going. People were buying kitchen equipment, like food processors, to use at home.

Wrong again. Today people are cooking less and buying more carryout.

In an effort to help those who still wanted to do some cooking but found it too time-consuming, my last three books were designed for quick, healthful, from-scratch meals: *Keep It Simple, 20-Minute Menus,* and *Eating Well Is the Best Revenge.* The theme has been that good food and healthful food are not mutually exclusive, a concept that many people still find hard to believe. In all of these books the ingredients and ideas of the flashy eighties and calmer nineties have found their way, but in simpler forms. There are recipes for fajitas, salsa, burritos, risotto, baba ghanouj, and sushi; in short, a reflection of what we are eating today with an emphasis on health.

The list of ingredients used in these books and in *The New Elegant but Easy* that were not available in 1960 is staggering. I couldn't help but make note of them as I was revising recipes. While we doubtless would be better off without potato chips made with Olestra, aspartame to sweeten our soft drinks, and fat-free cheeses and mayonnaise (ugh), and while we certainly would be better off without genetically engineered food and bovine growth hormone in cows' milk, there are many splendid ingredients that are now available thanks to the American chefs who demanded the best of both local and imported goods and organic ingredients, which taste better than commercially raised food.

Here are just a few things that were either nonexistent or very difficult to find forty years ago:

meat and fish—Pork tenderloin; fresh fish in many more varieties

dairy products—Parmigiano-Reggiano, mascarpone, goat cheese, fresh mozzarella; full-fat, low-fat, and nonfat yogurt; reduced-fat ricotta; and light sour cream

produce—Fresh herbs; fennel; sugar snap peas and snow peas; broccoli rabe; Vidalia and other sweet onions; purple potatoes, Yukon gold potatoes, tiny new potatoes; red, yellow, orange, and purple bell peppers; hot peppers; arugula, mesclun, radicchio, red leaf lettuces; tropical fruits like mango and papaya; dried cranberries, cherries, blueberries, and strawberries

condiments—extra-virgin olive, toasted sesame, walnut, hazelnut, and canola oils; raspberry, rice, balsamic, sherry, and champagne vinegars; imported soy sauces and reduced-sodium soy sauce; mustards—Dijon, grainy, sweet and hot; vanilla bean; top-quality baking chocolate

All of these treasures can now be purchased whether you live in Nome, Alaska, or New York City because if the local store doesn't have them they can be ordered by mail (see pages 21–24 for mail-order sources).

Equipment has changed, too. Food processors; superior pots and pans, many with excellent nonstick linings; and high-quality knives—each of these pieces of equipment makes it easier to put well-cooked food on the table. Stovetop grills provide the searing flavor from direct flame cooking formerly available only from an outdoor grill. And even though microwave ovens do not play a large role in good cooking or in this new version of *Elegant but Easy*, they are handy for reheating without thickening or burning the food.

The New Elegant but Easy is an idiosyncratic collection of the foods we love best that can be prepared in advance. We don't pretend to cover everything. We have taken out the fat where it doesn't affect the flavor and eliminated all but a couple of recipes that take a day to prepare, leaving the show-off dishes to the chefs. Comfort food, not all of it American, is on display along with the fusion cooking: coq au vin, grilled chicken with black bean and mango salsa, basil and garlic mashed potatoes, and sea bass with sake marinade.

Our cookbooks have always been considered accessible; this one follows in the same tradition. This *New Elegant but Easy* expands on ideas for getting meals on the table with a minimum of stress. Our earliest generalized suggestions for cook-ahead strategies have been turned into full-fledged game plans that still include the advice on the day of the party to "take a nap!" (See page 270 for the game plans.)

Before the recipes there are some helpful hints for ingredient choices, as well as suggestions for places to buy some that may not be available in the local super-market.

You can distinguish the recipes from the original *Elegant but Easy* and some of our other books by the headnotes that accompany them: each talks about how the recipe has been changed to update it.

Just as in the original *Elegant but Easy*, we have used symbols beside the title of each recipe to indicate how many days ahead it can be refrigerated and if it can be frozen: A snowflake (✳) stands for frozen; ☐2 means the dish can be prepared ahead and refrigerated for 2 days.

before you use this book

Take a moment to read the following information. All of it will make cooking even easier.

ingredients

Low-Fat Products

There are thousands of new prepared food items today that were not available in 1959. If you are interested in this book, you probably don't have any more use for most of them than we do. But some of the new low-fat or reduced-fat products can be used judiciously. Low-fat or light mayonnaise, low-fat or light sour cream, nonfat yogurt—these are examples of foods that have been reformulated, and when they are incorporated in dishes with high flavor it's difficult to tell they are missing some of their fat. They are suggested as alternatives in many recipes.

Nonfat products are a horse of another color. With the exception of nonfat yogurt, there are no nonfat dairy products that taste good.

Low-Sodium Canned Goods

Low-sodium canned goods are preferable to regular canned goods, because when you cook you want to do the seasoning yourself, not be dependent on what the manufacturer thinks is appropriate. Low-sodium or no-salt-added tomato products and low-sodium or no-salt-added stocks or broths are recommended in all dishes.

I also use reduced-sodium soy sauce instead of regular soy sauce.

Olive Oil

I use virgin olive oil in most of the recipes. For a few dishes where the olive oil flavor predominates, particularly uncooked dishes, use extra-virgin olive oil, preferably cold pressed. Recipes specify which type of oil is to be used.

Butter

I always use unsalted butter, not because of the salt content but because unsalted butter is always fresher than salted butter.

Cream

It's worth looking for pasteurized rather than ultrapasteurized cream. Ultrapasteurized has a burnt taste.

Gingerroot

If you always want to have gingerroot on hand, freeze a piece. When you want to use the ginger, simply grate it on the coarse side of the grater. It will defrost as it is grated.

Don't bother to peel ginger; it is not necessary.

Dried Fruits

There are many wonderful dried fruits available today that did not exist when *Elegant but Easy* first appeared: cherries, cranberries, blueberries, and strawberries. They are a lovely alternative to raisins and currants. But beware: some manufacturers are now adding oil to them, even sugar—ingredients that are not needed. Read the label.

Polenta

A product called instant polenta is nothing more than finely ground polenta. It cooks quickly, in less than 5 minutes, while regular polenta takes 45 minutes. You can take your choice.

Couscous

This North African pasta comes in an instant form, both regular and whole wheat. The whole wheat tastes better, but either will do in all the recipes.

Bulgur

Bulgur is a quick-cooking cracked whole wheat of the Middle East that comes fine, medium, and coarse. If the recipe does not specify, use fine or medium.

Chocolate for Baking

A chocolate tasting, conducted by The Bakers Dozen East, a group of professional bakers, was held in New York City in 1996 at Peter Kump's Cooking School. According to pastry chef and cooking teacher Nick Malgieri, the following sweetened dark chocolates were tasted and are listed in order of preference:

Valrhona
VanLeer bittersweet
Callebaut semisweet
Nestlé semisweet
Guittard bittersweet
Ghirardelli bittersweet
Hershey's
Baker's

It was a different story for unsweetened chocolates. In 1996 a panel of tasters at *Cook's Illustrated* magazine cited Nestlé as highly recommended. Guittard, Merckens, Ghirardelli, VanLeer, and Baker's were recommended.

Hershey's and Callebaut were not recommended.

Vanilla

Always use *pure* vanilla extract for baking. In some recipes I suggest using part of a vanilla bean because it gives a more intense flavor. Of course, the bean can be used in all recipes calling for vanilla. For 1 teaspoon vanilla extract, slit 1 inch of bean in half lengthwise, scraping the seeds into the other ingredients.

techniques

Measurements

Except for baked goods, the measurements of all ingredients are approximate. If your onions weigh 1 pound and 4 ounces and the recipe calls for 1 pound, don't worry about it.

Baking Times

Baking times in the recipes are approximate: all ovens differ. Begin to check for doneness 15 minutes before the end of the suggested baking time.

Recipe Yield

When only one number is listed for a recipe yield (6 servings) it means that is the minimum number of people the recipe will serve. There will be enough for some seconds. If a recipe yield is 4 to 6 servings, there will be seconds for 4 people but not for 6.

Wrapping for Storage

When you are refrigerating or freezing a dish, it is important to wrap it well. For the refrigerator, plastic or foil will do. For the freezer a combination of both is recommended to prevent freezer burn.

Pie Crusts

If there is one thing that turns off most people about making pies, it is making a crust and rolling it out, so all of the recipes in this book that call for pie crust offer a no-roll butter crust that is patted by hand into the pie plate (see page 81). If there are holes they don't show. Neither does the patching. It's very easy.

Raw Meat, Poultry, and Fish

Always rinse thoroughly before using. Marinades for raw meat, poultry, and fish can cause gastrointestinal problems if not handled properly. If you want to use the liquid in which the meat has been marinated on the finished dish as a sauce, boil it first. When brushing with the marinade, be sure that the last brushing is cooked thoroughly.

Don't put a utensil that has been in contact with the raw ingredients into cooked ingredients; don't use the plate on which the raw ingredients were placed for cooked ingredients.

Fruits and Vegetables

Always rinse well before using, even those that will be peeled.

Raw Eggs

A number of recipes in this book, particularly in the refrigerator and frozen dessert sections, call for uncooked eggs, which may contain hazardous bacteria called salmonella. Fifteen years ago no one gave any thought to such a problem with eggs, and there is plenty of blame to go around both in the government and among egg producers. Maybe in a few years the problem will have been solved and you can go back to making eggnog, preparing mayonnaise from scratch, and making any of these desserts with raw eggs and not a lot of rigmarole.

For now there are alternatives, and for those who feel they should be cautious, the extra effort required is worthwhile. Salmonella, which can cause serious illness, even death, is particularly a problem for people with compromised immune systems: the elderly, small children, and people who are ill with cancer or AIDS.

The simplest alternative is to choose organic eggs and then call the egg producer and find out if they test for salmonella. If they do not, the eggs, though less likely to contain the bacteria, cannot be guaranteed safe.

The next choice is your supermarket. Every day more and more are carrying pasteurized eggs. If not, call 1-800-HIS EGGS, the number of Pepetti's Hygrade Egg Productions of Elizabeth, New Jersey. This company can tell you where their refrigerated pasteurized egg whites are sold in your area. An alternative for pasteurized egg whites is Eggology, at 888-669-6557.

Finally you can pasteurize the raw eggs yourself. There is no question it is a nuisance, but it works. I have tried several different techniques and like these best:

To Pasteurize Egg Yolks

You must pasteurize at least three yolks at a time; if that is more than you need, save the extra for another time.

Have ready a pan of ice and water and an instant-read candy thermometer.

Blend 3 raw yolks with 2 tablespoons of sugar (you can use some of the sugar called for in a recipe) and place in a small, heavy pot over hot water. Use a double boiler if you have one.

Constantly stir the mixture until it reaches 160 degrees. Remove immediately and cool quickly, stirring over the ice bath. It is important to reduce the temperature quickly to stop the cooking. Then use the yolks as directed in the recipe.

It takes a split second for the liquid eggs to turn to scrambled eggs, so you must watch the mixture like a hawk and never stop stirring or taking its temperature. If the yolks are not being beaten in the recipe but added directly to another mixture, add 1 teaspoon of water for each 2 yolks along with the sugar.

It is not worth the trouble to pasteurize egg whites at home. Use the commercial egg products recommended above, or if you are confident that your eggs are salmonella-free and you are not serving the dish to anyone at risk, you may choose to use raw egg whites.

mail-order

Some ingredients mentioned in this book may not be readily available where you live. It's easy to order them by mail.

The sources listed below have appeared over the years in mail-order stories I have written in the *New York Times*, so I know they are reliable. If, however, you should have a problem, please let me know by writing to me care of the publisher.

Meat and Poultry

Chicken, lamb, veal, beef. These animals are raised humanely. The lamb is especially good.

Summerfield Farm, SR4, 195A, Brightwood, VA 22715; 540-948-3100; fax 948-6249.

Meat and chicken of all kinds. Superb ingredients, many of them organic.

D'Artagnan, Inc., 280 Wilson Avenue, Newark, NJ 07105; 800-DAR-TAGN; 973-344-0565; fax 465-1870.

Sausages. Low-fat chicken and turkey, filled with flavor but not with fat.

Aidells Sausage Company, 1625 Alvarado Street, San Leandro, CA 94577; 510-614-5450; 800-546-5795.

Fruits and Vegetables

Greens as good as or better than anything at the local farm market (all organic). Mesclun, arugula. Fruits and vegetables also available.

Diamond Organics, P.O. Box 2159, Freedom, CA 95019; 800-922-2396; fax 408-763-2444.

Wild mushrooms, dried and frozen berries. The choice of exotic mushrooms is spectacular: chanterelles, black trumpets, hedgehog among them.
Mushrooms and More, P.O. Box 532, Goldens Bridge, NY 10526; 914-232-2107.

Grains

Wild rice. Superbly nutty and truly wild, not cultivated.
Coteau Connoisseur Wild Rice, 218 West Warren, Dept. W1, Lucerne, MN 56156; 507-283-2338.

Cheese

Cheddar. The extra-sharp Cheddar is deeply flavored, one of the very best in the country.
Grafton Village Cheese Co., Townshend Road, P.O. Box 87, Grafton, VT 05146; 800-472-3866.

Parmigiano-Reggiano. The finest of these aged cheeses tastes nothing like the American version called Parmesan.
Todaro Brothers. Mail Order, 555 Second Avenue, New York, NY 10016; 212-679-7766; fax 212-689-1679.

Mascarpone. It is the best, and so is everything else from this place.
Egg Farm Dairy, 2 John Walsh Boulevard, Peekskill, NY 10566; 800-273-2637.

Goat. Low-fat and creamy; other versions as well.
Little Rainbow Chèvre, 15 Doe Hill, Hillsdale, NY 12529; 518-325-4628; fax 325-4409.

Goat. Cheddar and many wonderful others.
Vermont Butter and Cheese, Pittman Road, P.O. Box 95, Websterville, VT 05678; 800-884-6287.

Mozzarella. Once you've had fresh you will never want any other kind. There are dozens of other wonderful cheeses made by this company as well.
Mozzarella Company, 2944 Elm Street, Dallas, TX 75226; 214-741-4072; 800-798-2954.

Condiments

Chinese ingredients. Much of what you need to cook the Chinese-style recipes in this book can be found at one source: sesame oil, chile paste with garlic, hot chile oil, rice vinegar, hoisin sauce.

China Bowl Trading Company, 830 Post Road East, Westport, CT 06880; 203-222-0381; fax 203-226-6445.

Japanese ingredients.

Katagiri & Co., 224 East 59th Street, New York, NY 10022; 212-755-3566; fax 212-752-4197.

Japanese and Thai ingredients.

Anzen Importers, 736 Martin Luther King Boulevard, Portland, OR 97232; 503-283-1284.

Maple syrup.

Sugarwood Farm, RFD2, Box 158, Glover, VT 05839; 800-245-3718.

Olive oil. Especially for extra-virgin for salads as well as virgin olive oil for cooking.

See Todaro Brothers, page 22.

Olives. So many wonderful different kinds.

See Todaro Brothers, page 22.

Dried fruits. Cherries and cranberries as well as other dried fruits—such a nice alternative to raisins and currants.

American Spoon Foods, 1668 Clarion Avenue, P.O. Box 566, Petoskey, MI 49770; 616-347-9030; 800-222-5886.

Vinegar. Balsamic—the sweet rich vinegar called for in many recipes in this book.

See Todaro Brothers, page 22.

Baking

Chocolate for baking.

Paradigm Chocolate, 5777 SW Jean Road, Suite 106A, Lake Oswego, OR 97035; 503-636-4880

or

N.Y. Cake and Baking Distributor, 56 West 22nd Street, New York, NY 10010; 212-675-2253. (Callebaut, Valrhona, and VanLeer chocolate)

Williams-Sonoma, 800-541-2233. (Callebaut and Valrhona)

Savoiardi (Italian ladyfingers). Best for tiramisù.

> Providence Cheese Gourmet Foods, 178 Atwells Avenue, Providence, RI 02903; 401-421-5653.

Equipment

Stovetop grill. Many are available in kitchen shops but one of the best is the Max Burton grill. If you can't find it locally you can buy it by mail from: Max Burton, 2322 South Holgate Street, Tacoma, WA 98407; 800-272-8603.

hot
hors d'oeuvres

sherley's parmesan puffs

Sherley Koteen is my oldest friend in Washington and she has contributed recipes to almost every book I ever wrote.

"They disappear like soap bubbles" is what we said about these savory morsels in the original book, and the statement still holds. This time we have used Parmigiano-Reggiano instead of that horrible salty dry grated excuse for the real thing we had to use years ago.

If your cookie cutter is smaller than 1½ inches, use it and figure you will just get more!

1 cup finely grated Parmigiano-Reggiano
⅔ cup regular or light mayonnaise
2 tablespoons minced onion

40 white bread rounds about 1½ inches in diameter, cut from 20 slices of bread (2 loaves good firm white bread)

1. Mix the cheese, mayonnaise, and onion together and spread generously over each bread round. Refrigerate if desired.

2. To serve, preheat the broiler and broil the puffs about 4 inches from the heat source for 1 to 2 minutes, until the tops bubble and brown. Watch carefully: they burn quickly.

yield: forty 1½-inch rounds

cheese shorties

We've changed the cheese to extra-sharp Cheddar instead of sharp. A superb version is made by Grafton Village Cheese from Vermont (see mail-order sources, page 22).

The garlic salt in the original recipe has been sent packing, replaced by a little cayenne.

1 pound extra-sharp white Cheddar cheese, grated
½ pound (2 sticks) unsalted butter, softened

2 cups flour
Few dashes cayenne pepper

1. Cream the cheese and butter until thoroughly mixed, using an electric mixer or food processor. Add the flour and cayenne and mix thoroughly. Shape into rolls 1 inch in diameter, wrap in wax paper or plastic wrap, and chill at least 1 hour or overnight, or freeze. If freezing, wrap again with aluminum foil.

2. To serve, preheat the oven to 400 degrees. If frozen, let the rolls defrost in the refrigerator for at least a couple of hours or overnight. Cut into ⅓-inch-thick slices and place on cookie sheets 1 inch apart. Bake for about 10 minutes, until light brown on the bottom.

yield: 48 shorties

cheese cigarettes

4 tablespoons (½ stick) plus ¼ pound (1 stick) unsalted butter
¼ cup unbleached flour
2 cups milk (2% or whole)
Salt
⅔ cup heavy cream
Freshly ground pepper to taste

12 ounces Parmigiano-Reggiano cheese
3 egg yolks, beaten
½ teaspoon cayenne pepper
2 (22-ounce) or 3 (16-ounce) loaves very fresh sliced supermarket white bread (48 pieces), crusts trimmed

1. In a saucepan melt the 4 tablespoons butter. Remove from the heat and gradually whisk in the flour. Gradually add the milk and ¼ teaspoon salt, stirring. Return to medium heat and cook until thickened, whisking constantly. Remove from heat. Slowly add the heavy cream and season with black pepper. While the cream sauce is still hot, briskly stir in the cheese, egg yolks, and cayenne.

2. Place in a covered bowl in the refrigerator. Let the filling chill to spreading consistency, at least several hours or overnight.

3. Flatten each trimmed slice of white bread by rolling with a rolling pin. Make sure each slice is as thin as possible.

4. When the filling reaches the desired consistency, spread generously on each slice of flattened bread and roll tightly like a cigarette. Refrigerate or freeze.

5. To serve, let the rolls defrost if frozen. Preheat the oven to 400 degrees. Melt the remaining stick of butter and, using a pastry brush, coat each cigarette on all sides. Place on ungreased cookie sheets and bake for 10 to 15 minutes, or until golden brown. Cut in half. Serve hot or warm.

yield: 48 full cigarettes or 96 halves

brie and pesto

This would also be good for a salad course with a green salad.

1 whole 2-pound ripe brie   1 cup Basil Pesto (page 135)

1. Cut a circle in the top of the brie, leaving a ½-inch edge and cutting only deep enough to remove the white coating and a little of the cheese. Fill the circle with the pesto and refrigerate, if desired.

2. To serve, preheat the oven to 350 degrees. Let the brie come to room temperature and bake for 5 to 7 minutes, until the brie becomes soft and runny. Serve immediately with rounds of French bread or crackers.

yield: enough for 10 to 15 or more people, depending on the other hors d'oeuvres

toasted mushroom rolls

The changes in this recipe are minimal, but do take advantage of the fact that today cultivated wild mushrooms are available all over. The wild mushrooms add more flavor to the rolls, but the rolls are also superb with white button mushrooms.

Oh yes. The MSG has been eliminated, but the white bread should be the spongy white stuff we used to roll into spitballs. The bread has to be very soft to roll well.

These were served at my daughter's wedding in 1992.

½ pound white mushrooms or exotic mushrooms like portobello, cremini, shiitake, or some combination
4 tablespoons (½ stick) unsalted butter, plus melted butter for brushing
3 tablespoons flour

1 cup light cream or half-and-half
1 tablespoon minced chives
1 teaspoon lemon juice
Salt and freshly ground pepper to taste
21 slices white bread (two 16-ounce loaves), crusts removed

1. Wash, trim, dry, and finely chop the mushrooms. Sauté them in 4 tablespoons hot butter for about 3 or 4 minutes. Remove from the heat and blend in the flour. Stir in the cream and return to the heat, cooking until the mixture thickens. Remove from the heat. Stir in the chives and lemon juice. Season with salt and pepper. Let cool.

2. With a rolling pin, roll the bread slices thin. Spread each slice with some of the mushroom mixture; roll up and place, seam side down, on cookie sheets. Brush with additional melted butter. Leave on the cookie sheets and freeze, if desired, or refrigerate. After they are frozen or chilled, they can be removed from the sheets and stored in a plastic bag, if desired.

3. To serve, let the frozen rolls defrost; preheat the oven to 400 degrees. Toast on all sides for about 15 minutes, until the rolls are golden. Cut in half and serve warm, not hot.

yield: 42 rolls

mushroom-filled mushroom caps

A handsome first course as well as an hors d'oeuvre.

2 dozen medium plain white mushrooms
¼ pound cultivated exotic mushrooms
   such as shiitake, portobello, cremini,
   or others
1 tablespoon unsalted butter
1 teaspoon flour

½ cup crème fraîche
1 tablespoon marsala or Madeira
1 teaspoon chopped fresh tarragon or
   ½ teaspoon dried tarragon
Salt and freshly ground black pepper
   to taste

1. Wash, stem, and dry the white mushrooms. Wash, trim, and dry the exotic mushrooms. Finely chop the exotic mushrooms and the stems from the white mushrooms. Sauté the chopped mushrooms in hot butter until the mushrooms are tender, just a few minutes; remove from the heat and blend in the flour.

2. Return to the heat; stir in the crème fraîche, marsala, and tarragon, and season with salt and pepper. Cool and stuff the mushroom caps with the mixture. Arrange the stuffed mushrooms on a cookie sheet and refrigerate, if desired.

3. To serve, preheat the oven to 400 degrees and bake the mushrooms for 12 to 15 minutes, until the filling is bubbly and the mushroom caps are just beginning to soften. Serve at once.

yield: 2 dozen; for a first course, serve 4 per person on small plates decorated with sprigs of tarragon

crabmeat canapés

A lower-fat mayonnaise reduces some fat and calories, but this is still not health food!

1 clove garlic
6 ounces cream cheese
¼ cup heavy cream
¼ cup light or full-fat mayonnaise
2 tablespoons finely chopped onion
1 teaspoon Worcestershire sauce

A few sprinkles cayenne pepper
2 tablespoons fresh lemon juice
½ pound fresh crabmeat
Salt to taste
2 dozen very, very thin slices of a very
   narrow French baguette

1. With the food processor running, put the garlic through the feed tube to mince. Add the cream cheese and heavy cream and process until smooth. Add the mayonnaise, onion, Worcestershire, and cayenne and process.

2. Pick over the crabmeat to remove any shell bits and cartilage. Mix the crabmeat with the lemon juice, stir into the cream cheese mixture by hand, and season with salt.

3. Refrigerate or freeze.

4. To serve, let the mixture defrost in the refrigerator if frozen, and spread on the bread slices. Broil for a couple of minutes, until lightly browned.

yield: 2 dozen

chinese chicken wings

Good for a party when people are dressed in jeans, cutoffs, or the equivalent. For more decorous occasions, try skinless and boneless thighs and/or small skinless drumsticks. A favorite of Lois's.

24 small chicken wings with tips removed or 24 wingettes (tips already removed)
1 tablespoon coarsely grated fresh ginger

½ cup reduced-sodium soy sauce
2 large cloves garlic, crushed
⅓ cup packed dark brown sugar
1 teaspoon Dijon mustard
⅔ cup dry sherry

1. Cut the wings into two parts at the joint.

2. Combine the ginger, soy sauce, garlic, brown sugar, mustard, and sherry in a shallow nonreactive bowl and marinate the chicken wings in this mixture for at least 2 hours, preferably overnight, or as long as 3 days in the refrigerator. Or place in the freezer.

3. To serve, let come to room temperature and place the wings in a single layer in a roasting pan, adding the marinade. Preheat the oven to 375 degrees and roast the pieces for about 30 minutes, basting several times. Turn the wings once. Serve warm or at room temperature with plenty of napkins or plates and forks and knives.

yield: 48 pieces

spicy sausage balls

Using low-fat chicken or turkey sausage instead of regular pork sausage gives you the same amount of flavor but one-third to one-half less fat.

1 pound spicy chicken or turkey
  sausage
1 slightly beaten egg
1/3 cup unseasoned fine bread crumbs
1/2 teaspoon dried sage

1/4 cup chili sauce
1/4 cup catsup
1 teaspoon brown sugar
1 teaspoon reduced-sodium soy sauce
1 tablespoon white vinegar

1. Remove the sausage meat from the casings if necessary and put in a mixing bowl. Add the egg, bread crumbs, and sage and mix well. Shape into 4 dozen balls. Refrigerate or freeze.

2. Combine the chili sauce, catsup, brown sugar, soy sauce, and vinegar and refrigerate or freeze.

3. To serve, let the sausage balls and sauce defrost, if frozen, and brown the sausage balls in a skillet on all sides. Pour off any fat.

4. Combine the sausage balls with the catsup–chili sauce mixture and simmer the sausage balls in the mixture 10 to 15 minutes, until they are cooked through. Serve from a chafing dish or, if you gave your mother's away, place the balls in a bowl and keep warm on a hot tray.

yield: 4 dozen balls

spinach tarte

Many of the best recipes from *Pure and Simple*, a book I wrote in 1978, have been lost to new cooks because that book is out of print.

This one can be served as both an hors d'oeuvre and a side dish. I have reduced the fat by using light sour cream. The amounts of mushrooms and nutmeg have been increased, and garlic and black pepper have been added. It tastes marvelous.

Now, if you don't care a hoot about low fat, here's a way to make a very rich, exceptionally delicious version: sprinkle extra grated cheese on the bottom of the baking pan. Without that added cheese this makes a good side dish.

1 pound fresh loose spinach or 1 (10-ounce) package fresh spinach
2 tablespoons unsalted butter
1½ cups chopped onion (about 7 or 8 ounces)
1 large clove garlic, minced
½ pound fresh mushrooms (white, cremini, portobello), washed, trimmed, and sliced
1 cup nonfat yogurt

1 cup regular or light sour cream
4 ounces grated extra-sharp white Cheddar cheese, plus 2½ cups (about 7 or 8 ounces), coarsely grated sharp white Cheddar cheese (optional)
3 eggs, lightly beaten
1 teaspoon Worcestershire sauce
¼ teaspoon nutmeg
Freshly ground black pepper to taste

1. Wash the spinach and remove the tough stems. Steam the spinach, using only the water clinging to the leaves, and drain thoroughly. Chop coarsely with a knife.

2. In a medium skillet, melt the butter and sauté the onion and garlic until the onions begin to soften and turn golden. Add the mushrooms and cook until they release their liquid. Continue cooking until the liquid evaporates.

3. Stir in the yogurt, sour cream, grated extra-sharp Cheddar, eggs, Worcestershire, nutmeg, pepper, and spinach, and spoon into a 9x13-inch baking dish. (Or, as a richer alternative, sprinkle the optional 2½ cups grated sharp cheese in a single layer on the bottom of the baking dish and proceed.) Refrigerate, if desired.

4. To serve, let come to room temperature and bake at 350 degrees for about 40 minutes, until the filling is set and the mixture is firm. Allow to rest for about 10 minutes if serving warm. Serve warm or at room temperature.

yield: 30 squares for hors d'oeuvres; serves 8 as a side dish

phyllo with various fillings

It isn't difficult to work with phyllo, but you must be quick and you must follow directions; otherwise you will end up with scraps of dough that have turned to papyrus.

Try to buy phyllo that has never been frozen, available in Greek markets; it is much easier to work with. If you can find handmade phyllo, it is the best of all. If you use frozen phyllo, defrost it overnight in the refrigerator. Leftover phyllo that has never been frozen can be frozen and used later. For the recipes with smaller yields you will have leftover phyllo.

If you don't own one, it would be well worth your while to obtain a 2½- or 3-inch pastry brush or unused paintbrush for buttering the phyllo sheets. It will cut your preparation time virtually in half.

> 1 pound fresh phyllo dough or completely defrosted frozen phyllo dough
> ¼ to ¾ pound (1 to 3 sticks) unsalted butter, depending on the number of pastries you are making
> 1 recipe filling (pages 37–38)

1. About 2 hours before starting, remove the plastic-wrapped phyllo from its box and bring to room temperature. Adjust racks to the middle shelves in the oven.

2. Preheat the oven to 400 degrees. Melt the butter. Remove the plastic wrapper from the phyllo sheets. Unroll, lay out on a sheet of wax paper, and cover with a damp cloth to protect from drying. Be sure to cover unused phyllo with the damp cloth each time you use a sheet.

3. On a work surface, lay out a sheet of phyllo, short sides at your left and right. Lightly brush the phyllo with melted butter and fold in half from left to right like a book. Lightly brush the top of the "book" with melted butter. Cut the double layer of phyllo into 3 equal long strips from top to bottom (see illustration on page 38). Each strip will be about 12 inches long and approximately 2½ inches wide.

4. Place 2 to 3 teaspoons of filling on the bottom of each strip (you'll know better how much to use after you fold a few). Fold one corner diagonally over the filling to make a triangle, and continue folding "flag style" until the strip is all folded. Just tuck any excess underneath. Place, seam side down, on cookie sheets.

5. Continue to make triangles in this manner, using additional phyllo sheets, until all the filling is used. Lightly brush the tops of the pastries with melted butter and bake about 10 minutes, or until the tops are golden brown. Let cool; wrap well, and refrigerate or freeze.

6. To serve, let the pastries defrost if frozen, and preheat the oven to 325 degrees. Reheat for about 10 minutes, until bubbly. Serve warm.

seafood and basil filling

¼ pound cooked and peeled shrimp
¼ pound crabmeat, picked through
   for shells and cartilage
9 large fresh basil leaves
6 ounces cream cheese

½ cup freshly grated Parmigiano-
   Reggiano cheese
2 tablespoons dry sherry
Freshly grated nutmeg to taste

Place the shrimp in a food processor fitted with the metal blade and pulse until chopped. Place in a bowl, along with the crabmeat, and set aside. Put the basil in the processor bowl and pulse until minced. Add the cream cheese, Parmigiano-Reggiano, sherry, and nutmeg to taste. Pulse to mix well and stir into the crab and shrimp mixture.

yield: filling for about 3 to 4 dozen pastries

goat cheese and prosciutto filling

½ pound medium-sharp soft goat
   cheese
3 tablespoons cream cheese
½ cup large-curd cottage cheese
2 teaspoons chopped fresh thyme or
   ¾ teaspoon dried

Freshly ground black pepper to taste
2 eggs
¼ pound prosciutto, sliced thin, cut
   into ⅛-inch-wide strips and then into
   ½-inch pieces

In a food processor, whirl the cheeses with the thyme, pepper, and eggs until smooth. Stir in the prosciutto.

yield: filling for about 3 dozen pastries

tiropetas (cheese filling)

The traditional Greek filling.

½ pound good-quality feta cheese
8 ounces (scant 1 cup) large-curd cottage cheese
¼ cup freshly grated Parmigiano-Reggiano cheese

2 eggs
2 tablespoons finely chopped parsley
Freshly ground black pepper to taste

⅛ to ¼ teaspoon nutmeg

With a fork, cream together the feta, cottage cheese, and Parmigiano-Reggiano. Add the eggs, one at a time, beating until smooth. Mix in the parsley, pepper, and nutmeg.

yield: filling for about 6 dozen pastries

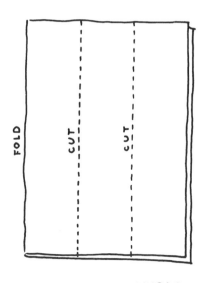

CUT PHYLLO INTO THIRDS
FROM TOP TO BOTTOM.

PLACE FILLING
ON BOTTOM
OF STRIP.

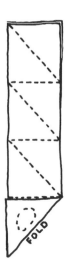

CONTINUE FOLDING
FLAG-STYLE UNTIL
ALL OF THE STRIP
IS FOLDED.

FINISHED
TRIANGLE

*⃞2 *sausage and mushroom filling*

Now here's how to make a vast quantity of phyllo pastries. You'll need some time, but once you start it's easy.

What has changed from my original recipe is the kind of sausage used: before it was pork, now it is turkey or chicken with much less fat and just as much flavor.

You could use Neufchâtel in place of full-fat cream cheese. It has a little less fat, but after all, how many of these are you going to eat?

Using phyllo sheets that are about 13 inches at the narrow end, you will have about 100 triangles. You will need a little more than 1 pound of phyllo.

1¾ pounds Italian chicken or turkey sausage
¼ pound hot Italian chicken or turkey sausage
½ cup minced shallots or green onions
2 pounds fresh white mushrooms

2 tablespoons olive oil
2 (8-ounce) packages cream cheese, softened and broken up into pieces
Salt and freshly ground black pepper to taste

1. Remove the sausage meat from the casings and sauté it until it is no longer pink; process in a food processor to break up; place in a bowl. Clean the processor bowl.

2. With the processor on, put the shallots through the feed tube, process, and measure. Wash, trim, dry, and halve the mushrooms and process in the food processor to mince. Place the mushrooms in a towel and squeeze dry. Sauté them and the shallots in hot olive oil until the liquid evaporates.

3. Combine the sausage meat with the mushroom mixture and the cream cheese and stir well to blend completely. Season with salt and pepper to taste.

yield: about 100

chafing dish meatballs

This is a direct quote from the first *Elegant but Easy:* "Probably the most popular hors d'oeuvre in the book." The recipe is reprinted just as it first appeared.

Well, no one is perfect, and it's included to prove how far we have come. It's not that sweet and sour meatballs aren't tasty, albeit cloyingly sweet. But grape jelly!

When Susan Simon, who worked on many of the recipes and read the manuscript, saw this recipe, she wrote this note in the margin: "I had the same recipe, too. And you're right—they were really popular."

2 pounds ground meat	1 (12-ounce) bottle chili sauce
1 slightly beaten egg	1 (10-ounce) jar grape jelly
1 large onion, grated	Juice of 1 lemon
Salt to taste	

1. Combine the meat, egg, onion, and salt, mix, and shape into small balls. Drop the balls into a sauce of chili sauce, grape jelly, and lemon juice. Simmer until brown. Refrigerate or freeze.

2. To serve bring to room temperature. Reheat in a chafing dish and serve with cocktail picks.

yield: 50 to 60 meatballs

cold

hors d'oeuvres

goat cheese marinated
in herbed olive oil

This is a twofer: you get marinated goat cheese and flavored olive oil, which can be used to dip toast in or for cooking other foods. The cheese also would be nice with a salad course.

1 cup extra-virgin olive oil
1 large clove garlic
10 whole black peppercorns
10 whole red peppercorns
1 teaspoon dried thyme

1 teaspoon dried rosemary
1 bay leaf
5 ounces plain, soft goat cheese log,
  regular or low-fat, cut in 5 slices

1. In a glass or plastic container with a cover, mix all the ingredients but the goat cheese. Then add the slices of cheese and cover. Refrigerate for 1 week.

2. To serve, let come to room temperature and serve the cheese with slices of toasted bread. You can also dip the toasted bread in the oil.

yield: 5 slices

brandied cheese roll

The logs taste better if made a few days ahead.
Don't use the food processor for this. It breaks down the cheese too much, and it won't get firm enough to hold its shape, even when refrigerated.

¾ pound Roquefort cheese, at room temperature
½ pound cream cheese, at room temperature

3 tablespoons brandy
2 cups finely chopped walnuts or toasted pecans

1. Using an electric mixer, beat the Roquefort cheese until creamy. Add the cream cheese and continue beating until smooth. Mix in the brandy.

2. Divide the mixture in half: place each half on a sheet of plastic wrap and form them into 2 roughly shaped logs, 1½ to 2 inches in diameter. Wrap tightly and refrigerate until firm, at least an hour.

3. When they are firm enough, roll each wrapped log back and forth on the counter to shape a more perfect log. Unwrap and roll in the nuts. Once again wrap tightly and refrigerate for at least several hours. Serve at room temperature either whole as a spread or sliced into rounds to put atop crackers or bread, or spread the mixture on crackers or bread, pop under the broiler a few minutes, and serve warm.

yield: about 24 rounds

roquefort almond spread

What's different about this new version is the seasonings, which offer a more interesting blending of flavors. You can also use some other good blue cheese like Gorgonzola or Stilton in place of the Roquefort.

In the new version the almonds are not added until the last minute so that they will not become soggy.

4 ounces Roquefort cheese, at room temperature
½ cup grated mild or medium-sharp white Cheddar cheese

1 cup light or regular sour cream
2 teaspoons lemon juice
2 teaspoons dry sherry
½ cup toasted slivered almonds

1. In a food processor blend the Roquefort, Cheddar, sour cream, lemon juice, and sherry. Refrigerate.

2. To serve, let come to room temperature and stir in the almonds; serve with little toasts or plain crackers.

yield: 2 cups

cheese crisps or frico

This is a fabulous hors d'oeuvre or a garnish for a salad or a soup—fried cheese. You can use other kinds of cheese for this, but if the cheese is aged and quite dry, it is easier to work with.

2 cups coarsely grated Parmigiano-Reggiano

Nonstick pan spray

1. Heat a nonstick pan, spray with nonstick spray, and sprinkle on ¼ of the cheese (½ cup) in a single even layer to form an 8-inch circle. Cook over low heat until the mixture melts and browns on the bottom; using a spatula, carefully lift the circle and flip it over. Continue cooking to brown on the second side. If it isn't perfectly shaped, it doesn't matter.

2. Remove from the pan to paper towels and allow to harden. Wipe out the pan and repeat. You only need to use pan spray once. If you are not using immediately, break the circles into jagged pieces, whatever size you wish, and wrap in aluminum foil, leaving at room temperature overnight if desired. Serve as an hors d'oeuvre or as a garnish for soups or salads.

yield: 24 or more pieces, depending on size

molded guacamole

Okay, so I slipped in a couple of molded salads (but no Jell-O). This creamy, savory green mixture always wins compliments.

To unmold a dish with gelatin, run some hot water into the sink; run a sharp knife around the edge of the molded dish. Quickly dip the mold into the hot water and twist back and forth until the mold is free of the sides. All of this must be done with speed or the gelatin will start to melt.

1 envelope unflavored gelatin
½ cup cold water
3 ripe, medium avocados
¼ cup finely minced onion
⅓ cup dry sherry
⅓ cup light sour cream

3 tablespoons lemon or lime juice
½ to 1 whole jalapeño, seeded and
  finely minced
2 tablespoons chopped cilantro
Salt to taste

1. Soften the gelatin in the cold water; then dissolve completely over low heat. Let cool to room temperature.

2. Coarsely mash the avocados and mix with the gelatin, onion, sherry, sour cream, lemon juice, jalapeño, cilantro, and salt. Spoon into a three-cup mold; cover and chill until firm, or overnight. To serve, unmold and serve with crackers or tortilla chips, or toasted pita bread that has been cut into small wedges.

yield: about 2½ cups

guac on the wild

When I first saw this recipe of Lois's my reaction was: why would anyone want guacamole that wasn't real guacamole? The answer, of course, was because this is lower in fat. Which is not *always* a good reason. Out of curiosity I tried it and found it very good. And, because it has lime juice, it doesn't turn brown when it is refrigerated overnight!

1 (10-ounce) package frozen peas, cooked and drained
1 ripe avocado, peeled and cubed
½ cup regular or light sour cream
¼ cup chopped green onions
2 tablespoons chopped cilantro
2 tablespoons lime juice
½ to 1 whole jalapeño pepper, seeded and coarsely chopped
1 small clove garlic, halved
Salt and freshly ground black pepper to taste

1. Place the peas, avocado, sour cream, green onions, cilantro, lime juice, jalapeño, garlic, salt, and pepper in a food processor and process until smooth.

2. Refrigerate, well covered, overnight, if desired. Serve with tortilla chips (the baked variety if you want to keep the dish low in fat).

yield: about 2 cups

hummus

I n the Middle East, hummus would be placed on the table at the beginning of dinner with a number of other small dishes to be sampled before the main course. In America we serve it as an hors d'oeuvre.

2 large cloves garlic	½ teaspoon ground cumin
1 (15-ounce) can garbanzos or chick-peas, drained and well rinsed	¼ teaspoon ground coriander
	Few sprinkles cayenne (optional)
2 tablespoons sesame paste	2 tablespoons minced parsley
¼ cup water	Lemon wedges and black Greek,
3 tablespoons lemon juice	Italian, or French olives for
1 teaspoon reduced-sodium soy sauce	garnish

1. With the food processor running, put the garlic through the feed tube and process to mince.

2. Add the garbanzos, sesame paste, water, lemon juice, soy sauce, cumin, and coriander, and the cayenne, if using, and process until the mixture is a well-blended paste. Refrigerate.

3. To serve, let the hummus come to room temperature and mix in the parsley. Decorate with lemon wedges and olives. Serve with warm pita wedges.

yield: 1⅓ cups

black bean dip

The rich and complex flavors of this dip are part of the enormous and delicious influence Mexico has had on American cooking.

1 medium onion (about 8 ounces), finely chopped
2 teaspoons olive oil
2 large cloves garlic, minced
3 cups cooked black beans—about 1½ cups dried beans or 2 (15-ounce) cans low-sodium black beans, rinsed and drained

1 tablespoon lime juice
2 tablespoons distilled white vinegar
1 teaspoon ground coriander
1 teaspoon cumin
½ to 1 whole serrano or jalapeño chile, trimmed, seeded, and coarsely chopped
Freshly ground black pepper to taste

1. Sauté the onion in hot oil in a nonstick pan until the onion softens. Add the garlic and cook for 30 seconds. Add the contents of the pan and the black beans, lime juice, vinegar, coriander, cumin, serrano pepper, and black pepper to a food processor and process to make a smooth paste. Add a little water if the mixture is too thick.

2. Refrigerate overnight to let the flavors meld. Serve with baked tortilla chips.

yield: about 2 to 2½ cups

olive lover's spread

This is a variation on olivada, an olive pesto beloved by Italians. You can also use it as a relish with grilled meats, fish, and poultry, and over any kind of pasta. But best of all, you can use it as an hors d'oeuvre. If you love olives you will love this.

1 large clove garlic, minced
3 tablespoons extra-virgin olive oil
2 cups pitted black and green Italian, French, Greek, and Moroccan olives (Gaeta, Kalamata, Nyons, Picholine, or others)
2 teaspoons grated lemon zest

1 teaspoon lemon juice
Freshly ground black pepper to taste
2 large roasted red peppers (page 183), coarsely chopped
Black pumpernickel rounds or squares OR crusty country bread

1. Sauté the garlic in 1 tablespoon of the olive oil for about 30 seconds, until the garlic is barely brown. Place the garlic, olives, lemon zest, and lemon juice in a food processor and pulse until the mixture forms a coarse paste.

2. Add the remaining 2 tablespoons of olive oil, the black pepper, and the roasted peppers and process until the mixture is blended. Refrigerate. To serve, let come to room temperature and spread on the bread.

yield: 1¾ to 2 cups

caponata

This flavor-filled mixture of finely cut sweet and tart vegetables is one of many variations of caponata.

The original recipe contained ¾ *cup* of oil.

2 medium eggplants
2 medium onions (about 1 pound), finely chopped
1 cup finely chopped celery (about 5 or 6 ounces)
3 tablespoons olive oil
2 large zucchini, scrubbed, trimmed, and finely chopped

1 cup coarsely chopped tomatoes (about 4 ounces)
¼ cup drained, chopped capers
¼ cup red wine vinegar
1 tablespoon sugar
3 tablespoons pine nuts
Freshly ground black pepper

1. Preheat the broiler and slice the eggplant into ½-inch-thick slices (do not peel) and arrange on cookie sheets. Spray both sides of the eggplant with pan spray and place the eggplant slices under the broiler. When the tops brown, in about 5 minutes, turn the slices and continue broiling until they begin to brown on the second side and have softened, another few minutes.

2. Sauté the onion and celery in the hot oil until the celery begins to soften. Add the zucchini and continue cooking a minute or two. Add the tomatoes, capers, vinegar, sugar, and pine nuts and continue to simmer.

3. Meanwhile, cut the broiled eggplant into small dice and stir into the mixture. Simmer a few minutes longer. Season with pepper to taste. Refrigerate or freeze. To serve, let the caponata come to room temperature and serve with small slices of black bread.

yield: 5 cups

tapenade with a difference

Tapenade is that Provençal spread that must contain olives, anchovy paste, and garlic. It often has a lot of other things, and here is one version with some of them. This is a very highly seasoned spread that would be wonderful in scooped-out cherry tomatoes or served spread thinly on slices of toasted baguette. It will keep for a week in the refrigerator.

1 clove garlic
1 medium-small onion (about 4 or 5 ounces), quartered
½ cup coarsely chopped parsley
6½- to 7-ounce can white meat tuna in water, rinsed and drained
6 canned sardines, drained (optional)
½ cup sesame paste

1 cup pitted Kalamata olives
¼ cup lemon juice
Grated zest of 1 lemon
2 tablespoons capers
1 tablespoon anchovy paste
1 tablespoon chopped fresh thyme or 1 teaspoon dried thyme

With the food processor running, put the garlic and onion through the feed tube. Turn off the processor; add the parsley, tuna, sardines, if using, sesame paste, olives, lemon juice, lemon zest, capers, anchovy paste, and thyme and process until well blended. Refrigerate and serve with thin toast or bread sticks, or as a filling for cherry tomatoes.

yield: 2¾ cups

variations on bruschetta

Bruschetta is toasted garlic bread with a variety of toppings. Below are three versions. One of each of these makes a nice first course.

The bread
18 slices of baguette-size bread,
   preferably a good peasant bread,
   but French baguettes will do

Extra-virgin olive oil
2 large cloves garlic

1. Lightly brush one side of each slice of bread with olive oil. Toast the bread on the side spread with the oil.

2. Cut the garlic in half and rub a cut side of the garlic on the toasted side of the bread while it is still warm. Set aside, covered, at room temperature.

3. To serve, refresh the bread: in a toaster oven place the slices of bread upside down so that the toasted tops are on the bottom and the untoasted sides are on the top, and toast. When the slices are warm, remove from the toaster oven and top the garlic-rubbed side with your choice of toppings.

yield: 18 bruschetta

mozzarella topping

1 pound fresh mozzarella
1 teaspoon hot red pepper flakes
3 cloves garlic
¼ cup olive oil
8 large leaves fresh basil, plus 18

small leaves fresh basil for
   garnish
Salt and freshly ground black pepper
   to taste
6 slices very thinly sliced prosciutto

1. Slice the mozzarella ½ inch thick and place in a shallow bowl. Sprinkle with the red pepper flakes. Slice the garlic into slivers and add to the bowl along with the olive oil, large basil leaves, and salt and pepper. Cover and refrigerate overnight.

2. To serve, top the refreshed slices of bread: cut up the prosciutto to fit the pieces of toast and arrange on top of each slice. Drain the mozzarella, cut to fit the bread slices, and place on top of the prosciutto. Garnish each with a small leaf of basil.

yield: 18 bruschetta

white bean topping

1 (15-ounce) can cannellini beans, rinsed in hot water and drained
1 large clove garlic, finely chopped
1 tablespoon finely chopped fresh rosemary

2 tablespoons extra-virgin olive oil
1 teaspoon balsamic vinegar
¼ teaspoon hot red pepper flakes

1. Mash the beans coarsely and stir in the garlic, rosemary, olive oil, vinegar, and hot pepper flakes. Cover and refrigerate overnight.

2. To serve, top the refreshed slices of the toasted bread with the bean mixture. (If there is more topping than bread, have it as a snack!)

yield: 18 bruschetta

tomato topping

One of the few instances where uncooked tomatoes taste wonderful after they have been cut up and refrigerated overnight.

1¼ pounds ripe plum tomatoes, seeded and chopped
1 small clove garlic, minced
1 tablespoon extra-virgin olive oil
1½ teaspoons balsamic vinegar

1 teaspoon chopped fresh thyme
3 large basil leaves, julienned
Salt and freshly ground black pepper to taste

1. Combine all of the ingredients; cover and refrigerate.

2. To serve, reheat toast as directed, top with the tomato mixture, and serve immediately.

yield: 18 bruschetta

smoked trout mousse

1 apple, peeled, quartered, and
  cored
2 (8-ounce) smoked trout, skinned and
  boned
2 tablespoons chopped green onions
⅛ teaspoon nutmeg
White pepper to taste

2 teaspoons chopped fresh dill plus
  additional dill for garnish
1 package unflavored gelatin
4 tablespoons cold water
1½ cups regular or light sour cream
1 tablespoon lemon juice

1. Finely chop the apple in a food processor. Remove about half of it and set it aside. Add the trout, green onions, nutmeg, pepper, and the 2 teaspoons of chopped dill to the food processor and process to make a smooth paste.

2. Sprinkle the gelatin over 1 tablespoon of cold water to soften. Add the 3 remaining tablespoons of water and dissolve the gelatin over very low heat. Add the gelatin, sour cream, and lemon juice to the trout mixture and process to combine thoroughly. Taste. If you prefer more apple taste, add some of the reserved apple.

3. Spoon the mixture into a decorative 3-cup mold or ring mold, cover, and refrigerate to jell. To unmold, run a knife around the edge. Fill the sink with hot water. Hold the mold in the water for a few seconds, shaking it until the mousse pulls away from the sides of the mold. Unmold on a serving dish and surround with melba toast. Sprinkle the top with more chopped dill.

yield: 2½ cups

nova scotia mousse

A favorite that has never been out of favor since it was published in 1970 in *Come for Cocktails, Stay for Supper.*

Only the smallest changes have been made. The red caviar has been eliminated. Enough is enough. I've tried this with reduced-fat cream cheese and light sour cream and the results are just as good. Half-and-half has replaced the light cream but, you know, I bet you could use milk instead. Of course, you could use heavy cream, too.

This makes a lovely first course on a bed of soft greens.

1 envelope unflavored gelatin
¼ cup cold water
½ cup half-and-half
1 clove garlic
2 tablespoons coarsely chopped red onion
1 (8-ounce) package light or regular cream cheese
1 cup light or regular sour cream
1 tablespoon prepared white horse-radish
1 teaspoon Worcestershire sauce
Few sprinkles cayenne pepper
1 teaspoon lemon juice
1 tablespoon finely chopped parsley
½ pound smoked salmon, coarsely chopped
½ cup pitted, coarsely chopped oil-cured olives

1. Sprinkle the gelatin over the cold water to soften.

2. Heat the half-and-half, stir in the softened gelatin, and stir to dissolve.

3. With the food processor running, put the garlic and onion through the feed tube to chop. Add the cream cheese, sour cream, horseradish, Worcestershire, cayenne, and lemon juice, and process until smooth. Stir in the gelatin mixture.

4. Stir in the parsley, salmon, and olives, pour into a 3-cup mold, and refrigerate, covered, until firm, at least a couple of hours but as long as 2 days. To serve, unmold onto a plate and serve with small, thin slices of pumpernickel or rye bread.

yield: 3 cups, serves 8 to 10 as a first course

pickled shrimp

½ cup virgin olive oil
½ cup red wine vinegar
2 tablespoons capers
2½ teaspoons celery seed
⅛ to ¼ teaspoon hot red pepper
  flakes

4 bay leaves
1 large clove garlic, sliced
2 pounds cooked, peeled medium or
  large shrimp
1 large onion (about 12 ounces),
  thinly sliced into rings

1. In a large nonreactive bowl, whisk the oil and vinegar together; stir in the capers, celery seed, hot pepper flakes, bay leaves, and garlic.

2. Stir in the shrimp and the onion rings; cover and marinate the shrimp for at least a day, stirring occasionally. To serve, drain, arrange on a platter, and provide toothpicks.

yield: about 4 dozen shrimp, depending on size

shrimp dip

This used to be called fruit of the sea, but the only fruit of the sea in this recipe is shrimp. I added more shrimp, more onion, lemon juice, and Worcestershire sauce, and eliminated the cream. I've tried it with light mayonnaise and regular mayonnaise, and one is as good as the other.

⅔ cup light or regular mayonnaise
¼ cup chili sauce
1 tablespoon grated onion
1 tablespoon Worcestershire sauce

2 tablespoons lemon juice
2 tablespoons drained pickle relish
2 tablespoons catsup
1 pound cooked shrimp, finely cut up

1. Combine the mayonnaise, chili sauce, onion, Worcestershire, lemon juice, pickle relish, and catsup in a nonreactive bowl. Stir in the shrimp and mix thoroughly.

2. Refrigerate, if desired. Serve with crackers, vegetable chips, or potato chips.

yield: 2½ cups

mollie dickenson's caviar pie

The first time I met this pie, it was made with hard-cooked eggs, mayonnaise, and full-fat sour cream and cream cheese. It was gobbled up by all the guests present each time it was served. I asked my friend Mollie for the recipe, and she gave me her new low-fat version. I have taken a few liberties with it, but when I served it to several people, including Mollie and her husband, Jim, it was a huge hit, just as good as the full-fat version.

2 teaspoons olive oil
3 whole eggs, lightly beaten
4 egg whites, lightly beaten
Juice of ½ lemon plus 1 tablespoon
1 cup chopped green onions (about 1 bunch)
1 (8-ounce) package light or regular cream cheese, at room temperature

⅔ cup light sour cream
1 (4-ounce) jar black whitefish caviar (or sturgeon caviar if you are feeling flush)
Lemon wedges and parsley for garnish

1. Heat the oil in a nonstick pan and scramble the eggs and egg whites. Spoon them into a shallow serving bowl. Squeeze the juice from the ½ lemon over the eggs. Sprinkle the green onions over the eggs.

2. Beat the cream cheese and sour cream together with the 1 tablespoon of lemon juice and spread over the eggs and green onions, using a combination of a spatula and your fingers. Cover and chill for at least 1 hour, but overnight is fine, too.

3. To serve, spread the caviar evenly over the cheese mixture. Garnish with the lemon wedges and decorate with parsley. Serve with thin, unsalted crackers.

yield: 8 servings

gravlax with mustard sauce or horseradish cream

Nothing has been changed in this fabulous recipe for marinated salmon except the mustard sauce. There, instead of using 6 tablespoons of oil, only 2 are really needed.

Great for brunch or as a first course at dinner. If you like, you can serve the gravlax and sauces on a bed of arugula. If you have the time, make both sauces and drizzle a little of each on the gravlax.

2½ pounds center-cut fresh salmon, skinned
4 teaspoons sugar
4 teaspoons salt
5 teaspoons coarsely ground black pepper

2 large bunches dill, coarsely cut (reserve 12 sprigs for serving)
2 lemons, thinly sliced
Mustard Sauce (recipe follows)
Horseradish Cream (recipe follows)

1. Cut the fish in half. Remove all the bones. Combine the sugar, salt, and pepper, and sprinkle over the top halves of the flesh. Sprinkle on the dill and place the two salmon halves flesh side together.

2. Place the fish in an enamel or glass container and cover tightly with plastic wrap. Put a brick or other heavy weight on top of the salmon and refrigerate for 3 to 4 days, turning the salmon occasionally.

3. To serve, remove the dill and scrape off the seasonings. Thinly slice the salmon, garnish with fresh dill and lemon slices, and serve with mustard sauce drizzled over the salmon, or with a dab of horseradish cream on the side.

yield: 12 servings

mustard sauce

2 tablespoons Dijon mustard
1 tablespoon sugar

2 tablespoons white vinegar
2 tablespoons canola oil

Mix the mustard with the sugar and vinegar; slowly whisk in the oil. Refrigerate until serving time. Let come to room temperature and drizzle over the gravlax.

horseradish cream

3 heaping tablespoons prepared
white horseradish, thoroughly
squeezed to remove liquid
1 tablespoon confectioners' sugar

½ teaspoon dry mustard
2 tablespoons white wine vinegar
Salt and white pepper to taste
1 cup heavy cream, whipped

1. Mix the horseradish, sugar, mustard, vinegar, salt, and pepper together.

2. Fold in the whipped cream and chill the sauce at least several hours or overnight before serving. Serve the gravlax with horseradish cream on the side.

note: This would also be delicious with grilled beef.

mozzarella, salmon, and basil pinwheels

The original recipe for this handsome presentation comes from the Villa d'Este, the magnificent hotel in Italy, and I served it at my daughter's wedding. There are always lots of oohs and ahhs.

The mozzarella must be fresh. Follow the directions for handling the cheese to the letter. And the better the salmon, the better the pinwheels.

This makes a handsome first course.

1 pound fresh, unsalted mozzarella
1 cup milk (whole, 2 percent, 1
   percent, or nonfat)

6 ounces smoked salmon, very thinly
   sliced
20 large basil leaves, plus additional
   basil leaves for garnish

1. Arrange two pieces of plastic wrap about 15 inches long on a counter, overlapping the sheets.

2. Dice the mozzarella and place it in a heavy-bottomed pot with the milk. Cook slowly over medium-low heat until the mozzarella begins to melt and all the pieces blend together into a mass. Stir often and watch carefully. *Immediately* remove the mozzarella from the milk with a slotted spoon and place directly on the plastic wrap, using your hands and the spoon.

3. Quickly spread the mozzarella into a thin rectangle, using your hands to shape it as long and thin as you can make it without creating holes. If there are any, fit pieces of mozzarella over them. And don't worry if there is milk around the edges or if the shape is irregular.

4. Arrange the salmon on top of the mozzarella, and arrange the basil leaves on top of and in between the salmon slices.

5. Roll up the mozzarella from the long side into a tight roll. Trim off the ragged edges. Wrap tightly in plastic, securing the ends, and refrigerate at least several hours or overnight.

6. To serve, slice into 28 to 32 pinwheels and arrange on a serving platter, decorating with additional basil leaves. To serve as a first course, arrange 3 or 4 pinwheels on each plate and decorate with the basil leaves.

yield: 28 to 32 slices

fish

There are a few things you should keep in mind when cooking fish.

For each fish recipe, the Canadian rule is invoked. It is a foolproof method for cooking fish that James Beard, the father of American cooking, popularized. Fish is measured at its thickest point. It is then cooked 8 to 10 minutes to the inch.

No form of fish should ever be cooked twice—that is, reheated. This form of protein is too delicate to survive that kind of treatment with taste and texture intact. So do all the preparation in advance and cook the fish just before serving.

If you wish to use the liquid in which a piece of fish, chicken, or meat has been marinated after the protein has been cooked, bring the marinade to a boil so that any bacteria that may have been on the raw protein will be killed.

Never put a cooked piece of fish, chicken, or meat back on the plate that held the raw product, and don't use a utensil that has been in contact with the raw product with anything that will not be cooked again.

See page 24 for information about stovetop grills.

scrod with sweet and sour peppers

2 tablespoons olive oil
1 pound onions (2 medium), sliced
 into ½-inch strips
3 pounds assorted red, yellow, orange,
 brown, or purple bell peppers, cored,
 seeded, and cut into ½-inch strips
2 tablespoons chopped fresh thyme or
 2 teaspoons dried
6 tablespoons balsamic vinegar

4 teaspoons sugar
½ cup water
1 ½ pounds scrod, monkfish, rockfish,
 or catfish fillets, about 6 ounces each
 fillet
Salt and freshly ground black pepper
 to taste
Chopped fresh parsley for garnish
 (optional)

1. Preheat a large nonstick skillet over high heat until the pan is hot. Pour the olive oil into the hot pan and reduce the heat to medium-high. Add the onion strips and sauté until they have just begun to soften and brown. Add the bell peppers and sauté 1 minute to coat well.

2. Reduce the heat to medium-low and stir in the thyme, vinegar, sugar, and water. Cover and cook 4 to 5 minutes, until the peppers are soft. Refrigerate.

3. To serve, reheat the onion and pepper mixture briefly. Wash and dry the fish fillets. Place the fish in the skillet, spoon the pepper-onion mixture over the fish, and cook until the fish is done, following the Canadian rule: Measure the fish at its thickest point and cook 8 to 10 minutes to the inch. Season with salt and pepper, sprinkle with chopped parsley, if desired, and serve at once.

yield: 4 servings

grilled salmon
and
tabbouleh salad

This recipe is adapted from a dish I ate at Meadowood, a gracious resort in St. Helena, California.

Though lemongrass is found increasingly in supermarkets, it is not easy to find everywhere. It is worth a trip to a Thai or Vietnamese grocery store to pick it up. It can be kept for months in the freezer.

To use the lemongrass, whose citrusy fragrance and flavor cannot be duplicated, cut the stem from the bulb and remove the tough outer leaves of the bulb. Use only the soft part of the bulb for this recipe.

2 cups coarse bulgur
6 cups water
4 bulbs lemongrass
2 tablespoons reduced-sodium soy sauce
2 tablespoons olive oil plus additional oil for brushing
6 (8-ounce) salmon fillets with skin on
¼ cup balsamic vinegar
1 teaspoon ground cumin
2 large shallots, minced

2 small cloves garlic, minced
¼ cup chopped chives
8 peeled baby carrots, finely sliced
2 stalks celery, finely diced
½ pound Kirby cucumbers, unpeeled, finely diced
Salt and freshly ground black pepper to taste
2 large ripe tomatoes (about 2 pounds)
12 leaves red leaf lettuce, washed and dried

1. Combine the bulgur with the water and boil for about 15 minutes, until the bulgur is tender. Meanwhile, finely slice the soft bulbs of the lemongrass, combine with the soy sauce and 1 tablespoon of the oil, and spoon over the salmon. Refrigerate.

2. Mix the remaining 1 tablespoon oil with the vinegar, cumin, shallots, garlic, and chives in a nonreactive bowl large enough to hold the bulgur and all the salad ingredients. Mix the carrots, celery, and cucumber and stir into the oil and vinegar dressing. When the bulgur is cooked, drain thoroughly and stir into the dressing. Season with salt and pepper. Refrigerate.

3. To serve, preheat the broiler or prepare a stovetop grill. Remove the salmon from the refrigerator 30 minutes before cooking and brush the flesh with oil. Broil or grill the salmon, skin side up first, following the Canadian rule: measure the fish at its thickest part and cook for a total of 8 to 10 minutes to the inch, turning once.

4. Meanwhile, chop the tomatoes and stir them into the dressed bulgur. Line a large shallow serving bowl with the lettuce leaves. Spoon the bulgur mixture into the center; cut each piece of salmon into 3 pieces and place on top of the bulgur.

yield: 6 servings

cold poached salmon with green coriander or dill mayonnaise

This dish, ideal for a summer buffet, can be served with either one or both of the sauces. If you are serving both sauces, halve those recipes. It makes an excellent first course.

3 pounds salmon fillet
½ bottle dry white wine
2 to 3 cups fish stock or broth

1 recipe Green Coriander Mayonnaise or 1 recipe Dill Mayonnaise or ½ recipe of each (recipes follow)

1. If you do not have a fish poacher or a large pan, cut the salmon into 2 or 3 pieces and place in a stovetop pan large enough to hold them without folding. Pour on the wine and stock, adding water if necessary to cover the fish. Place parchment paper or a double thickness of wax paper on top of the fish. Cover the pan and bring the liquid to a boil; reduce to a simmer and cook the fish according to the Canadian rule: measure the fish at its thickest point and cook 8 to 10 minutes to the inch.

2. The salmon will cook in about 10 to 12 minutes. Remove from the heat, uncover, and allow to cool in the liquid. Remove the skin; then cover the fish and chill overnight.

3. Serve with either one or both of the green sauces.

yield: 6 to 8 servings

green coriander mayonnaise

1 ounce young spinach leaves (1 cup firmly packed)
2 ounces parsley, stems removed (1 cup firmly packed)
2 medium cloves garlic
2 ounces cilantro (1½ cups firmly packed)

1½ teaspoons ground coriander seed
1 teaspoon lemon juice
1 cup light or regular mayonnaise
½ cup nonfat plain yogurt
Salt to taste

1. In a small pot, bring water to boil and blanch the spinach and parsley for 5 seconds. Drain and run under cold water; squeeze dry in a dishcloth.

2. In the food processor with the motor running, put the garlic through the feed tube and mince. Add the spinach, parsley, and cilantro and process to chop. Add the coriander, lemon juice, mayonnaise, and yogurt and process until the greens are well blended and the mayonnaise is bright green. Season with salt. Chill to meld the flavors, at least a couple of hours or overnight. Serve over the chilled salmon.

yield: 1½ cups

dill mayonnaise

1 large (8-ounce) bunch dill
1 cup light or regular mayonnaise

½ cup nonfat plain yogurt
Salt to taste

Wash and dry the dill and remove just the top greens from the stems. Process the greens in a food processor to chop. Add the mayonnaise and yogurt and process to chop the dill further and blend it into the mixture. Season with salt. Chill at least several hours or overnight. Serve over the chilled salmon.

yield: 1½ cups

red snapper veracruzana

Red snapper is the fish of choice in Veracruz, Mexico, where this dish originated. The combination of the cinnamon, olives, capers, and peppers gives the sauce heat and depth.

This is a quick, light dish, good with boiled potatoes or rice.

1 pound onions (2 medium), chopped
1 tablespoon olive oil
3 cloves garlic, minced
½ to 1 whole jalapeño or serrano pepper, seeded and minced
1 tablespoon chopped fresh oregano or 1 teaspoon dried
8 large Spanish or Italian green olives, pitted and chopped
⅛ teaspoon cinnamon
2 tablespoons capers, chopped if large (tiny ones can be left whole)
2½ cups peeled canned low-sodium tomatoes
1 bay leaf
1½ pounds red snapper, sea bass, halibut, or cod
Juice of 1 lime

1. In a nonstick pan, sauté the onions in hot oil until they begin to soften and color. When they color, add the garlic and jalapeño and cook for 30 seconds.

2. Add the oregano, olives, cinnamon, and capers to the onion mixture and stir. Squeeze the tomatoes between your fingers and add, with the bay leaf. Simmer for 10 minutes. Refrigerate.

3. To serve, wash the fish and squeeze the lime juice over it. Refrigerate for no more than 1 hour.

4. Reheat the sauce slowly. Arrange the fish in a large skillet, spoon the sauce over it, and cook according to the Canadian rule: measure the fish at its thickest part and allow 8 to 10 minutes to the inch. Remove the bay leaf and serve the fish with its sauce over boiled potatoes or rice.

yield: 4 servings

grilled swordfish with lemon-ginger marinade

The fish can be marinated in advance and cooked just before serving. This dish is full of flavor but very light.

Buy a thick piece of swordfish so that it can be cooked medium-rare.

1 tablespoon grated lemon zest	¼ cup minced green onions
2 tablespoons lemon juice	1 tablespoon coarsely grated ginger
¼ cup dry white wine	Freshly ground black pepper to
1 tablespoon olive oil	taste
1 tablespoon reduced-sodium soy sauce	2 pounds swordfish cut 1 inch thick

1. Combine the lemon zest, juice, wine, olive oil, soy sauce, green onions, ginger, and pepper for the marinade. Place the swordfish in a shallow, nonreactive container and cover with the marinade. Let stand for 3 to 4 hours or overnight in the refrigerator.

2. To serve, remove the fish from the marinade and pour the marinade into a small saucepan.

3. Using a stovetop grill, an outdoor grill, or a preheated broiler, cook the swordfish following the Canadian rule: measure the swordfish at its thickest point and cook it 8 to 10 minutes to the inch, brushing with the marinade occasionally. Turn once.

4. Meanwhile, bring the marinade to a boil and remove it from the heat. After the swordfish is cooked, spoon the remaining boiled marinade over it and serve.

yield: 4 to 6 servings

broiled sake-marinated sea bass

This superb light dish is from Terra, a restaurant in St. Helena, California. After eating it there, I adapted it for use in the *New York Times* and decided that it ought to be in this book, too. It may seem complicated, but almost all of it can be done in advance.

You will need access to a Japanese or Asian market to buy the shiso, wonderfully fragrant green leaves. Mirin (sweet rice wine) can often be found in the Asian food section of a good supermarket, and sake (rice wine) in a well-stocked liquor store. (See Mail Order, page 23, for some of the ingredients.) You can make the marinade and the soy mix two days ahead; marinate the sea bass one day ahead, and make the sauce one day ahead. All that has to be done before serving is to reheat the sauce and broil the fish.

Marinade
½ cup reduced-sodium soy sauce
¼ cup mirin
¼ cup sake
6 tablespoons sugar

1 teaspoon coarsely grated fresh ginger
1 teaspoon minced garlic

6 sea bass fillets, 6 to 7 ounces each

Soy mix
¼ cup reduced-sodium soy sauce
2½ tablespoons mirin
2½ tablespoons rice vinegar
¼ teaspoon minced garlic

¼ teaspoon grated ginger
1½ teaspoons sugar
¼ cup toasted sesame oil

Sauce
½ cup of the soy mix
1½ cups low-sodium chicken stock or broth
6 ounces washed, sliced shiitake mushrooms, stems removed

1 inch white part of leek, julienned
6 baby carrots, sliced into thin disks

Finishing the dish
3 ounces spinach leaves
1 tablespoon toasted white sesame seeds

2 tablespoons chopped chives
6 shiso leaves, sliced

1. Prepare the marinade: In a nonreactive bowl, mix the soy sauce, mirin, sake, sugar, ginger, and garlic. Place the sea bass in the marinade. Marinate overnight in the refrigerator.

2. Prepare the soy mix: In a nonreactive container, combine the soy sauce, mirin, vinegar, garlic, ginger, sugar, and oil, and refrigerate.

3. Prepare the sauce: Boil the ½ cup of soy mix and the chicken stock in a medium saucepan. Add the shiitake mushrooms, leek, and carrots and simmer for 1 to 1½ minutes. Refrigerate.

4. To serve, preheat the broiler. Remove the sea bass fillets from the marinade, pat dry, and place them on a jelly-roll pan. Broil for about 10 minutes, turning once. The top part of the sea bass should be golden brown.

   Reheat the sauce. Add the spinach and simmer 30 seconds.

   Divide the sauce among 6 serving bowls. Place a broiled sea bass fillet on top of the sauce in each bowl and sprinkle with the sesame seeds, chives, and shiso.

   yield: 6 servings

note: The little bit of leftover soy mix can be used on a small piece of fish for two another day.

grilled tuna with lemon and capers

This is a simple, light dish to put together for last-minute company.

3 large cloves garlic, minced
3 tablespoons drained and chopped capers
6 tablespoons lemon juice

1 ½ tablespoons olive oil
Freshly ground black pepper to taste
1 ½ pounds tuna steaks

1. Mix the garlic, capers, lemon juice, oil, and pepper. This can be done a day ahead and refrigerated, well covered, overnight.

2. To serve, place the tuna in a nonreactive bowl and marinate with the mixture for 1 hour only.

3. Preheat the broiler, or stovetop or outdoor grill, and grill the tuna, spooning the marinade over the fish as it cooks. Follow the Canadian rule: measure the tuna at its thickest point and cook 8 minutes to the inch for medium, less if you like rare tuna and more if you prefer it well done.

yield: 4 servings

spaghetti alla puttanesca

For those who are not anchovy fans, or to please the vegetarians in your midst, omit the anchovies and add 2 more tablespoons of capers and 6 more olives. This is Lois's version—a fast, light meal for unexpected guests.

4 cloves garlic, minced
3 tablespoons olive oil
½ cup minced fresh basil, plus additional basil for garnish
1 tablespoon chopped fresh oregano
2 pounds ripe tomatoes, chopped
½ cup chopped parsley
½ teaspoon hot red pepper flakes

Freshly ground black pepper to taste
2 dozen small black Italian, French, or Greek olives, pitted and chopped
¼ cup drained capers
1 (2-ounce) can flat anchovies, drained, patted dry, and minced
1 pound spaghetti

1. Sauté the garlic in hot oil without browning. Add the ½ cup minced basil and the oregano, tomatoes, parsley, and hot pepper flakes. Season with black pepper and bring to a boil. Add the olives, capers, and anchovies and simmer for 20 to 30 minutes. Refrigerate.

2. To serve, cook the spaghetti and slowly reheat the sauce. When the spaghetti is done, drain it and top with the sauce; garnish with the remaining fresh basil.

yield: 4 servings

shellfish

clam, corn, and potato chowder

Sometimes you want a very simple supper for your guests. A filling chowder like this with very good bread and salad to follow will fill the bill. This is a wonderful dish for summer, but if you want to make it when corn is not in season, use frozen corn kernels. Allow about 1 to 1½ cups frozen corn for every 2 ears.

½ cup chopped shallots
2 tablespoons unsalted butter
5 cups clam juice
1 quart water
4 medium potatoes, peeled and
cubed
1½ tablespoons chopped fresh thyme
or 1½ teaspoons dried thyme

6 ears fresh corn
1½ cups chopped clams
1 teaspoon sugar (optional, depending on sweetness of corn)
Freshly ground black pepper to
taste
¼ cup chopped parsley
½ cup chopped chervil

1. In a large pot, lightly brown the shallots in the butter. Add the clam juice, water, potatoes, and thyme and cook for about 10 minutes, until the potatoes are tender. Refrigerate.

2. To serve, scrape the kernels from the corn. Reheat the soup, add the corn, clams, and sugar, if using, and cook about 2 minutes. Season with pepper and add the parsley and chervil.

yield: 5 or 6 servings

maryland crab cakes

The best. Just crabmeat and seasonings, not a lot of fillers. Marylanders do make good crab cakes because there are wonderful blue crabs in our Chesapeake Bay. Just a few changes from the original in *The Summertime Cookbook* that have no effect on the flavor: only 1 whole egg, and light mayonnaise (if you choose) to replace full-fat mayonnaise. The crab cakes can be sautéed in olive oil, but there is a subtle difference in taste and I prefer butter.

This is also a fine first course or brunch dish, and it is very quick.

2 pounds backfin crabmeat
1 cup fine bread crumbs
6 tablespoons regular or light mayonnaise
2 tablespoons Dijon mustard
1 whole egg, lightly beaten

2 egg whites, lightly beaten
2 tablespoons minced parsley
2 teaspoons Worcestershire sauce
4 green onions, finely chopped
2 tablespoons unsalted butter

1. Pick over the crabmeat and remove any bits of shell and cartilage; lightly mix the crabmeat with the bread crumbs.

2. Mix the mayonnaise, mustard, egg, egg whites, parsley, Worcestershire sauce, and green onion and fold carefully into the crabmeat so that nice chunks of crabmeat remain.

3. Shape into 10 crab cakes, cover, and refrigerate.

4. To serve, heat the butter in a nonstick skillet and sauté the crab cakes on both sides until they are golden brown, about 4 minutes total. You may have to do them in two batches.

yield: 10 crab cakes; 5 servings

chesapeake crab

Marylanders love their crab and always have at least a half-dozen dishes that call for it. Here is an old favorite of mine that has been updated. Nice for brunch, made with either regular or light mayonnaise

¾ cup regular or light mayonnaise
1 tablespoon Worcestershire sauce
¼ cup finely chopped green pepper
¼ cup finely chopped onion
1 roasted red pepper (page 183), rinsed and chopped

2 teaspoons Dijon mustard
3 tablespoons dry sherry
1 egg, lightly beaten
1 pound lump or backfin crabmeat

1. Mix together the mayonnaise, Worcestershire, green pepper, onion, roasted red pepper, mustard, and sherry. Stir in the egg.

2. Pick over and remove the shell bits and cartilage from the crabmeat. Gently fold the crabmeat into the sauce mixture, leaving the lumps.

3. Spoon into an ovenproof casserole, cover, and refrigerate, if desired.

4. To serve, preheat the oven to 350 degrees and bake the uncovered casserole for 20 to 25 minutes, until bubbly and hot all the way through. Serve at once.

yield: 4 servings

shrimp fra diavolo

Easterners, particularly those who live in and around New York and Boston—if they are old enough—will remember an Italian dish we thought the most exotic thing we'd ever eaten: lobster fra diavolo. Lobster was cooked in its shell in a simple but spicy tomato sauce. No one knows who invented it—it was probably an Italian-American creation—and no one has ever figured out how to eat it without creating one godawful mess. But what a delicious mess!

Here's an easier and less expensive version made with shrimp. It is very quick and quite light.

2 cups chopped onion (about 10 ounces)
2 tablespoons olive oil
3 large cloves garlic, minced
4 cups canned Italian plum tomatoes
½ cup dry red wine
1 tablespoon fresh oregano or 1 teaspoon dried
½ teaspoon hot red pepper flakes, or more
1 pound fresh or dried linguine
1 pound large raw peeled shrimp
Freshly ground black pepper to taste

1. In a nonstick pan, sauté the onion in hot oil until it begins to soften. Add the garlic and sauté for 30 seconds. Then stir in the tomatoes, which should be crushed in your hand as you add them, and the wine, oregano, and hot pepper flakes. Cook over high heat until the mixture begins to thicken a little, just a few minutes.

2. Refrigerate. To serve, boil the water for the linguine and cook just al dente. Reheat the sauce until it is very hot; add the shrimp and cook 2 to 3 minutes, depending on the size of the shrimp. Season with black pepper and serve over the linguine.

yield: 4 servings

shrimp with feta, tomatoes, and fusilli

Like a number of other recipes in this book, this one comes from my "Plain and Simple" column in the *New York Times*. Those recipes are designed to be made very quickly and to be quite healthful. I have revised them for the book so that most of the work can be done in advance, with just a little work left for the last moment.

Feta is now available from Greece, Bulgaria, Israel, and locally. The Bulgarian is the strongest, the American the mildest. It's your choice.

2 tablespoons olive oil
4 cups chopped onion (about 20 ounces)
4 large cloves garlic, minced
4 pounds ripe plum tomatoes, coarsely chopped
1½ cups dry white wine
2 tablespoons minced Italian parsley

6 tablespoons minced fresh oregano or 2 tablespoons dried
1½ pounds dried fusilli
½ cup chopped fresh basil
3 pounds shelled raw shrimp
Salt and freshly ground black pepper to taste
2 tablespoons brandy
2½ cups crumbled feta cheese

1. Heat the oil in a nonstick pan large enough to hold all the sauce ingredients. Sauté the onion until it begins to soften and brown. Add the garlic and cook another 30 seconds. Add the tomatoes, wine, parsley, and oregano; reduce the heat and simmer, uncovered, until thickened, about 20 to 30 minutes. Refrigerate.

2. To serve, cook the pasta. Reheat the sauce until it is very hot. Then add the basil and the shrimp and cook 2 to 3 minutes, depending on the size of the shrimp. Season with salt and pepper. Heat the brandy; pour over the sauce and ignite. When the flames die, pour the sauce over the pasta and top with the crumbled feta.

yield: 8 servings

seafood stew over linguine

I t's easy, it's delicious, and it looks as if you went to a lot of trouble.

1 pound onions (2 medium), finely
  chopped
2 tablespoons olive oil
1 pound green peppers, seeded,
  cored, and finely chopped
2 stalks celery, finely chopped
2 cloves garlic, minced
2 pounds ripe plum tomatoes, coarsely
  cubed, or 6 cups canned drained
  tomatoes
2½ cups dry red wine
2 cups fish stock or clam juice
1 bay leaf

¼ cup tomato paste
4 teaspoons fresh thyme leaves or 1
  teaspoon dried thyme
¼ cup chopped Italian parsley
1 pound fresh spinach linguine
1 pound firm fillets of white fish such
  as black sea bass or cod, cut into
  large chunks
½ pound shrimp, shelled and left
  whole if small, or cut in half or thirds,
  depending on size
Freshly ground black pepper to
  taste

1. Sauté the onions in hot oil in a nonstick pan. When they have softened and started to brown, add the green peppers, celery, and garlic and continue cooking until the peppers and celery begin to soften. Add the tomatoes, wine, stock, bay leaf, tomato paste, thyme, and parsley and continue cooking for about 5 minutes. Refrigerate or freeze.

2. To serve, let the sauce defrost if frozen; bring the water for the pasta to a boil; reheat the sauce until very hot. Cook the pasta al dente. Add the fish and shrimp to the tomato mixture and cook for 2 or 3 minutes. Remove the bay leaf and serve the seafood stew over the linguine.

yield: 4 servings

seafood quiche

Described in the original *Elegant but Easy* as "Excellent! Lois's mother's best recipe." Even though it has been given a new no-roll crust, and the Swiss cheese has been changed to imported Gruyère, it is basically the same—only better.

   The biggest change in the recipe is that the quiche is partially baked, then refrigerated, and the baking finished just before serving. This prevents a soggy crust.

Crust

1½ cups unbleached flour
⅛ teaspoon salt
¼ pound (1 stick) unsalted butter

1 egg
2 tablespoons ice water

Filling

½ pound imported Gruyère cheese,
   cut into slices ⅛ inch thick
1 cup fresh crabmeat, picked over
   carefully to remove bits of shell and
   cartilage
½ cup cooked, shelled shrimp, cut in
   small pieces
1½ cups light cream
4 eggs, beaten

2 tablespoons butter, melted and
   cooled
2 tablespoons dry sherry
1 tablespoon flour
⅛ teaspoon salt
Freshly ground black pepper to taste
Few dashes cayenne pepper or to
   taste
¼ teaspoon nutmeg

1. The crust can be made a day or two ahead and refrigerated, or it can be frozen and defrosted before use. Blend the flour, salt, and butter, using a pastry blender or your fingers to make a crumbly mixture. Whisk the egg and ice water together and add to the flour mixture, blending until the pastry is smooth and holds together in a ball.

2. Pull pieces of dough from the ball and press them evenly over the bottom and sides of a 10-inch pie plate, using the heel of your hand. Be sure the dough is not too thick around the bottom edge. Don't worry about the patching: none of it will show when baked.

3. Preheat the oven to 375 degrees. Adjust a rack to the lower third of the oven.

4. Prepare the filling: Line the unbaked shell with slices of cheese. Cover with the crabmeat and shrimp. Thoroughly mix the cream, eggs, butter, and sherry. Stir a little of this liquid into the flour to make a paste. Return the paste mixture to the cream mixture and

mix well. Season with the salt, black pepper, cayenne, and nutmeg and pour the mixture over the seafood.

5. Bake for about 30 minutes, until the filling is almost set. Let cool and refrigerate as long as overnight.

6. To serve, preheat the oven to 375 degrees and let the quiche come to room temperature. Bake for 15 to 20 minutes longer, until the center is set. Remove from the oven and let the quiche stand for 20 minutes before serving.

yield: 8 servings as a main dish, 14 servings as a first course

shrimp and black beans with orzo

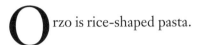rzo is rice-shaped pasta.

¾ cup dried black beans or 1 (15-ounce) can, rinsed and drained

⅔ cup orzo

1 tablespoons plus 2 teaspoons olive oil

½ pound red onions, chopped into ¼-inch dice (about 1⅔ cups)

5 ounces yellow bell pepper, cored, seeded, and chopped into ½-inch dice (about 1 cup)

1 large clove garlic, minced

⅓ cup currants

¼ cup dry red wine

3 tablespoons balsamic vinegar

¼ cup freshly squeezed lemon juice

2½ teaspoons ground cumin

Salt and freshly ground black pepper to taste

¾ pound cooked, peeled shrimp

2 tablespoons chopped fresh parsley or thyme

1. Rinse the dried beans. Soak overnight in enough water to cover the beans by 2 inches. Drain. Place the beans in a pot of water, bring slowly to a boil, and cook until tender.

2. Cook the orzo al dente. Rinse and drain.

3. Heat a medium-size nonstick skillet over high heat until very hot. Reduce the heat; add 1 tablespoon of the olive oil and the chopped onion. Sauté until the onion softens and begins to brown. Add the pepper and cook a few minutes, until the pepper is not quite fork-tender. Then add the garlic and sauté 30 seconds more. Stir in the currants and red wine. Reduce the heat to a simmer, cover the pan, and cook until the vegetables are tender, just a few minutes longer. Set aside to cool.

4. In a large serving bowl, combine the balsamic vinegar, lemon juice, cumin, and the remaining 2 teaspoons of olive oil. Add the beans, orzo, and cooked vegetables. Season with salt and freshly ground pepper. Refrigerate, if desired.

5. To serve, add the shrimp and let sit at room temperature for 30 minutes. Sprinkle with chopped parsley or thyme.

yield: 4 to 6 servings

note: Three-quarters of a cup of dried beans produces about 2 cups of cooked beans, about ½ cup more than the contents of a 15-ounce can. Reserve ½ cup of the home-cooked beans for another use. Or you can cook a larger amount and freeze what you don't use. Cooked beans freeze very well.

lemon-dill seafood salad

Ideal for supper or lunch on a warm day.
  The lemon mayonnaise and the yogurt dill sauce are delicious on their own, over grilled or poached seafood or chicken.

Salad base
1 cup dry white wine or vermouth
1 bay leaf

1 ½ pounds raw, peeled medium
  shrimp
1 ½ pounds bay or calico scallops

Lemon mayonnaise
1 cup low-fat or light mayonnaise
¼ cup freshly squeezed lemon juice
1 teaspoon finely grated lemon zest

2 teaspoons Dijon mustard
1 teaspoon dry mustard
Few shakes of cayenne pepper

Yogurt-dill sauce
¾ cup plain low-fat yogurt
¼ cup minced fresh dill, plus some
  extra sprigs for garnish
2 tablespoons minced green onions
1 small clove garlic, minced

2 teaspoons freshly squeezed lemon
  juice
Few shakes of cayenne pepper

Salad greens of your choice

1. To poach the shrimp and scallops: Put the wine and bay leaf in a large shallow skillet. Bring to a gentle simmer. Add the shrimp, scallops, and a little water if necessary; the liquid should almost but not totally cover the seafood. Cover the pan. (If you don't have a lid, cut a wax paper or parchment circle the diameter of the pan, make a ½-inch hole in the center, and place it directly on top of the seafood.) Bring the liquid back to a gentle simmer and cook just until the shrimp are barely pink and the scallops feel slightly springy. This will only take about a minute. Remove the pan from the heat and allow the seafood to cool in the cooking liquid for 10 to 15 minutes, so it will pick up flavor. Drain thoroughly, remove the bay leaf, and refrigerate while making the dressings.

2. To make the lemon mayonnaise, whisk together the mayonnaise, lemon juice, zest, mustards, and cayenne in a small bowl until smooth. Adjust the seasoning and set aside.

3. To make the yogurt dill sauce: In a medium bowl, combine the yogurt, minced dill, green onions, garlic, lemon juice, and cayenne for the yogurt dill sauce. Adjust the seasonings. Add the lemon mayonnaise to the dill sauce and blend well.

4. In a large bowl combine the poached seafood with some of the lemon dill sauce. Don't feel obligated to use all the sauce. Start by dressing the salad lightly, taste, and add more sauce to taste. (If there is extra sauce, it will keep for a day or two.) Refrigerate, covered, until serving time.

5. To serve, arrange the greens of your choice on plates, with the seafood mixture on top. Garnish with fresh dill sprigs.

> *yield: 6 to 8 servings as dinner, 8 to 10 as lunch, 10 to 12 as a first course*

germaine's scallop salad

Germaine Swanson serves this at her fine Washington restaurant, Germaine's. I love this dish so much that it was the first course at my daughter Ann's wedding. This is excellent for a buffet, lunch, or first course.

2 pounds bay scallops, cleaned and rinsed
¾ cup lemon juice
Freshly ground white pepper to taste
¼ cup vegetable oil
3 tablespoons white wine vinegar
1 clove garlic

1 small onion, quartered
¾ teaspoon sugar
2¼ teaspoons Dijon mustard
¼ cup chopped fresh dill
6 cups shredded iceberg lettuce
30 snow peas, blanched and halved
5 tablespoons pine nuts

1. Combine the scallops, lemon juice, and white pepper in a large glass bowl. Cover and marinate for at least 2 hours or overnight in the refrigerator.

2. In a blender or food processor, combine the oil, vinegar, garlic, onion, sugar, mustard, and 2 tablespoons of the dill, and purée until smooth. Refrigerate.

3. To serve, drain the scallops of their marinade and mix them with the dressing. Arrange the shredded lettuce on a serving plate and spoon the scallops and dressing over the lettuce. Trim with the snow peas and sprinkle with the remaining 2 tablespoons dill and the pine nuts.

yield: 8 servings

chicken

chicken cacciatore

In the original *Elegant but Easy*, this recipe called for canned tomato sauce and onions that had not been browned. It used an assortment of herbs. For a pure, simple, and fresh-tasting dish with robust old-fashioned flavor, this version is superior. You may need two pans for this amount of chicken; it would make sense to cook the breasts in one pan and the thighs in another. You could also do this in batches. If you're concerned about fat and calories, just don't eat the skin. Serve the cacciatore with spaghetti.

¼ cup olive oil
3 cups thinly sliced onions, about 1 pound
4 cloves garlic, thinly sliced
6 pounds bone-in chicken breasts and thighs (in any ratio you prefer)

Salt and freshly ground black pepper to taste
1 cup dry red wine
4 cups low-sodium canned Italian tomatoes, crushed

1. In a skillet or two skillets large enough to hold the chicken in a single layer, heat the olive oil and sauté the onions until they are well browned; add the garlic and cook for 30 seconds.

2. Push the onions and garlic to the side and add the chicken, in one layer, skin side down, and cook over medium-high heat until the pieces are well browned on both sides. Place the onions and garlic on top of the chicken as the chicken browns.

3. Season with salt and pepper and add the wine. Briskly simmer the wine until it is reduced by half. Add the tomatoes, reduce the heat to low, cover, and simmer until the chicken is tender, another 5 to 7 minutes for the breasts; remove the breasts and continue cooking the thighs another 5 to 7 minutes. If the mixture becomes too thick, thin with a little water.

4. Refrigerate or freeze, well wrapped.

5. To serve, let the dish return to room temperature and reheat it in a 325-degree oven, well covered with aluminum foil, for about 20 minutes, until heated through, or heat in the microwave. Add a little water as necessary to keep the sauce from getting too thick.

yield: 8 to 10 servings

breezy barbecued chicken

Years ago, this recipe took a prize at the Delmarva chicken contest, the forerunner of the national chicken cooking contest. This is the New Age version. The additional salt has been removed; there's enough in the catsup, mustard, and Worcestershire sauce. The oil has been reduced from 1 cup to 4 teaspoons. Using skinless, boneless chicken breasts reduces the fat content further. But there's no reason a whole cut-up chicken can't be used, if you increase the cooking time.

4 teaspoons canola oil
¾ cup red wine vinegar
1 cup catsup
½ cup finely grated onion
2 teaspoons dry mustard
3 tablespoons Worcestershire sauce

4 large cloves garlic, minced
⅛ to ¼ teaspoon hot red pepper flakes
2 pounds skinless, boneless chicken breasts, halved

1. Mix together the oil, vinegar, catsup, onion, mustard, Worcestershire sauce, garlic, and pepper flakes.

2. Wash and dry the chicken breasts and place them in the marinade in a shallow, nonreactive container for several hours or overnight. Refrigerate or freeze.

3. To serve, let the chicken and marinade defrost if frozen, and either cook the breasts outdoors over charcoal, basting with marinade and turning often, cooking about 10 to 15 minutes, or grill on a stovetop grill, basting and turning. If there is leftover marinade, bring to a boil and serve with the chicken.

yield: 5 or 6 servings

chicken breasts piquant

In the original *Elegant but Easy*, this dish was baked in the oven, and the flavor and aroma imparted by browning were missing.

1½ cups dry red wine
¼ cup reduced-sodium soy sauce
¼ cup plus 2 tablespoons canola oil
2 tablespoons water
3 large cloves garlic, sliced
2 tablespoons coarsely grated fresh ginger or 2 teaspoons ground ginger

1 tablespoon chopped fresh oregano or 1 teaspoon dried oregano
1 heaping tablespoon brown sugar
3 pounds skinless, boneless chicken breasts

1. Combine the wine, soy sauce, ¼ cup oil, water, garlic, ginger, oregano, and brown sugar in a nonreactive bowl large enough to hold the chicken.

2. Cut the chicken breasts in half, wash and dry, and place the pieces in the marinade, turning to coat both sides; spoon marinade over the breasts occasionally. Marinate overnight in the refrigerator, or freeze.

3. To serve, let the chicken defrost if frozen. Heat a large nonstick sauté pan and add the remaining 2 tablespoons oil. Remove the chicken from the marinade and sauté the breasts on both sides in hot oil until they begin to brown. Add the marinade. Cover and simmer about 10 minutes, depending on the thickness of the breasts, until they are cooked through. Serve with the marinade over rice.

yield: 8 servings

chicken gloriosa

Did we really need 1 cup of oil to brown 2 chickens? Could we substitute a cup of orange juice to be used in its place for the liquid? If fresh mandarin oranges are available, why use canned? And for a tart, sweet change, what about dried cranberries instead of raisins? After all these questions were answered, Lois's en-lightened recipe emerged.

2 pounds skinless chicken breasts and thighs	¼ teaspoon or more hot red pepper flakes
3 tablespoons lime juice	½ cup dried cranberries
Salt and freshly ground pepper to taste	¼ cup tomato paste
2 tablespoons canola oil	½ cup dry sherry
2 large cloves garlic, thinly sliced	1 cup orange juice
6 slices very ripe fresh pineapple, cut into bite-size wedges (save the juices)	2 large or 3 small seedless tangerines, peeled and segmented
½ cup coarse bread crumbs	

1. Wash and dry the chicken and cut the breasts into quarters. Sprinkle the breasts and thighs with 2 tablespoons of the lime juice and the salt and pepper and allow to sit in the refrigerator for 2 hours or more.

2. Drain and reserve the juices. Sauté the chicken pieces in a nonstick pan in the hot oil, browning well on both sides. About 30 seconds before removing the chicken from the pan, add the garlic and sauté. In a 9x13-inch pan, arrange the chicken and garlic.

4. Stir the pineapple wedges and bread crumbs into the pan in which the chicken was cooked; add the remaining 1 tablespoon lime juice, any pineapple juice from the cut-up pineapple, and the hot pepper flakes, cranberries, tomato paste, sherry, and orange juice. Spoon this mixture over the chicken pieces. Strew the tangerine segments around the chicken and cover with aluminum foil. Refrigerate, if desired.

5. To serve, preheat the oven to 350 degrees and bake the chicken for about 1 hour. Serve with saffron rice.

yield: 4 servings

curried chicken and apples

A simple dish with Indian flavors for a quick dinner.

1 ½ pounds skinless, boneless chicken breasts and thighs, cut on the diagonal into ½-inch strips
3 tablespoons olive oil
1 pound onions (2 medium), chopped
2 large cloves garlic, minced
4 large tart apples (such as Granny Smith), peeled, cored, and cut in eighths
2 teaspoons ground cumin
1 teaspoon ground coriander
¼ teaspoon turmeric
¼ teaspoon cinnamon

⅛ teaspoon cloves
⅛ teaspoon nutmeg
⅛ teaspoon cardamom
Salt and freshly ground black pepper to taste
¼ to ½ teaspoon hot red pepper flakes
2 cups reduced-sodium chicken stock or broth
2 tablespoons cornstarch
1 tablespoon lime juice
1 cup nonfat plain yogurt (or more, if desired)

1. In a nonstick pan, brown the chicken strips on both sides in hot oil. Remove and set aside.

2. Add the onions to the pan and sauté, cooking until they begin to brown and soften. Add the garlic and cook 30 seconds. Reduce the heat to medium and add the apples, all the spices, and the salt, pepper, and hot pepper flakes. Return the chicken to the pot, cover, and cook over low heat until the apples begin to soften, just a few minutes.

3. Mix a little of the stock with the cornstarch to make a smooth paste and stir the paste into the remaining chicken stock. When the chicken is almost cooked, add the cornstarch mixture and cook over low heat, stirring, until the mixture thickens a little. Add the lime juice. Refrigerate, if desired.

4. To serve, let the chicken return to room temperature and reheat very slowly over low heat or in the microwave. Serve over rice, with yogurt on the side.

yield: 4 servings

marinated grilled chicken with black bean and mango salsa

This was the main course for my daughter Ann's wedding. It is light, colorful, and makes for a handsome presentation. In a pinch (but not for anything as important as a wedding!), use canned beans, well rinsed.

¾ cup olive oil
½ cup white wine vinegar
3 tablespoons coarsely grated ginger
1 tablespoon ground coriander
1 tablespoon ground cumin
3 tablespoons Dijon mustard

Freshly ground black pepper to taste
12 small whole skinless, boneless
  chicken breasts, halved
Black Bean and Mango-Pineapple
  Salsa (recipe follows)
Sprigs of fresh cilantro for garnish

1. Combine the oil, vinegar, ginger, coriander, cumin, mustard, and pepper; blend well. Place the chicken breasts in a glass or ceramic baking dish and pour all but ¼ cup of the marinade over the chicken pieces, making sure they are all coated. Cover and refrigerate and marinate up to 2 days, turning the pieces a few times. Refrigerate the remaining marinade.

2. To serve, prepare a charcoal grill; remove the chicken from the marinade and discard what's left in the dish. Grill the chicken over medium heat, basting with the reserved (refrigerated) marinade, until the chicken pieces are cooked through, 6 to 10 minutes, depending on size.

3. Spread the salsa on a serving platter and arrange the chicken on top. Decorate with sprigs of cilantro.

yield: 12 servings

black bean and mango-pineapple salsa

8 cups cooked black beans (recipe follows)
2 large cloves garlic, minced
2 jalapeños, seeded and minced
6 tablespoons lime juice
1 cup finely chopped red onion (about 4 ounces)

6 cups chopped ripe mango (about 5 mangoes)
2 cups finely chopped fresh pineapple
½ teaspoon or more hot red pepper flakes
Salt to taste
½ cup chopped fresh cilantro

1. Combine the cooked black beans with the garlic, jalapeños, lime juice, onion, mangoes, pineapple, hot pepper flakes, salt, and cilantro and mix well. Refrigerate.

2. Let the salsa return to room temperature to serve as a bed for the chicken.

yield: 12 cups, serving 12 with some seconds

black beans

3 cups uncooked black beans
1 large onion (about 12 ounces)

6 small cloves garlic

1. Soak the beans overnight in water to cover.

2. Chop the onion and garlic and cook with the beans in plenty of fresh water to cover for about 30 minutes, until the beans are tender but slightly firm; drain.

yield: 8 cups

arroz con pollo

Arroz con pollo is Spanish, a superb blending of simple ingredients. Originally in *Freeze with Ease*, it has been nutritionally streamlined here: less fat has been used for browning the chicken; skinless breasts have been used instead of parts; the amount of vegetables has been increased; and cumin and hot pepper flakes have been added. If you do not have saffron, you can use turmeric for the rice; the flavor will be a little different.

¼ cup olive oil
6 skinless chicken breast quarters (1½ whole chicken breasts)
6 skinless chicken thighs
1 large onion (about 12 ounces), chopped
2 large cloves garlic, minced
1 large red pepper and 1 large green pepper (1 pound total), cored, seeded, and chopped
1 large, ripe tomato (about 1 pound), seeded and chopped
1 large bay leaf

1 teaspoon ground cumin
¼ teaspoon hot red pepper flakes, or more
1 teaspoon saffron threads or 1 teaspoon turmeric
4 cups low-sodium chicken stock or broth
2 cups arborio or other short-grain rice
Salt and freshly ground black pepper to taste
2 cups frozen tiny peas
1 large roasted red pepper (page 183), julienned

1. In the hot oil in nonstick skillet(s), sauté the chicken pieces until they are golden brown on both sides. Be sure the chicken is dry and the pan is hot enough before sautéing so it won't stick to the pan. Set the chicken aside.

2. Sauté the onion until it begins to soften and brown; add the garlic and peppers and continue cooking until the peppers are soft. Add the tomato, bay leaf, cumin, hot pepper flakes, and saffron and place in a large flameproof casserole along with the stock, chicken, and rice. Stir well and season with salt and black pepper. Refrigerate, if desired.

3. To serve, preheat the oven to 325 degrees. Bring the casserole to a boil on top of the stove; place in the oven, uncovered, and cook 15 to 17 minutes, or until the rice is tender. After 10 minutes check the chicken and if it is cooked, carefully scrape off any clinging rice, remove the chicken from the casserole, and set aside so that it does not overcook. Return the casserole to the oven. Two minutes before the rice is ready, stir in the peas and return the chicken to the casserole to heat through. Adjust the seasonings; remove the bay leaf and serve the dish topped with strips of roasted red pepper.

yield: 6 servings

coq au vin

Unlike traditional coq au vin, which had to be simmered for hours because the birds used were old and tough, this version cooks in a very short time. The vegetables retain their character, and, as long as you brown the breasts quickly, they won't become stringy and dry. Remember, you will also be reheating this, so don't overcook. Pearl onions can be peeled more easily if blanched in boiling water about 2 minutes. Run them under cold water; slice off the root ends. When the onions are squeezed, the skins will pop right off.

5 pounds skinless chicken breasts and thighs
1 to 2 cups unbleached flour
Salt and freshly ground black pepper to taste
¼ cup olive oil
¼ cup Cognac or brandy, plus an additional 3 to 4 tablespoons
2 tablespoons fresh chopped thyme
1 bay leaf

3 tablespoons minced parsley, plus extra for garnish
2 tablespoons tomato paste
1 pound small whole mushrooms, washed and stems trimmed
24 pearl onions, peeled
1 bottle (750 ml) good-quality dry red wine
1 to 2 tablespoons Madeira or marsala

1. Wash and dry the chicken pieces thoroughly. Season 1 cup of the flour with salt and pepper and flour the chicken lightly. (Season additional flour if 1 cup is not enough.)

2. Preheat a large, heavy-bottomed pot over high heat for 3 or 4 minutes. (Enameled cast-iron pots and pans are perfect for this.) Add 2 tablespoons of the olive oil and continue to heat until the oil just begins to smoke. Quickly brown the chicken pieces on all sides, cooking the thighs and then the breasts in batches to avoid overcrowding and to ensure even cooking. Add the remaining 2 tablespoons olive oil as needed.

3. Return all the browned chicken to the pot. Add the ¼ cup of Cognac or brandy, heat briefly, and then carefully flame. Add the thyme, bay leaf, parsley, tomato paste, mushrooms, onions, and wine. Stir to combine. Cover the pot, bring to a boil, then reduce the heat to a simmer. Cook about 15 minutes, or until almost tender. Refrigerate or freeze. This is one of those dishes that tastes even better when reheated.

4. To serve, let the dish defrost if frozen. Reheat slowly. Just before serving, add the remaining Cognac, the Madeira, lots of fresh parsley, and salt and pepper. Remove the bay leaf, taste, adjust the seasonings, and serve.

yield: 6 to 8 servings

chicken breasts stuffed with goat cheese

A perfect party dish. Don't worry if some of the filling leaks; it will simply thicken and flavor the sauce.

2 large cloves garlic

6 ounces soft goat cheese, regular or reduced fat, cut into chunks

4 teaspoons minced fresh rosemary or 2 tablespoons minced fresh oregano

2 tablespoons lemon juice

4 large whole skinless, boneless chicken breasts, halved

Salt and freshly ground black pepper to taste

2 tablespoons olive oil

½ cup low-sodium chicken stock or broth

½ cup dry white wine

1. With the food processor running, put the garlic through the feed tube and mince. Add the goat cheese, rosemary or oregano, and lemon juice and process to a paste.

2. Between two sheets of wax paper, pound the chicken breast halves to about ⅛-inch thickness. Divide the cheese mixture into 8 portions and place a portion on one side of each chicken breast half, leaving a margin around the edge. Fold the uncovered half of the breast over the cheese mixture and press the edges together to seal. Freeze, if desired, or refrigerate.

3. To serve: If the breasts are frozen, let them defrost. Season them with salt and pepper and sauté in hot oil. After they have been browned, add the stock and wine to the pan; reduce the heat and simmer the breasts for about 10 minutes, turning once or twice, until they are no longer pink inside. Serve with the sauce left in the pan. (If the sauce seems too thin, remove the chicken and boil the sauce until it thickens slightly.)

yield: 4 to 6 servings

alice's barbecued chicken

If you remember the song "Alice's Restaurant," written by Arlo Guthrie, then you will remember there is a real Alice. Alice really *can* cook, and it was quite an occasion when the counterculture icon once came to Washington to cater a dinner given by a member of the Reagan administration. This is an adaptation of a dish she cooked for that dinner. It has an Asian flavor and would be nice served with rice.

Marinade
½ cup reduced-sodium soy sauce
½ cup dry sherry
1 tablespoon grated fresh ginger

2 large cloves garlic, minced
4 pounds bone-in chicken breasts,
 halved

Sauce
½ cup hoisin sauce
1 cup dry sherry
½ cup catsup

2 tablespoons brown sugar
1 clove garlic, minced

1. Prepare the marinade: Combine the soy sauce, sherry, ginger, and garlic and pour over the chicken pieces in a shallow pan. Marinate overnight at least, well covered, in the refrigerator, occasionally turning the pieces.

2. Prepare the sauce: Combine the hoisin sauce, sherry, catsup, brown sugar, and garlic and set aside.

3. To serve, preheat the oven to 350 degrees. Remove the chicken from the marinade a half hour before baking and place in a shallow pan; cover with the sauce. Bake for 20 to 30 minutes, depending on the size of the breasts; baste several times.

yield: 6 servings

baked imperial chicken

This is very close to the original recipe. We've substituted egg whites for some of the whole eggs, and of course now we use fresh Parmigiano-Reggiano.

1 cup grated Parmigiano-Reggiano
2 cups fine unseasoned bread crumbs
1 teaspoon dried basil
1 teaspoon dried thyme
1 teaspoon dried rosemary
Salt to taste
¼ cup sesame seeds

3 eggs, lightly beaten
3 egg whites, lightly beaten
3 pounds bone-in chicken breasts, skin
  removed
Nonstick pan spray
Cumberland Sauce (recipe follows)

1. Stir the cheese, bread crumbs, basil, thyme, rosemary, salt, and sesame seeds until well mixed.

2. Mix the whole eggs and egg whites together in a medium bowl.

3. Wash and dry the chicken breasts and dip them into the egg mixture, then into the cheese-crumb mixture, and place the pieces in a shallow greased baking pan. Refrigerate or freeze.

4. To serve, let the chicken defrost, if frozen. Preheat the oven to 350 degrees. Spray the tops of chicken with nonstick pan spray. Bake in the lower third of the oven for about 45 minutes. Serve with Cumberland Sauce.

yield: 4 to 6 servings

note: Boneless chicken breasts can be substituted for the bone-in breasts. Reduce the cooking time to 20 to 25 minutes. Allow 1 small whole chicken breast per person.

cumberland sauce

¾ cup red currant jelly
¾ cup defrosted frozen orange juice
  concentrate, undiluted
2 tablespoons lemon juice
¼ cup dry sherry

¼ cup water
½ teaspoon ground ginger
1 teaspoon dry mustard
⅛ teaspoon cayenne

1. In a small saucepan over medium heat, combine the jelly, orange juice, lemon juice, sherry, water, ginger, mustard, and cayenne and cook, stirring occasionally, until smooth. Refrigerate.

2. To serve, reheat.

yield: 2 cups

glazed orange chicken

A favorite from Lois. This is quick!

12 boneless, skinless chicken breast
 halves
½ cup freshly squeezed orange juice
1 tablespoon frozen orange juice concentrate (optional, for a more intense
 orange flavor)
2 tablespoons freshly squeezed lemon
 juice
2 tablespoons honey

2 tablespoons Worcestershire
 sauce
2 tablespoons grainy Dijon mustard
1 tablespoon canola oil
1 tablespoon grated orange zest
1 tablespoon chopped fresh tarragon
 (preferred) or 1 teaspoon dried
1 or 2 bunches of watercress
12 thin slices of orange for garnish

1. Place the chicken in a 9x13-inch glass or ceramic baking dish in a single layer.

2. Combine the orange juice, concentrate, if using, lemon juice, honey, Worcestershire, mustard, oil, zest, and tarragon and pour over the chicken. Cover the pan and marinate overnight or longer in the refrigerator, turning the chicken a few times.

3. When ready to cook, adjust the racks to the middle and broil positions in the oven. Preheat the oven to 375 degrees.

4. Bake the chicken, uncovered, in its marinade for 12 to 16 minutes, or until almost done. It should still be very slightly pink inside. Check by making a slit. Be careful not to overcook. Adjust the heat to broil, move the pan of chicken under the broiler, and broil a few more minutes, with the door partially open, until the breasts are golden. Do not permit them to brown too much.

5. While the chicken is cooking, line a plate with a bed of watercress. Remove the breasts from the oven, arrange on top of the watercress, and garnish each with the orange slices. Spoon the marinade over the chicken.

yield: 8 to 10 servings

note: If at the end of broiling, the marinade sauce is thinner than you'd like it, just pour it into a small saucepan, bring to a boil, and reduce to the desired consistency.

chicken and smoked sausage jambalaya

One of the great successes of lower-fat foods is sausages. For every variation of full-fat pork sausages there is a version of excellent chicken and turkey sausages with all the flavor and one-third to one-half less fat.

You can easily turn this dish into a seafood jambalaya by eliminating the chicken breasts and sautéing an equal amount of seafood of your choice, setting it aside, and returning it to the pot just before you stir in the green onions. If the dish is being refrigerated or frozen, do not sauté the seafood until you are ready to reheat the rest of the dish.

¾ pound low-fat smoked chicken or turkey kielbasa, quartered lengthwise, then sliced ¼ inch thick

1 pound skinless, boneless chicken breasts, cut into ¾-inch dice (or skinless, boneless thighs for moister meat)

Seasoning Mix (recipe follows)

1 to 2 tablespoons oil

3¼ cups low-sodium chicken stock or broth

1 tablespoon dark brown sugar

4 cups diced onions (about 20 ounces)

2 cups cored, seeded, and diced green bell pepper (about 10 ounces)

1 cup diced celery

1 bay leaf

5 cloves garlic, minced

1⅔ cups (one 14½-ounce can) low-sodium diced tomatoes

2 cups long-grain rice

1½ cups chopped green onion tops

1. In a 5-quart nonstick pan or enameled cast-iron pot, sauté the smoked sausage over high heat to release a little fat. Add the chicken (if your pot isn't nonstick, you may need to add a little oil), plus one-half of the seasonings, and continue sautéing over high heat until the chicken is browned. Remove the sausage and chicken from pan and set aside.

2. Deglaze the pan with ¼ cup chicken stock; add 1 tablespoon oil plus brown sugar and stir. Add the 2 cups of the onions, and sauté until they soften and begin to brown. Add the remaining 2 cups of onion, the green pepper, the celery, the bay leaf, and the remaining seasoning mix. Sauté until the vegetables are barely fork-tender. Add the garlic and cook 30 seconds more.

3. Return the chicken and sausage to the pot. Add the tomatoes and cook a few minutes. Remove the bay leaf. (This dish may be made ahead up to this point and refrigerated a few days.)

4. To serve, rinse the rice and add the remaining 3 cups chicken stock to the sausage mixture. Bring to a boil, stir in the rinsed rice, and return to a boil.

5. Cover and reduce the heat to a simmer. Cook 10 minutes, then stir the rice quickly, turning completely from top to bottom. Cook, covered, for another 10 minutes, and then turn the rice completely again. Cook for another 10 to 15 minutes, or until the liquid is absorbed.

6. Taste and adjust the seasonings if necessary. Stir in the green onions and serve.

yield: 6 to 8 servings

seasoning mix

1½ tablespoons chopped fresh thyme or 1 teaspoon dried
1 tablespoon paprika
½ teaspoon salt
¼ to ½ teaspoon cayenne pepper, or to taste
½ teaspoon dry mustard
¼ teaspoon black pepper
¼ teaspoon oregano
¼ teaspoon basil
Dash of white pepper

Mix together.

red lentil and chicken sausage stew

Red lentils, which cook much more quickly than green lentils, are often used in Indian cooking. Their one drawback is that if they are not watched carefully, they turn to mush in a flash. This would be the perfect last-minute company supper, a very satisfying cold weather dish that is quite low in fat.

2 cups red lentils
4 cups low-sodium chicken or vegetable stock or broth
¾ pound onions, chopped (2½ to 3 cups)
1 tablespoon olive oil
4 large cloves garlic, minced
2 large carrots, finely chopped
2 stalks celery, finely chopped

1 pound low-fat spicy chicken or turkey sausage, like hot Italian or New Mexican, thinly sliced
2 cups dry white wine
½ pound short pasta, like fusilli, rigatoni, or penne
Salt and freshly ground black pepper to taste

1. Combine the lentils with the stock in a large saucepan and bring to a boil; reduce the heat and simmer for 12 to 15 minutes, until the lentils have begun to soften. Set aside.

2. Meanwhile, sauté the onion in hot oil in a nonstick pan until it begins to soften. Add the garlic and cook 30 seconds. Then stir in the carrots and celery and continue sautéing until the vegetables are cooked. Add the sausages and cook them until they have lost their pink color. Add the wine and remove from the heat. Transfer the lentils and their cooking liquid to the sausage mixture and refrigerate.

3. To serve, cook the pasta in boiling water until just al dente; reheat the lentil-sausage mixture slowly until it is hot. Stir in the drained cooked pasta and season with salt and pepper.

yield: 4 to 6 servings

tortellini and smoked turkey or grilled chicken

There are so many different fillings in commercially prepared tortellini today, and many of them are good enough, so who cares if you don't make them at home? For this recipe mushroom tortellini were used, but cheese- or other vegetable-filled varieties would be equally appropriate.

¾ pound onion (1 large onion), chopped
1½ tablespoons olive oil
1 pound red and yellow peppers, cored, seeded, and chopped
¼ to ½ teaspoon hot red pepper flakes
2 large cloves garlic, coarsely chopped
2 tablespoons lemon juice
⅓ cup nonfat plain yogurt
⅓ cup light sour cream
¼ cup good-quality mango or other chutney

2 teaspoons Dijon mustard
1-pound piece smoked turkey cut in bite-size chunks, or 1 pound grilled skinless, boneless chicken breasts, cut into bite-size chunks
½ pound cooked green beans or haricots verts, cut in 1-inch lengths
½ pound fresh mushroom tortellini, cooked and drained
¼ pound soft salad greens, washed and dried

1. Sauté the onions in hot oil in a nonstick pan until they begin to soften and brown. Add the peppers and hot pepper flakes and cook until the peppers soften. Set aside.

2. With food processor running, put the garlic through the feed tube and process. Add the lemon juice, yogurt, sour cream, chutney, and mustard and process until the blended. Combine this dressing with the sautéed onions, peppers, and pepper flakes, plus the turkey chunks, green beans, and tortellini, and mix gently to coat thoroughly. Refrigerate.

3. To serve, allow the tortellini mixture to sit at room temperature for 30 minutes. Arrange the salad greens on a serving plate and top with the tortellini mixture.

yield: 4 servings

chicken and potatoes with blue cheese dressing

A light, luscious salad with a strong savory flavor from a lower-fat version of pesto.

1 pound skinless, boneless chicken breasts
2 cups low-sodium chicken stock or broth
2 cups dry white wine
2 cloves garlic, coarsely chopped
2 cups tightly packed fresh basil leaves
1 cup reduced-fat ricotta
1 cup nonfat plain yogurt
¼ pound blue cheese—Gorgonzola, Roquefort, or Stilton
2 tablespoons sherry wine vinegar
2 pounds unpeeled cooked new potatoes, halved or quartered
2 cups cored, seeded, and chopped red bell pepper, about 10 ounces
Salt and freshly ground black pepper to taste
½ pound salad greens, washed and dried

1. Poach the chicken breasts in the stock and wine for 10 to 15 minutes, depending on the thickness of the breasts, until they are no longer pink. Drain and cut the chicken into julienne strips.

2. With the food processor running, put the garlic through the feed tube and process to mince. Turn off the processor and add the basil leaves, ricotta, yogurt, blue cheese, and vinegar. Process to blend thoroughly.

3. Combine the julienned chicken, the dressing, the potatoes, and the red peppers and season to taste with salt and pepper; refrigerate. To serve, remove from the refrigerator 15 minutes before serving to take off the chill. Serve on a bed of greens.

yield: 4 to 6 servings

asparagus, chicken, and portobello rice salad

This light, colorful spring salad makes a delicious lunch or light dinner entrée.

1½ cups long-grain rice
1½ pounds skinless, boneless chicken breasts
2 pounds asparagus
¾ pound portobello mushrooms, trimmed and thickly sliced
3 tablespoons extra-virgin olive oil
7 tablespoons balsamic vinegar

2 dozen medium Greek, Italian, French, or Moroccan black olives, pitted and chopped
½ cup chopped red onion
2 large cloves garlic, minced
2 tablespoons chopped fresh oregano
Salt and freshly ground black pepper to taste

1. Combine the rice and 3 cups of water and bring to a boil. Reduce the heat, cover, and simmer the rice, cooking a total of 17 minutes. Reserve.

2. Spray the chicken breasts with nonstick pan spray. Grill or broil the breasts, browning on both sides, cooking 10 to 15 minutes, depending on the thickness of the breasts. Meanwhile, break the asparagus at the point where the tough stem meets the tender part; discard the tough stems. Steam the asparagus 5 to 7 minutes depending on the thickness of the spears.

3. After grilling and setting aside the chicken, grill or broil the mushrooms on both sides until they are soft, about 5 minutes.

4. Whisk together the oil and vinegar and stir in the olives, onion, garlic, and oregano. Cut the chicken into julienne strips and add to the dressing. Cut the asparagus into 1-inch lengths and add. Add the mushrooms. Stir in the rice and season with salt and pepper. Refrigerate.

5. To serve, remove from the refrigerator 15 to 30 minutes before serving.

yield: 6 servings

indian pilaf

This pilaf is a delicious way to use up leftovers. It's actually so good it is worth sautéing 1 pound of boneless chicken breasts, or 1 pound of boneless leg of lamb, cut in slices, if you have no leftover chicken.

1 cup long-grain rice
2 cups low-sodium chicken or beef stock or broth
1 small bay leaf
¾ teaspoon good-quality curry powder
½ teaspoon ground cumin
1½ pounds onions (about 3), chopped
1½ tablespoons olive oil

2 green peppers (about 10 ounces), seeded and finely chopped
½ cup currants
½ teaspoon cinnamon
¼ teaspoon nutmeg
4 cups julienne strips cooked chicken or lamb
Salt to taste
Freshly ground black pepper to taste
¼ cup toasted slivered almonds

1. Combine the rice, stock, bay leaf, curry powder, and cumin, and bring to a boil; reduce the heat, cover, and cook for a total of 17 minutes, until the rice is tender and the liquid has been absorbed. Remove the bay leaf and set aside.

2. In a nonstick pan, sauté the onions in hot oil until they begin to soften. Add the peppers and sauté until the onions are golden and the peppers are soft. Stir in the currants, cinnamon, and nutmeg. Mix with the rice.

3. Combine the rice mixture with the chicken and season with salt and black pepper. Refrigerate or freeze.

4. To serve, defrost if frozen. Stir in the almonds and reheat in the microwave.

yield: 4 servings

meat

beef and veal

teriyaki

The marinade calls for significantly less soy sauce, and the water has been replaced by dry sherry. The amount of sugar has been cut in half, and the onion eliminated because it doesn't really belong in teriyaki.

Our original recipe called for sirloin steak, but if you want a good juicy cut of meat, use a strip steak, and if you want to be more frugal with your fat, use top round steak. The marinade will tenderize it.

2 tablespoons coarsely grated ginger
4 cloves garlic, minced
2 tablespoons sugar

⅓ cup reduced-sodium soy sauce
5 tablespoons dry sherry
2 pounds strip steak or flank steak

1. Mix the ginger, garlic, sugar, soy sauce, and sherry in a nonreactive bowl large enough to hold the beef. Cut the beef lengthwise into ¼-inch-thick strips. Marinate the beef overnight, well covered, in the refrigerator.

2. To serve, either grill over a charcoal fire outside or on top of a stovetop grill (see page 24) until browned on both sides and rare or medium-rare inside, about 3 to 5 minutes.

yield: 6 servings

meat sauce for spaghetti

This was my mother's recipe. We added more vegetables and more herbs, and replaced the chuck with very lean ground beef. My mother would not recognize her recipe, I'm afraid.

It's best if you grind the beef yourself. You'll know what you are getting. Or ask the butcher to grind it for you. Use round—top or bottom.

1 pound extra-lean ground beef
1 tablespoon olive oil
¾ pound onions, chopped (1 large)
2 large cloves garlic, minced
½ cup chopped carrots
1 pound white mushrooms, chopped
1 (28-ounce) can no-salt-added whole
  tomatoes

1 (6-ounce) can tomato paste
1 tablespoon chopped fresh basil or
  1 teaspoon dried basil
1 tablespoon chopped fresh oregano
  or 1 teaspoon dried oregano
Salt and freshly ground pepper

1. In a nonstick skillet, brown the meat in its own fat, stirring the meat to break it up. Push to the side of the pan. Add the oil and sauté the onions until they begin to soften. Add the garlic and cook another 30 seconds. Then add the carrots and mushrooms and cook until the mushrooms begin to give up their juices. Cook until the liquid evaporates.

2. Add the tomatoes, breaking them up with your fingers as you put them in the pan, along with the tomato paste, basil, and oregano. Season with salt and pepper. Cover and simmer over low heat at least 30 minutes, but preferably 1 hour. Let cool and refrigerate or freeze.

3. To serve, defrost if frozen. Reheat slowly and serve over spaghetti.

yield: 4 servings

pot roast

The changes in this recipe are so great that it really isn't the same. The preferred meat is bottom round—less fat—but you can use brisket (the original). Carrots and stock have been added, and catsup and tomato soup removed. The results are tender and delicious.

2 large onions (about 1½ pounds), chopped
2 tablespoons olive oil
½ pound carrots, peeled and thinly sliced
3 pounds bottom round roast, fat removed

Salt and freshly ground black pepper to taste
2 cups low-sodium beef stock or broth
2 tablespoons lemon juice
2 tablespoons brown sugar

1. Sauté the onions in hot oil in a nonstick pan until they are golden. Push to the side, add the carrots, and cook them until they begin to color, about 5 minutes. Set the vegetables aside.

2. Meanwhile, season the meat with salt and pepper and brown in the pan on all sides and at both ends. Return the onions and carrots to the pan along with the beef stock; reduce the heat, cover, and simmer the meat about 2 to 2½ hours, turning occasionally.

3. Remove the meat from the liquid and slice thin; stir the lemon juice and brown sugar into the stock and return the slices to the pan, making sure the stock covers the meat. Add more, if necessary. Refrigerate, if desired.

4. To serve, slowly reheat the meat and stock and serve with potatoes or noodles.

yield: 6 to 8 servings

beef stew with burgundy
(boeuf bourguignonne)

Our original recipe contained celery, tomato sauce and tapioca, canned water chestnuts, canned mushrooms, and canned potatoes. All have been banished, and the result is much closer to the real thing.

¼ cup plus 1 tablespoon canola oil
4 pounds extra-lean or lean beef round, cubed
5 medium carrots, peeled and cut into cubes
4 onions (about 2 pounds), sliced
4 cloves garlic
1 large bay leaf
4 cups canned low-sodium tomatoes, preferably Italian

1 bottle (750 ml) good Burgundy, * Cabernet, or pinot noir
2 cups low-sodium beef stock or broth
Salt and freshly ground black pepper to taste
1½ pounds white mushrooms or cremini or portobello, or a mixture, washed, dried, and trimmed
¼ cup flour

1. In one or two large, deep nonstick pans or a Dutch oven, heat ¼ cup oil and sauté the beef until it is well browned on all sides. Add the carrots and onions and sauté until the vegetables are lightly browned. Add the garlic and sauté for 30 seconds.

2. Add the bay leaf and tomatoes, crushing them between your fingers before adding, along with the wine and beef stock. Cover and simmer for about 2 hours, until the beef is tender. Season with salt and pepper and refrigerate or freeze, well wrapped.

3. To serve, let the stew defrost if frozen. Depending on the size of the mushrooms, leave them whole, quarter them, or halve them. In a skillet, sauté them in the remaining tablespoon of oil until they are soft and brown. Stir into the beef. (This can be done earlier on the day the stew will be served).

4. Mix a little of the stewing liquid with the flour to make a paste. Add more liquid to blend well, then stir into the stew. Reheat the beef over very low heat until it is simmering and the liquid is slightly thickened. Remove the bay leaf and serve over noodles or with boiled or mashed potatoes or rice.

yield: 12 servings

*At today's prices almost no one would use Burgundy.

picadillo

If you do not like sweet and savory food, you may not want to use the dried cherries. The dish is delicious without them, but dried fruit (raisins actually) is traditional in a picadillo. I found the dried cherries to be much more interesting than raisins.

Using ground turkey instead of all beef reduces the fat content substantially without affecting the flavor.

Grind the beef and turkey yourself or ask the butcher to grind it.

1 pound onions, chopped (2 medium)
1½ tablespoons olive oil
2 large cloves garlic, minced
1 pound extra-lean ground beef
1 pound ground white-meat turkey
½ teaspoon cinnamon
¼ teaspoon cloves
1 teaspoon dried oregano
¼ to ½ teaspoon hot red pepper flakes

½ of a (28-ounce) can crushed low-sodium tomatoes
20 medium Greek, Italian, or French olives, pitted and chopped
⅓ cup dried cherries (optional)
3 tablespoons dry sherry
1 tablespoon white vinegar
Salt and freshly ground black pepper to taste

1. Sauté the onions in hot oil in a nonstick pan until they are soft and begin to brown. Add the garlic and cook another 30 seconds. Push the onions and garlic to the side, add the ground beef and ground turkey, and cook, stirring to break up the pieces. Brown thoroughly.

2. While the meat cooks, stir in the cinnamon, cloves, oregano, and hot pepper flakes. When the meat is brown, add the tomatoes, olives, cherries if using, sherry, and vinegar. Reduce the heat and simmer for about 10 minutes. Season with salt and pepper. If the mixture becomes too thick, add a few more crushed tomatoes. Refrigerate or freeze.

3. To serve, let the mixture defrost if frozen; reheat slowly, thinning with more tomatoes if necessary, and serve over rice or orzo, the rice-shaped pasta.

yield: 8 servings

bob jamieson's best meat loaf

This recipe was used for quick-cooking meat loaf hamburgers in my cookbook *20-Minute Menus*. Now it can go back to its original form with only a few alterations to remove some of the fat. The beef is lower in fat; the veal is now turkey breast;and the pork is from the tenderloin. Instead of 2 eggs I use 1 egg and 2 whites. The meat loaf is still delicious comfort food. Grind your own beef, turkey, and pork. Use low-fat beef such as round.

8 ounces finely chopped onion (about 1½ cups)
1 tablespoon olive oil
1½ pounds lean ground beef
⅓ pound ground turkey breast
⅓ pound ground pork tenderloin
2 tablespoons Worcestershire sauce
2 tablespoons Dijon mustard

¼ cup fine bread crumbs
1 egg, lightly beaten
2 egg whites, lightly beaten
Salt and freshly ground black pepper to taste
3 tablespoons catsup, plus 5 tablespoons for glazing

1. Sauté the onion in the oil in a nonstick pan until it is quite soft and golden. In a bowl, mix the onions with the beef, turkey, pork, Worcestershire sauce, mustard, bread crumbs, egg, egg whites, salt, and pepper and 3 tablespoons of catsup. Spoon into 9x5-inch loaf pan; pat gently and spread the remaining 5 tablespoons of catsup over the top to glaze. Refrigerate or freeze.

2. To serve, let the meat loaf defrost if frozen, and return to room temperature. Preheat the oven to 350 degrees. Bake the meat loaf for 1 hour, slice, and serve warm.

yield: 6 servings

veal parmigiana

A real veal parmigiana has no ground beef in the tomato sauce, an ingredient in the original *Elegant but Easy*. Parmigiano-Reggiano, not salty pre-grated Parmesan cheese, and fresh mozzarella make a big difference here.

You can also use chicken or turkey cutlets to make this recipe, and the sauce can be made three days ahead and refrigerated, if desired. If you are preparing the dish in advance, the meat should not be browned until the day before serving.

½ cup chopped onion
6 tablespoons olive oil
1 (28-ounce) can low-sodium Italian
  plum tomatoes with basil
1 bay leaf
1 (6-ounce) can tomato paste
1 teaspoon sugar
Salt and freshly ground black pepper
  to taste

1 egg
2 egg whites
⅔ cup fine bread crumbs
½ cup finely grated Parmigiano-
  Reggiano
1 pound veal scallops
8 ounces fresh mozzarella, sliced

1. Sauté the onion in 1 tablespoon of the hot oil in a nonstick pan until the onion begins to brown. Add the tomatoes, crushing them between your fingers while adding, and the bay leaf, tomato paste, and sugar. Season with salt and pepper. Simmer over low heat for 30 minutes. When the sauce is ready, remove the bay leaf. Refrigerate, if desired.

2. Beat the egg and whites together in a small bowl. In another bowl, stir the bread crumbs, Parmigiano-Reggiano, and salt and pepper to taste together and place on a plate.

3. Dip the veal scallops into the egg mixture and allow the excess egg to drip off. Then dip the scallops into the bread crumb mixture.

4. Heat a couple of tablespoons of the remaining oil in a large skillet and brown the veal quickly on both sides. Don't cook long or the veal will be tough, and don't crowd in the pan. Repeat, using more oil if necessary, until all the veal is cooked.

5. In a shallow baking dish, arrange a single layer of the veal; top with half the tomato sauce, then with half the mozzarella, and cover with the remaining tomato sauce and remaining mozzarella. Refrigerate.

6. To serve, let the dish return to room temperature. Preheat the oven to 350 degrees. Bake for about 20 minutes, until the cheese is melted, browned, and bubbling.

yield: 4 servings

saltimbocca

Saltimbocca means "jump into the mouth," and that's what this old-fashioned Italian dish does.

Once upon a time, veal was cheap. Now it's very expensive and turkey breast is sometimes substituted for veal. It is not as tender, but the flavor is still quite good.

The mozzarella of the original version has been replaced by provolone, and the amounts of oil and butter have been reduced. This dish tastes better with fresh sage, but dried will do.

1½ pounds (8 pieces) thin veal steak, pounded to make thinner, or 1½ pounds turkey fillet (8 thin slices)

4 paper-thin slices prosciutto (about 2 ounces)

8 very thin slices aged provolone (about 5 ounces)

4 teaspoons chopped fresh sage or 1½ teaspoons dried sage

Salt to taste

2 tablespoons unsalted butter

2 tablespoons olive oil

⅓ cup dry white wine

1. To flatten the veal (or turkey), place each piece between 2 pieces of wax paper and pound with a rolling pin until the pieces are very thin but not torn. Top 4 slices of veal with 4 slices of prosciutto and the provolone (2 slices on each). Sprinkle with sage. Place remaining 4 slices of veal on top and press edges to seal. Season with salt. Cover and refrigerate or freeze.

2. To serve, let the saltimbocca defrost if frozen and return to room temperature. Heat the butter and oil in a large sauté pan and brown the veal packages on both sides, cooking quickly, about 1½ minutes on each side for the veal and 2½ minutes on each side for the turkey. Reduce the heat to a simmer and stir in the wine; simmer about 30 seconds. Do not overcook or the meat will become dry.

yield: 4 servings

lamb

rack of lamb

Allow 2 racks for 5 or 6 people, depending on whether you will be feeding them 2 or 3 chops each (there are 8 chops per rack).

Ask the butcher to "french" the chops, that is, scrape the bones, removing the excess fat and thin strips of meat. The butcher can also provide you with "panties" or "booties" to decorate the bones of the finished racks.

2 racks of lamb	3 cloves garlic, minced
Salt and pepper	

1. Trim any remaining fat from the lamb and wash and dry the racks. Season with salt and pepper and rub the lamb with the garlic. Wrap the exposed bones with aluminum foil; cover the racks tightly and refrigerate overnight if desired.

2. To serve, allow the racks to return to room temperature. Preheat the oven to 450 degrees. Place the racks, meat side up, in a roasting pan. Do not crowd. Roast the lamb for 20 to 30 minutes, depending on how rare you want it; check by cutting a small slit in the middle between chops. Remove the foil from the exposed bones and put the "panties" or "booties" on the bones. Let the lamb rest for 5 minutes and slice the between the bones.

yield: 5 or 6 servings

moroccan spice rub

If you want to add something a little extra to a rack of lamb or a leg of lamb you can rub some of this on the meat, to your taste.

2 tablespoons ground cumin
1 tablespoon paprika
1 tablespoon ground coriander
1 teaspoon salt
1 teaspoon freshly ground black pepper

1 teaspoon cinnamon
1 teaspoon allspice
¼ teaspoon cloves
⅛ teaspoon cayenne, or to taste
2 tablespoons minced fresh garlic, or to taste

Mix the cumin, paprika, coriander, salt, pepper, cinnamon, allspice, cloves, and cayenne thoroughly. Rub on the surface of the meat. Rub the garlic over the spices and refrigerate overnight. Without the garlic the spices will keep for months in a tightly covered container in the pantry.

yield: 5-plus tablespoons of rub, enough for a large leg of lamb or 4 or 5 racks of lamb

pork

how to cook a whole pork tenderloin

Pork tenderloin is an American cut that is found between the loin and the spareribs. It is very tender, very lean, very fast-cooking, and perfect for entertaining.

Heat 1 tablespoon of oil in a nonstick pan large enough to hold the tenderloin and brown the meat on all sides thoroughly, about 6 minutes. Preheat the oven to 400 degrees. Place the tenderloin in an ovenproof pan and roast for 15 minutes, or until the pork is slightly pink in the center. (It may take another 5 minutes, at the most.)

Any of the following marinades (pages 123 and 124) can be used on the whole tenderloin.

yield: 3 or 4 servings

pork tenderloin with mustard and thyme

A quick main dish.

About 2 pounds pork tenderloins	Freshly ground black pepper to taste
½ cup whole-grain mustard	2 tablespoons balsamic vinegar
4 large cloves garlic, crushed	¼ cup dry red wine
2 tablespoons dried thyme	2 tablespoons olive oil

1. Remove the fat from the tenderloins and wash and dry them. Cut off each tip and reserve. Cut the remaining tenderloins into 1-inch-thick slices.

2. Combine the mustard, garlic, thyme, pepper, vinegar, red wine, and oil in a bowl large enough to hold the tenderloins and tips and mix thoroughly, coating the pork slices and the tips well. Marinate overnight or at least 1 hour in the refrigerator, turning occasionally.

3. To serve, allow the meat to sit at room temperature for 30 minutes. Remove from the marinade. Prepare a stovetop grill or preheat the broiler. Broil or grill the pork tenderloin pieces on both sides for 5 to 7 minutes total, until just slightly pink inside, brushing with marinade. This can also be done over a charcoal grill. Watch carefully. It goes from pink to dry in a flash. If there is leftover marinade, boil it and brush the cooked pork with it before serving.

yield: 5 or 6 servings

grilled pork with lime-ginger marinade

Easy, light, and delicious.

6 tablespoons lime juice	6 tablespoons maple syrup
2 large cloves garlic, minced	About 2 pounds pork tenderloins
3 tablespoons coarsely grated ginger	Freshly ground black pepper to taste

1. Combine the lime juice, garlic, ginger, and maple syrup and place in a bowl large enough to hold the pork.

2. Wash the tenderloins, trim the fat, and cut off the tips of the pork. Cut the remaining tenderloins into 1-inch-thick slices and add to the marinade, along with the cut-off tips. Turn to coat.

3. Refrigerate in the marinade overnight or at least 1 hour.

4. To serve, remove pork from the refrigerator and let sit at room temperature for 30 minutes. Prepare a stovetop grill or preheat the broiler. Grill or broil the pork until it is slightly pink inside, 5 to 7 minutes, basting with marinade and browning on both sides. This can also be done on a charcoal grill. Watch carefully. It goes from pink to dry in a flash.

yield: 5 or 6 servings

pork and potatoes in coriander wine sauce

Pork and potatoes sound so nice and old-fashioned; coriander adds a modern flavor.

A very quick dish.

1 ½ cups dry red wine
2 tablespoons ground coriander
1 ¼ pounds pork tenderloin
3 tablespoons olive oil
1 ½ pounds onions, chopped (about 5 or 6 cups)

1 ½ pounds new potatoes, unpeeled, thinly sliced
Salt and freshly ground black pepper to taste
¼ cup chopped parsley

1. Combine the wine and coriander in a bowl large enough to hold the pork. Trim the fat from the pork and cut off the tip. Slice the rest of the pork into ¼-inch-thick slices and add with the tip to the wine mixture, stirring to coat.

2. Heat the oil in a large nonstick pan and sauté the onions until they begin to soften and brown. Add the potatoes and cook until they just begin to soften and brown. Add the pork and sauté until it is brown on both sides.

3. Add the wine-coriander mixture and remove from the heat. Refrigerate.

4. To serve, let return to room temperature and cook slowly to finish cooking the potatoes. Season with salt and pepper and sprinkle with parsley.

yield: 4 servings

lasagna

The MSG went immediately! A more flavorful combination of ground pork tenderloin and Italian turkey sausage replaced the ground beef, reduced-fat ricotta and part-skim mozzarella replaced full-fat versions, the Parmesan cheese is now Parmigiano-Reggiano, and oh, yes, there is no more canned tomato sauce. Eggplant, browned in a very hot oven, has been added as a layer. What a difference!

There's no question that this dish is a project, but it can be made far in advance and is absolutely scrumptious.

2 tablespoons plus 1 teaspoon olive oil
¾ pound hot and sweet turkey or chicken Italian-style sausages, removed from casings
¼ pound ground pork tenderloin
2 medium onions (about 1 pound), chopped
4 large cloves garlic, thinly sliced
1 (28-ounce) can low-sodium crushed tomatoes or tomato purée
1 (28-ounce) can low-sodium Italian plum tomatoes
1 cup dry red wine

¼ cup chopped fresh basil or 1½ tablespoons dried basil
¼ cup chopped fresh oregano or 1 tablespoon dried oregano
Salt and freshly ground pepper to taste
9 lasagna noodles, fresh or dried
2 pounds eggplant
1 pound reduced-fat ricotta
1 pound part-skim mozzarella, thinly sliced
¾ cup finely grated Parmigiano-Reggiano (about 2½ ounces)

1. Bring 6 quarts of water to a boil in a covered pot for the lasagna noodles, and preheat the oven to 500 degrees.

2. Heat 1 tablespoon of the oil in a large nonstick skillet and sauté the sausage and ground pork, stirring often to break apart and brown. Remove the meats with a slotted spoon and set aside.

3. Add 2 teaspoons of the oil to the skillet and sauté the onions until they are golden. Add the garlic and cook for 30 seconds. Stir in the tomato purée (or crushed tomatoes) and the plum tomatoes, crushing the tomatoes between your fingers before adding them to the pot along with the wine, basil, and oregano. Simmer for 5 minutes. Add the sausages and pork to the tomato sauce and simmer for 45 minutes, covered; season with salt and pepper.

4. Meanwhile, add the remaining 2 teaspoons of oil and a little salt to the pasta cooking water; add the noodles carefully so they do not stick together. Cook dried noodles 7 to 10 minutes, until they are tender but not mushy; cook fresh noodles about 1½ minutes. When the noodles are ready, drain them and run under cold water to stop the cooking. Spread the noodles out on a dishcloth or cookie sheet so they don't stick together.

5. Wash and trim the eggplant but do not peel it; cut it into ¼-inch-thick slices. Spray a large cookie sheet with nonstick pan spray. Arrange the eggplant slices on the tray; spray them with the nonstick spray and season with salt on both sides. Bake at 500 degrees for 10 to 15 minutes on the bottom rack of the oven, until they are golden on both sides. Remove and set aside.

6. To assemble: Spread a 9x13-inch baking dish with a very thin layer of the sauce. Then lay 3 lasagna noodles side by side on top of the sauce; top with one-third of the ricotta, half of the eggplant, one-third of the mozzarella, and enough sauce to cover well. Repeat with 3 noodles, another third of the ricotta, the remaining eggplant, and another third of the mozzarella. Then finish with sauce, the remaining noodles, ricotta, mozzarella, and sauce and sprinkle with Parmigiano-Reggiano. Wrap well and refrigerate or freeze.

7. To serve, defrost if frozen. Let the lasagna return to room temperature. Preheat the oven to 375 degrees, cover the pan with a single layer of foil, and bake for about 45 minutes, until browned and bubbling. Allow to rest 10 minutes before cutting.

yield: 12 servings

vegetarian dishes

asparagus and zucchini pancakes with cheese

Originally there were two variations: all zucchini and all asparagus. This combination is even better, and one of those vegetarian dishes that can also be served as a first course for a dinner party instead of as a main course for vegetarians.

2 ounces Neufchâtel or regular cream cheese, softened
¼ cup freshly grated Parmigiano-Reggiano
2 tablespoons flour
1 tablespoon chopped chives
2 teaspoons chopped fresh thyme
2 eggs

3 egg whites
½ pound zucchini, coarsely shredded and squeezed dry in a towel
½ pound cooked asparagus, cut into ½-inch lengths
Salt and freshly ground black pepper to taste
1 tablespoon or more olive oil

1. In a large bowl, beat together the cream cheese, Parmigiano-Reggiano, flour, chives, thyme, eggs, and egg whites. Mix in the zucchini and asparagus. Season with salt and pepper.

2. Heat a large nonstick skillet until it is very hot. Film with a little of the oil. Drop heaping tablespoonsful of batter into the skillet and cook over medium-high heat until the pancakes are brown. Turn and brown on the second side. Repeat the process, filming with a little oil, if necessary. Be sure to stir the batter before making each batch. Refrigerate.

3. To serve, let the pancakes return to room temperature and reheat in a skillet that has been filmed with a little oil, by cooking on both sides. Or reheat in a 400-degree oven on cookie sheets for 5 to 10 minutes. Serve the pancakes with sour cream, Crème Fraîche (page 223), or yogurt.

yield: about twenty 3-inch pancakes, 4 servings as main course

patricia's market mélange

What went into this vegetable dish was determined entirely by what was available from the local farmers in Northeast Vermont, where I spend many summer weekends.

½ pound (1 medium) red onion, chopped
½ pound (1 medium) white or yellow onion, chopped
1½ tablespoons olive oil
¼ to ½ teaspoon hot red pepper flakes
2 stalks celery, sliced
2 red bell peppers (about 10 ounces), chopped
4 small carrots, sliced

1 large leek, white part only, sliced
3 julienned sun-dried tomatoes
3 sprigs thyme leaves
12 Kalamata olives, pitted and sliced
2 ripe medium tomatoes, coarsely chopped
3 small zucchini, cut into cubes
3 small yellow squash, cut into cubes
Salt and freshly ground black pepper to taste
10 large basil leaves

1. Sauté the onions in hot oil in a nonstick pan until they soften and begin to turn golden.

2. Add the hot pepper flakes, celery, bell peppers, carrots, and leek and continue cooking over medium heat until the vegetables begin to soften.

3. Add the sun-dried tomatoes, thyme, olives, and tomatoes and continue cooking until the tomatoes soften.

4. Add the zucchini and yellow squash and season with salt and pepper. If not serving immediately, refrigerate at this point.

5. To serve, reheat slowly, cooking until the mixture is hot and the zucchini has softened but is not limp. Add the basil leaves, cook about 2 minutes longer, and serve.

yield: 4 servings

spicy eggplant and peppers

Chinese in feeling, this lovely vegetarian dish is served over rice.

Sautéing eggplant requires vast quantities of oil because the vegetable soaks it up. You can eliminate a considerable amount of oil and achieve the same results by broiling the eggplant.

Toasted sesame oil is oil from the toasted seeds.

3 pounds eggplant, washed, trimmed, and sliced ¼ inch thick but not peeled
1½ tablespoons toasted sesame oil
2 large cloves garlic, minced
2 tablespoons coarsely grated fresh ginger
2 pounds red and yellow peppers, trimmed, seeded, and chopped
4 teaspoons hot chile paste with garlic* (or less if you don't like it spicy)

4 teaspoons hoisin sauce*
2 tablespoons rice vinegar*
¼ cup dry sherry
2 tablespoons reduced-sodium soy sauce
2 tablespoons dark brown sugar
6 green onions, trimmed and finely sliced
2 cups low-sodium vegetable stock
4 teaspoons cornstarch

1. Cover two broiler pans with aluminum foil and preheat the broiler. Arrange the sliced eggplant on the foil and lightly spray with pan spray on both sides. Broil 2 to 3 inches from the heat, turning the pieces after they begin to brown, 7 to 10 minutes. Continue broiling until the eggplant pieces are soft. Watch carefully so they don't burn. You may have to do this in two batches to accommodate all the slices.

2. Meanwhile, heat the sesame oil in a wok or nonstick skillet, stir in the garlic, ginger, and peppers, and sauté over medium-high heat until the peppers soften.

3. When the eggplant is cooked, cut it into bite-size pieces and add to the peppers, along with the chile paste, hoisin sauce, rice vinegar, sherry, soy sauce, and brown sugar. Stir well. At this point the dish can be refrigerated.

4. To serve, reheat slowly. Add the green onions. Stir a little of the stock into the cornstarch to make a paste; then add the paste to the rest of the stock and mix well. Stir into the skillet and cook over low heat until the mixture thickens. Serve over rice.

yield: 6 servings

*Can be found in Asian markets, or the Asian food section of a well-stocked supermarket, or by mail (see page 23).

potatoes, peas, and corn curry

1½ pounds tiny thin-skinned potatoes
1½ pounds onions (3 medium) chopped
3 tablespoons olive oil
4 large cloves garlic, minced
2 tablespoons grated ginger
½ to 1 teaspoon hot red pepper flakes
2 teaspoons ground coriander
1 teaspoon turmeric
2 teaspoons cumin
2 pounds fresh ripe tomatoes, cut up, or 1 (14- to 15-ounce) can low-sodium tomatoes
2 cups low-sodium vegetable stock or broth
2 cups fresh corn kernels (2 ears) or 2 cups frozen corn kernels
2 cups frozen peas
Salt and freshly ground black pepper to taste

1. Scrub and boil the unpeeled potatoes in water to cover for about 20 minutes, depending on the size of the potatoes, until tender.

2. Meanwhile, sauté the onions in hot oil in a large nonstick pan until they begin to soften and color. Add the garlic, ginger, and hot pepper flakes and cook 30 seconds. Stir in the coriander, turmeric, and cumin.

3. Add the tomatoes, squeezing the canned ones between your fingers to crush; add the stock and cook quickly over high heat to reduce the liquid a little. Set aside.

4. When the potatoes are cooked, drain and add to the skillet. Refrigerate, if desired.

5. To serve, reheat slowly; stir in the corn and peas and cook a couple of minutes longer. Season with salt and pepper. Serve with yogurt and chutney over rice.

yield: 6 servings

polenta with fennel, peppers, tomatoes, and cheese

❄ 🄵

Polenta may be associated with Italy, but this dish has been freely adapted from one I had in Paris at Michel Rostang's bistro.

What is often called instant polenta is simply fine-grained polenta. If you prefer to use coarse-grained polenta, just follow the package directions for cooking it and allow for about 45 minutes' additional cooking time.

2 pounds fennel
2 tablespoons olive oil
2 pounds red peppers, cored, seeded, and finely chopped
1 pound ripe tomatoes, cut into small chunks
16 large black Greek olives, pitted and chopped

7 cups low-sodium vegetable stock or broth
1½ cups instant or fine-ground polenta
1½ cups coarsely grated Parmigiano-Reggiano (about 5 ounces)
Salt and freshly ground black pepper to taste

1. Trim the fennel and cut the bulbs into julienne strips. Sauté the fennel in hot oil in a large nonstick pan until it begins to brown and soften. Add the peppers and continue sautéing until they begin to soften. Add the tomatoes and olives and continue cooking over medium-low heat while making the polenta.

2. Meanwhile, bring the stock to a boil and stir in the polenta slowly so that it doesn't clump. Cook, stirring, over medium heat until the mixture begins to thicken. This is a matter of minutes. When the polenta and vegetables are cooked, combine them and stir in the cheese; season with salt and pepper. Spoon into a large shallow baking dish and refrigerate or freeze.

3. To serve, let defrost and return to room temperature if frozen. Preheat the oven to 350 degrees. Reheat for 20 to 30 minutes until heated through.

yield: 6 servings

traditional basil pesto

There are so many different so-called pestos now: made with arugula, with sun-dried tomatoes, or with parsley and coriander, for example. But pesto with basil is still the best, and this is one of the best recipes.

The most time-consuming part of making pesto is picking the basil leaves.

Pesto is not only good over pasta. It is superb over fish or meat, or boiled potatoes, mixed into a bowl of minestrone, combined with tomato sauce, or drizzled over fresh mozzarella. There is a lower-fat version of pesto, called Blue Cheese Dressing, on page 108.

10 cups fresh basil leaves, tightly
  packed
1½ cups extra-virgin olive oil
4 large cloves garlic, halved
1 cup pine nuts

½ cup finely grated Parmigiano-
  Reggiano for each ¾ cup pesto
Salt and freshly ground black pepper
  to taste

1. Wash and drain the basil leaves. Combine them with the oil, garlic, and nuts in a food processor and process until a rough paste is formed. The mixture should not be completely smooth.

2. If you are not using the pesto immediately, it can be preserved in either of two ways: Place the pesto in a plastic or glass container with a tight-fitting lid. Pour ½ inch of olive oil over the top of the pesto and refrigerate. This method of storing permits you to use a little pesto at a time, after draining off some of the oil. Pesto stored this way will keep for weeks. You can also place the pesto in a tightly covered container and freeze, or freeze it in ice cube trays. When frozen, remove the pesto cubes and wrap individually. In all cases, to serve, let return to room temperature and stir in the cheese. Season to taste with salt and pepper.

3. After the pesto and cheese have been combined, allow ¾ cup of the pesto-cheese mixture for every ½ pound of pasta. Stir 3 tablespoons of the pasta cooking water into the pesto-cheese mixture before spooning over the pasta.

yield: 2-plus cups of pesto, enough for 1¼ pounds pasta, to serve 5 people

sun-dried tomato pesto with pasta

Sun-dried tomatoes, despite their overuse in many dishes, make a good pesto-type sauce.

2 cloves garlic
48 large basil leaves
1 cup regular or reduced-fat ricotta
1 cup nonfat plain yogurt
36 sun-dried tomatoes, packed in oil,

rinsed in warm water and patted dry on towels
Freshly ground black pepper to taste
1 ¼ pounds fresh pasta

1. With the food processor running, put the garlic through the feed tube to mince.

2. Turn off the food processor and add the basil, ricotta, yogurt, and 32 of the tomatoes and process until the mixture is fairly smooth. Season with pepper. Coarsely chop the remaining sun-dried tomatoes and set aside. Refrigerate the "pesto," if desired.

3. To serve, let return to room temperature and serve the sauce over freshly cooked hot pasta, decorated with the chopped sun-dried tomatoes. If the sauce is too thick, thin with a little of the pasta water.

yield: 5 servings

sesame noodles and broccoli

One of the hundreds of variations on everyone's favorite sesame noodles, this one has much less fat in it than the kind your local Chinese carryout is serving, but just as much flavor.

4½ pounds broccoli
1½ pounds very thin noodles such as angel hair, preferably fresh, or fresh oriental egg noodles
6 cloves garlic, halved
6 green onions, coarsely chopped
½ cup toasted sesame paste*
5 tablespoons reduced-sodium soy sauce

5 teaspoons sugar
1 tablespoon hot chile paste,* or less if you don't like it spicy
¼ cup toasted sesame oil*
3 tablespoons red wine vinegar
¼ cup dry vermouth
3 tablespoons coarsely grated ginger
¼ cup chopped cilantro
¼ cup toasted sesame seeds

1. Trim the tough stems from the broccoli. Cut the broccoli tops into bite-size florets and steam 5 to 7 minutes, until tender but firm. Cook the noodles according to package directions, drain, and rinse under cold water.

2. Place the garlic, green onions, sesame paste, soy sauce, sugar, chile paste, sesame oil, vinegar, vermouth, and ginger in a food processor and process to make a smooth sauce. If the sesame mixture is too thick—that depends on the oil content of the sesame paste—add additional vermouth and sesame oil a tablespoon at a time to reach the right consistency so the sesame mixture will mix well with other ingredients and not be too dry.

3. Mix the sauce with the cooked noodles and broccoli; cover and refrigerate.

4. When you are almost ready to serve, let the mixture return to room temperature and serve topped with chopped cilantro and toasted sesame seeds.

yield: 8 servings

*These ingredients can be found in Asian markets, specialty food stores, in the Asian foods section of a well-stocked supermarket, or by mail (see page 23).

tortellini vinaigrette

So many tortellini stuffings—so little time! Any type of tortellini—cheese, vegetable, even chicken or meat, if you aren't making a vegetarian meal—may be used in this recipe.

¼ cup olive oil
3 tablespoons white wine vinegar
2 teaspoons Dijon mustard
2 tablespoons finely minced
 parsley
2 teaspoons minced fresh thyme
2 tablespoons minced fresh basil
1 large clove garlic, crushed
1 pound fresh tortellini stuffed with
 your choice of filling, cooked according to package directions, drained,
 and rinsed under cold water

2 cups broccoli florets, steamed
2 cups asparagus spears, cut into
 1-inch lengths, steamed
1½ cups finely julienned carrots (about
 1½x⅛x⅛ inch), steamed
3 tablespoons minced scallions
Salt and freshly ground black pepper
 to taste

Whisk the oil, vinegar, and mustard in a bowl large enough to hold all the ingredients. Stir in the parsley, thyme, basil, and garlic. Add the tortellini, broccoli, asparagus, carrots, and scallions and stir gently. Season with salt and pepper. Refrigerate. To serve, return to room temperature.

yield: 4 servings

mediterranean couscous salad

Couscous, both regular and whole wheat, is available in most supermarkets. If you want to turn this into a nonvegetarian main dish, poach 1 pound of chicken breasts in 2 cups of dry white wine. Cube the chicken and add it with the vegetables.

Never add raw tomatoes to a dish that is going to be refrigerated. Cut-up tomatoes lose their flavor in a half hour and actually take on an unpleasant taste if they sit in the refrigerator, so always add them at the last minute.

3 cups low-sodium vegetable stock or broth
2 cups instant whole wheat or regular couscous
3 tablespoons olive oil
6 tablespoons balsamic vinegar
4 teaspoons Dijon mustard
2 large cloves garlic, minced
Grated zest of 2 oranges
1 to 2 whole jalapeños, trimmed, seeded, and finely minced
2 dozen green or black medium Italian or French olives, pitted and finely chopped
¼ cup chopped capers
2 cups (about 10 ounces) julienned red bell pepper
1 pound zucchini, cut into julienne strips
½ cup finely diced red onion
1 cup diced fennel
Salt and freshly ground black pepper to taste
2 medium-large ripe tomatoes

1. Bring the vegetable stock to a boil in a covered pot. Add the instant couscous; remove from the heat and allow to sit for 5 minutes, until the liquid has been absorbed.

2. Whisk the oil, vinegar, mustard, and garlic in a serving bowl. Add the orange zest, jalapeños, olives, and capers and mix well. Stir in the red pepper, zucchini, onion, and fennel, and season with salt and pepper. Refrigerate.

3. To serve, let stand at room temperature for 30 minutes. Cut up the tomato and stir it in; adjust seasoning if necessary.

yield: 6 to 8 servings

macaroni and cheese,
the canal house

The Canal House restaurant is in the SoHo Grand Hotel, a very New York, very downtown place where everyone wears black and everyone is very thin and very chic. But not from eating this grown-up version of macaroni and cheese.

The quality and the sharpness of the cheese are all-important to the success of this dish. Choose a white Cheddar that has been aged at least two years. (See page 22.)

Other corkscrew-shaped pastas can be substituted for the cavatappi; the sauce adheres beautifully to this shape.

This makes a perfect side dish for simply grilled chicken or meat, too.

1 cup diced onion (about 4 ounces)
2 tablespoons unsalted butter
2 tablespoons unbleached flour
2 cups low-fat milk
1 tablespoon Dijon mustard
10 ounces extra-sharp aged white Cheddar cheese, grated, plus 2 ounces, grated

Salt and freshly ground white pepper to taste
1/8 teaspoon ground nutmeg
1/4 to 1/2 teaspoon hot pepper sauce
8 ounces cavatappi
2 tablespoons grated Parmigiano-Reggiano

1. In a large saucepan, cook the onion over low heat in the melted butter until the onion is soft but not browned, 5 to 7 minutes. Stir in the flour. Remove from the heat and whisk in the milk until thoroughly blended. Return to medium heat and cook, stirring, until the mixture *begins* to thicken. Remove from the heat and stir in the mustard and the 10 ounces of Cheddar cheese, the salt, pepper, nutmeg, and hot pepper sauce.

2. Meanwhile, cook the cavatappi according to package directions until just al dente. Drain but do not rinse. Stir immediately into the prepared cheese sauce until well blended. Adjust seasonings.

3. Spoon the mixture into a 9x13-inch baking dish. Top with the remaining 2 ounces of Cheddar cheese and the Parmigiano-Reggiano. Refrigerate, if desired.

4. To serve, let the dish return to room temperature. Preheat the oven to 400 degrees. Bake about 30 minutes, until the mixture is hot, bubbling throughout, and golden.

yield: 3 to 4 servings as a main dish, 6 servings as a side dish

prepare-ahead cheese soufflé

This is an exciting concept lifted from an out-of-print cookbook of mine. Though the soufflé does not rise as high as the traditional prepared-at-the-last-minute version, its advantage is that it can be made a week or two in advance and frozen. This is one of those dishes that impresses company: your vegetarian friends will thank you and the rest of the dinner company will want the same thing. Just remember that people wait for hot soufflés; soufflés do not wait for people. This falls *immediately*.

You can double the recipe.

2 tablespoons plus 2 teaspoons unsalted butter
5 tablespoons plus 1 teaspoon unbleached flour
½ teaspoon salt
Freshly ground black pepper to taste

⅛ to ¼ teaspoon cayenne
¼ to ½ teaspoon dry mustard
1⅓ cups 2 percent milk, heated
2 cups grated extra-sharp white Cheddar cheese
8 eggs, separated

1. Prepare three 3-cup soufflé dishes: Line the dishes with aluminum foil, fitting the foil as snugly as possible and allowing for 5- to 6-inch overhangs, which will be used to cover the soufflé tops during freezing.

2. Melt the butter; remove it from the heat and blend in the flour and salt, pepper, cayenne, and dry mustard. Return to low heat and cook for 1 minute. Remove from the heat; slowly stir in the hot milk until the mixture is smooth. Return to the burner and cook and stir over medium heat until the sauce thickens. Reduce the heat; add the cheese and stir until the cheese is melted and blended. Let cool for 5 minutes.

3. Beat the yolks well. Slowly add a little of the cooled cheese mixture to the yolks, stirring vigorously. Then pour the remaining yolk mixture into the cheese mixture and mix well.

4. Beat the egg whites until stiff but not dry. Fold the whites into the cheese base. Pour into the prepared soufflé dishes and freeze immediately. After the mixture has frozen, remove it from the dishes and wrap the soufflés in additional foil.

5. To serve, preheat the oven to 300 degrees. Remove the soufflés from the aluminum foil. (It takes a bit of work to remove the foil from the frozen soufflés.) Place the frozen soufflés back in the (clean) soufflé dishes. Bake for 40 to 50 minutes, until the soufflés have puffed up. Serve *immediately*.

yield: 3 servings

black bean and corn chili

This is a handsome-looking dish that derives its pleasant, slightly yeasty flavor from the beer. If you would rather not use alcohol, try one of the widely available nonalcoholic brews instead.

1 pound (2 medium) onions, chopped
1½ tablespoons olive oil
2 large cloves garlic, minced
½ to 1 whole jalapeño, seeded and
 finely minced
2 teaspoons ground cumin
½ to 1 teaspoon hot chili powder
3 cups cooked black beans or 2
 (15-ounce) cans low-sodium black
 beans, rinsed and drained
2 tablespoons chopped fresh oregano
 or 2 teaspoons dried oregano

1 (28- to 32-ounce) can low-sodium
 puréed tomatoes
2 (12-ounce) cans beer (3 cups)
2 teaspoons white vinegar
Salt and freshly ground black pepper
 to taste
4 cups fresh (about 4 ears) or frozen
 corn kernels
4 green onions, chopped
½ cup regular or light sour cream

1. Sauté the onions in hot oil in a nonstick pan until they begin to soften and brown. Add the garlic, jalapeño, cumin, and chili powder and cook for about 1 minute. Add the black beans, oregano, puréed tomatoes, beer, and vinegar and cook for another 5 minutes. Season with salt and pepper. Refrigerate.

2. To serve, reheat for 5 minutes or until hot. When the mixture is very hot, add the corn and cook for about 2 minutes, until the corn is cooked through. Serve topped with the green onions and sour cream.

yield: 4 to 6 servings

black bean cakes

There is no question that canned beans are not as firm-textured as home-cooked beans, and unless you buy the kind found in natural-food stores, they will be very salty even if well rinsed. So if you are not going to cook your own, look for the brands like Eden or American Prairie, which are low in sodium and usually a little firmer in texture. They can be found in health- and natural-food stores as well as in well-stocked supermarkets.

For bean cakes, however, texture is not very important.

½ pound onions, chopped (1⅔ cups)
2 tablespoons olive oil
4 large cloves garlic, minced
½ to 1 whole jalapeño or serrano
 chile, seeded and minced
2 teaspoons ground cumin
2 teaspoons ground coriander
¼ to ½ teaspoon hot red pepper flakes

1½ cups chopped carrots
4 (15-ounce) cans no-salt-added black
 beans, well rinsed and drained, or
 home-cooked beans (see page 95)
Salt and freshly ground black pepper
 to taste
½ cup nonfat plain yogurt or Crème
 Fraîche (page 223)

1. Sauté the onions in a nonstick pan over medium-high heat in 1 tablespoon of the oil until they begin to brown. Add the garlic, jalapeño, cumin, coriander, and hot red pepper flakes and cook 30 seconds; stir well. Add the carrots and black beans; season with salt and pepper and stir well.

2. Purée the bean mixture in a food processor, and if it is too thick, add a little bit of vegetable stock or water. The beans should be thick enough to make into 8 or 10 cakes that will hold their shape. Form and refrigerate the cakes.

3. To serve, heat a nonstick skillet and add the remaining tablespoon of oil. Sauté the bean cakes over medium-high heat until they brown; turn and brown on the second side and heat through. Serve with yogurt or crème fraîche.

yield: 4 or 5 servings

bulgur with tomatoes, olives, and cheese

Bulgur, or cracked wheat, is a grain known to most Americans in a dish called tabbouleh, a Middle Eastern salad with tomatoes, mint, oil, and lemon juice. It has a delightful nutty taste.

3 cups low-sodium vegetable stock or broth, or water
1 cup coarse bulgur
1½ pounds (3 medium) onions, chopped
2 tablespoons olive oil
2 large cloves garlic, minced
1 pound assorted cultivated exotic mushrooms including shiitake, portobello, cremini (whatever you can find), or plain white if the others aren't available, washed, dried, trimmed, and sliced

2 dozen Moroccan or other oil-cured olives, pitted and chopped
1½ pounds ripe plum tomatoes, diced
½ cup dry sherry
4 teaspoons chopped fresh oregano or 1 heaping teaspoon dried oregano
Salt and freshly ground black pepper to taste
2 cups coarsely grated extra-sharp white Cheddar cheese

1. Bring the stock to a boil in a covered pot and add the bulgur. Reduce the heat and simmer, uncovered, for about 10 minutes, until the bulgur is almost tender. Remove from the heat and allow to sit for 10 minutes longer, until the liquid has been absorbed.

2. Meanwhile, sauté the onions in hot oil in a large skillet until they begin to soften and brown. Stir in the garlic and cook for 30 seconds. Add the mushrooms and cook over medium heat until the mushrooms release their liquid.

3. Add the olives and tomatoes and continue cooking for a minute or two. Then stir in the sherry, oregano, and bulgur and season with salt and pepper. Spoon into a shallow baking dish. Refrigerate.

4. To serve, let the bulgur come to room temperature. Preheat the oven to 350 degrees. Sprinkle the bulgur mixture with grated cheese and bake for 10 to 15 minutes, or until the dish is heated through and the cheese has melted and begun to brown.

yield: 4 servings

vegetables

sesame asparagus

This can be made several hours before dinner and served at room temperature.

2 pounds asparagus
1 tablespoon toasted sesame oil

1 tablespoon toasted sesame seeds
1 teaspoon reduced-sodium soy sauce

1. Trim the tough part of the asparagus stems from the tender part by bending and breaking at the point where the stems break easily. Depending on thickness, steam the asparagus 3 to 7 minutes and drain. Set aside.

2. In a pot large enough to hold the asparagus, heat the oil until it is warm. Add the sesame seeds and asparagus, stirring to coat and warm the asparagus slightly. Stir in the soy sauce and serve.

yield: 4 servings

piquant asparagus

Like other green vegetables, asparagus cannot be marinated in advance in an acid mixture: they will lose their bright color. So make the dressing ahead; cook the asparagus and refrigerate the remaining ingredients separately.

If you cannot find a jar of cornichons, the tiny sour French pickles, you can use sweet and sour pickles.

1 tablespoon tarragon vinegar
2 tablespoons cider vinegar
3 tablespoons extra-virgin olive oil
1 tablespoon chopped cornichons

1 tablespoon chopped parsley
1 teaspoon chopped chives
3 pounds asparagus

1. Combine and mix well the vinegars, olive oil, cornichons, parsley, and chives; refrigerate.

2. Trim the tough part of the asparagus stems from the tender part by bending and breaking at the point where the stems break easily. Depending on thickness, steam the asparagus 3 to 7 minutes and drain; refrigerate, well wrapped.

3. To serve, pour the dressing over the asparagus and mix well just before serving.

yield: 6 servings

asparagus with roasted red pepper salsa

81

The salsa can be prepared almost completely a day in advance. The asparagus can be prepared in the morning and mixed with the sauce later.

12 roasted red bell peppers
(page 183)
2 to 3 tiny hot red peppers, such as
bird peppers or Thai peppers
3 medium cloves garlic, minced

¾ cup minced red onion
2 tablespoons lime juice
3 pounds asparagus
1½ cups chopped cilantro (1 or 2
bunches)

1. Rinse the peppers and slice into ⅛-inch-wide strips. Trim and seed the hot peppers and mince. Combine the roasted peppers, hot peppers, garlic, and onion. Add the lime juice a few teaspoons at a time, until the desired tartness. Cover and refrigerate, if desired.

2. The morning of the day the asparagus will be served, cook them. Trim the tough part of the asparagus stems from the tender part by bending and breaking at the point where the stems break easily. Depending on thickness, steam the asparagus 3 to 7 minutes. Drain. Refrigerate the asparagus separately, well covered.

3. Remove from the refrigerator 1 or 2 hours before serving and stir the salsa into the asparagus. Just before serving, mix in the cilantro.

yield: 6 servings

green beans provençal

They were called string beans in the first book and they were frozen, but there are no strings on modern-day green beans, and fresh beans taste so much better. Haricots verts are the very thin version, quite tender and much more expensive.

Dislike anchovies? Omit and use another tablespoon of capers.

2 tablespoons olive oil
10 flat anchovy fillets, rinsed, drained, and finely chopped
3 tablespoons capers
3 cloves garlic, crushed

2 pounds fresh green beans or haricots verts
Salt and freshly ground black pepper to taste

1. Heat the olive oil in a small nonstick pan and add the anchovies, capers, and garlic, cooking about 30 seconds. Set aside and cover.

2. Wash and trim the green beans; place in a plastic bag and refrigerate.

3. To serve, steam the green beans 7 to 10 minutes, depending on their size; drain and mix immediately with the anchovy mixture; season with salt and pepper and serve.

yield: 6 servings

golden beets

O kay. If you can't find golden beets, and it's not worth running all over town in pursuit, use regular red beets instead. The dish isn't as pretty but it tastes just as good.

8 large gold or red beets
3 finely chopped shallots
1 clove garlic
6 tablespoons extra-virgin olive oil

¼ cup balsamic vinegar
Salt and freshly ground black pepper
  to taste
1 tablespoon Dijon mustard

1. Wash the beets and remove the tops, leaving a little of the green stem on. Boil in water to cover until tender but still firm, about 1 hour. Cut off the tops; peel the beets under cold running water and cut them in quarters lengthwise. Cut into slices ½ inch thick.

2. Make the dressing by combining the shallots, garlic, oil, vinegar, salt, pepper, and mustard. Add the beets and refrigerate if desired. Serve chilled or at room temperature.

yield: 8 servings

baby bok choy with sesame sauce

Bok choy is Chinese cabbage. It has green leaves and a white stalk. If your local supermarket doesn't carry it, try a specialty food shop or an Asian market.

1 tablespoon sesame seeds
1½ pounds baby bok choy
2 tablespoons toasted sesame oil*
1 tablespoon grated fresh ginger
3 tablespoons dry sherry

1 tablespoon reduced-sodium soy
 sauce
¼ teaspoon chile paste with garlic*
3 tablespoons sliced green onions

1. In a toaster oven, bake the sesame seeds at 325 degrees until golden. Set aside.

2. Trim the stems off the bok choy and cut the bok choy in half lengthwise. Rinse very well and drain. Brush the bottom of a large skillet with 1½ teaspoons of the sesame oil; set the skillet over medium-high heat. Place part of the bok choy in the pan in a single layer, cut sides down. Add 2 tablespoons water. Cover and cook until wilted, about 4 or 5 minutes. Lift out of the pan, drain, and arrange, cut side up, in a 9x13-inch oblong baking dish.

3. Remove the water, if any, from the skillet, brush the bottom with more sesame oil, and repeat the entire cooking process until all the bok choy has been steamed. Add the second batch to the baking dish, let cool, cover, and refrigerate.

4. Add the remaining tablespoon of sesame oil and the grated ginger to the skillet. Stir over high heat until the ginger is lightly browned. Add the sherry and bring to a boil. Remove from the heat and add the soy sauce and chile paste. Pour the sauce into a small bowl, cover, and keep at room temperature.

5. To serve, let the bok choy return to room temperature. Pour on the reserved sauce. Cover with plastic wrap, make several slits with a knife to vent, and microwave on reheat about 3 minutes or until hot, turning the baking dish halfway through, if necessary. Sprinkle with the green onions and sesame seeds and serve.

yield: 8 servings

*These ingredients can be found at an Asian market, specialty food store, the Asian food section of a well-stocked grocery store, or by mail (see page 23).

gingered broccoli

2 pounds broccoli, trimmed of tough
  stems, florets cut into bite-size pieces
2 tablespoons toasted sesame oil
2 large cloves garlic, minced
2 tablespoons reduced-sodium soy
  sauce

¼ cup low-sodium chicken stock or
  broth
2 tablespoons chopped candied ginger
Salt and freshly ground black pepper
  to taste
4 green onions, chopped

1. Sauté the broccoli in the oil over low heat until it is deep green. Add the garlic and cook 30 seconds. Remove from the heat; stir in the soy sauce, chicken stock, and ginger and refrigerate.

2. To serve, let the broccoli return to room temperature. Reheat slowly for a few minutes in a covered pot, or heat in the microwave. Season with salt and pepper. Top with the chopped green onions and serve.

yield: 6 to 8 servings

sicilian carrots

Around the corner from where I live in New York City, there is a wonderful grocery carryout shop called Agata and Valentina. The recipe for these superb carrots comes from the store's prepared food counter.

The quality of the olive oil makes a tremendous difference in the flavor of the dish. Don't stint; use the best you can afford.

2 pounds peeled baby carrots or regular carrots, thinly sliced
4 tablespoons extra-virgin olive oil
4 tablespoons dried cranberries
3 tablespoons pine nuts

9 medium basil leaves, cut in julienne strips
Salt and freshly ground black pepper to taste

1. Preheat the oven to 400 degrees. Spray two large roasting pans with nonstick olive oil spray and arrange the carrots in a single layer on the pans, mixing with 2 tablespoons of oil. Bake the carrots for 30 to 40 minutes, occasionally mixing them so they don't burn. They should become soft and start to brown. Remove and let cool.

2. In a bowl, mix the carrots with the cranberries, pine nuts, basil, and remaining 2 tablespoons olive oil, and allow to sit overnight in the refrigerator.

3. To serve, let return to room temperature.

yield: 6 to 8 servings

note: The easy way to julienne basil is to stack several leaves one on top of the other, roll them up like a cigarette, and then slice crosswise into strips.

michele's corn pudding

Michele's corn pudding is an often-requested favorite at Occasions, a catering firm in Washington, D.C. When I tasted it I asked for seconds and permission to use the recipe in the book.

No wonder I liked it so much: the original contained 3 cups of heavy cream!

My version substitutes whole milk for the cream and 4 whole eggs and 4 whites for the 6 whole eggs. You can't tell the difference, believe me. Try it yourself. (P.S.: It's not so bad with 2 percent milk either!)

The cooks at Occasions use a local brand of Silver Queen corn, Hanover, but other really sweet corn, fresh or frozen, will work.

3 cups corn kernels scraped from fresh uncooked corn (about 3 ears) or 3 cups frozen Silver Queen corn kernels, defrosted
4 whole eggs
4 egg whites

2 teaspoons baking powder
1 tablespoon flour
¼ cup sugar
½ teaspoon salt
3 cups whole milk
1 tablespoon unsalted butter, melted

1. Pulse the corn kernels in a food processor about 10 times and then place in a colander for about an hour to drain.

2. Preheat the oven to 350 degrees.

3. Stir together and lightly beat the eggs and egg whites. Thoroughly mix the corn with the baking powder, flour, sugar, and salt and then stir in the milk, the beaten eggs and whites, and the butter. Butter a 10-cup baking dish and fill it with the pudding. Bake for about 1 hour in the middle of the oven, or until the pudding is baked through and a knife inserted in the center comes out clean. Cover and refrigerate when the pudding is cool.

4. To serve, let return to room temperature. Preheat the oven to 325 degrees, cover the dish with foil, and heat through, about 20 minutes.

yield: 6 servings

eggplant parmigiana

The eggplant is baked, not fried, considerably reducing the amount of oil, and real Parmigiano-Reggiano adds a lot of flavor.

The delicate flavor of fresh whole-milk mozzarella is wasted in this dish; use skim-milk mozzarella instead.

1 (29-ounce) can low-sodium tomatoes
2 tablespoons tomato paste
4 teaspoons olive oil
1 teaspoon dried basil
1 teaspoon dried oregano
1 teaspoon sugar
Freshly ground black pepper

3½ pounds eggplant
1 cup chopped onions (about 4 ounces)
2 large cloves garlic, minced
8 ounces skim-milk mozzarella, sliced
½ cup coarsely grated Parmigiano-Reggiano (about 2 ounces)

1. Preheat the oven to 400 degrees. In a saucepan, combine the tomatoes, the tomato paste, 1 teaspoon of the oil, and the basil, oregano, sugar, and pepper and simmer, uncovered, for 20 to 30 minutes.

2. Peel and trim the eggplant and cut into ¼-inch-thick slices. Spray slices on both sides with pan spray, place in a single layer on cookie sheets, and bake in the oven, turning once, until the slices take on color, 20 to 30 minutes.

3. Meanwhile, heat the remaining oil in a nonstick sauté pan and sauté onions until they soften and become golden. Add the garlic and sauté for 30 seconds. Add to the tomato sauce.

4. Arrange the eggplant on the bottom of a 9x13-inch pan, add a layer of mozzarella, using all the mozzarella, and then spread the sauce over the top. Sprinkle with Parmigiano-Reggiano and refrigerate.

5. To serve, allow the eggplant to sit at room temperature for 30 minutes. Preheat the oven to 375 degrees. Bake for 20 to 35 minutes, until it bubbles and browns.

yield: 8 to 10 servings

parmesan-braised fennel

This is incredibly simple and absolutely fabulous. Cooking brings up the licorice flavor of the fennel, and the combination of fennel and Parmigiano-Reggiano is a marriage made in culinary heaven.

3 pounds fennel
2 tablespoons olive oil
2½ cups low-sodium chicken stock or broth

Salt and freshly ground black pepper
6 tablespoons grated Parmigiano-Reggiano

1. Trim the feathery tops from the fennel and slice off the tough core at the bottom. Quarter the fennel bulbs lengthwise and brown in the olive oil in a nonstick sauté pan, turning and cooking about 5 minutes.

2. Add the chicken stock and cover. Cook about 30 minutes, until the fennel is very tender. The liquid should be syrupy, but if it is not, remove the fennel and set aside. Boil the liquid in the sauté pan until it becomes syrupy. If the pan can go in the oven, return the fennel to it and spoon on the syrup; otherwise place the fennel in a shallow baking dish and pour on the syrup. Season with salt and pepper and refrigerate.

3. To serve, remove the fennel from the refrigerator and let sit at room temperature for 30 minutes. Preheat the oven to 375 degrees. Sprinkle the fennel with the cheese and bake for about 15 minutes, until the fennel is heated through and the cheese has melted and is beginning to brown.

yield: 4 servings

roasted fennel, potatoes, and onions

2½ pounds red onions (5 medium),
  cut into eighths
4 large fennel bulbs, trimmed and cut
  into eighths
3 pounds tiny new potatoes, red or
  white, scrubbed but not peeled

4 large unpeeled cloves garlic
⅔ cup olive oil
Leaves from 5 sprigs fresh rosemary
Salt and freshly ground black pepper
  to taste

1. In a very large roasting pan, mix the onions, fennel, potatoes, unpeeled garlic, oil, and rosemary. Season with salt and pepper. Cover and refrigerate uncooked.

2. To serve, let the vegetables return to room temperature; preheat the oven to 425 degrees. Stir the vegetable mixture and roast for about 40 to 50 minutes, until all the vegetables are soft. Stir once while roasting. Remove the garlic and serve.

yield: 10 servings

basil-garlic mashed potatoes

A simple variation on the classic theme.

4 pounds scrubbed, unpeeled thin-skinned potatoes (Yukon golds, if possible), sliced ¼ inch thick
6 large cloves garlic
1 cup chopped fresh basil leaves

2 cups or more low-fat or nonfat buttermilk
Salt and freshly ground black pepper to taste

1. Cook the potato slices and garlic in water to cover until the potatoes are tender, about 10 minutes. Mash (peel and all) in a food mill, or use some other mashing tool. (The little bit of skin that goes through is not a problem.) Stir in the basil and buttermilk to a creamy consistency; season with salt and pepper. Refrigerate, if desired.

2. To serve, place in a glass dish; cover with plastic wrap and reheat in a microwave about 8 minutes on high. Stir once or twice while reheating. If the potatoes become too dry, stir in a little additional buttermilk.

yield: 10 servings

mashed potatoes with corn and chives

This is especially good during the summer when sweet, fresh corn is available.

4 pounds thin-skinned potatoes (Yukon golds if possible), scrubbed but not peeled, sliced ¼ inch thick
6 large cloves garlic
2 cups fresh or frozen corn kernels (about 2 ears if fresh)

2 to 3 cups nonfat or low-fat buttermilk
Salt and freshly ground black pepper to taste
1 cup chopped chives (about 4 bunches)

1. Cook the potatoes and garlic in water to cover until the potatoes are tender, about 10 minutes. When they are cooked, remove from the water with a slotted spoon, add the corn to the water, and cook 2 minutes.

2. Using a potato masher or a food mill, mash the potatoes and garlic. (If you use a food mill, much of the skin will be left behind.) Drain the corn and stir it into the potatoes with enough buttermilk to make a medium-firm mixture. Season with salt and pepper and stir in the chives. Refrigerate, if desired.

3. To serve, place the potato mixture in a glass dish; cover with plastic wrap and reheat in a microwave about 8 minutes on high. Stir once or twice while reheating. If the potatoes become too dry, stir in a little additional buttermilk.

yield: 10 servings

layers of potato and smoked mozzarella

82

If you prefer a more delicate flavor, use plain fresh mozzarella instead of smoked. Nonfat buttermilk makes this dish creamy with little added fat and cholesterol. The amount of buttermilk depends on the moisture in the potatoes.

If you can find Yukon gold potatoes, use them, but any thin-skinned potato will do. This dish is good without the basil, but it adds a depth of flavor that turns a very good dish into one that is outstanding.

2 pounds Yukon gold or other thin-skinned potatoes
4 large cloves garlic
1 to 1½ cups nonfat or low-fat buttermilk

½ cup chopped fresh basil
Salt and white pepper to taste
1 (8-ounce) package smoked mozzarella or fresh mozzarella, thinly sliced

1. Scrub but do not peel the potatoes and boil with the garlic until tender. Mash the potatoes and garlic with a potato masher or in a food mill. Stir in 1 cup of the buttermilk and the basil. Add more buttermilk until you reach a creamy consistency. Season with salt and pepper.

2. Spoon half of the mashed potatoes into a shallow casserole and top with half of the mozzarella slices. Top with the remaining mashed potatoes and arrange the remaining mozzarella slices on top. Refrigerate or freeze.

3. To serve, let defrost if frozen. Preheat the oven to 375 degrees. Bake the casserole for 20 to 25 minutes, or until the mixture is bubbly and the top is browning.

yield: 6 servings

note: This dish can be made without the cheese for a simple side dish that can go with more complicated entrées.

sweet potato pudding

Lots of interesting flavors, and not all of them sweet, make for an excellent sweet potato pudding. Maple syrup in place of sugar complements the seasonings, while low-fat sour cream and nonfat yogurt instead of full-fat sour cream cut fat and calories without sacrificing texture or taste.

2 pounds sweet potatoes	¼ teaspoon ground cloves
1 egg	⅛ teaspoon salt
2 egg whites	2 teaspoons grated lemon zest
2 tablespoons maple syrup	1 teaspoon grated lime zest
1 teaspoon cinnamon	3 tablespoons low-fat sour cream
½ teaspoon ground ginger	5 tablespoons plain nonfat yogurt

1. Peel the sweet potatoes and slice ⅛ inch thick. Cook in water to cover for about 10 minutes, until the potatoes are soft.

2. In a food processor, process the potatoes slightly, then add the egg, egg whites, maple syrup, cinnamon, ginger, cloves, salt, lemon and lime zests, sour cream, and yogurt and process until smooth. (If the food processor is small, this may be done in batches.) Place the mixture in a greased baking dish and refrigerate or freeze.

3. To serve, let defrost if frozen. Preheat the oven to 350 degrees and bake the dish for 30 to 40 minutes, until completely heated through.

yield: 6 servings

green and gold squash

Here's another entry from the original *Elegant but Easy*, but with significant changes. The original recipe had so much liquid that all the baking in the world could not evaporate it without incinerating the vegetables.

Egg whites have replaced some of the whole eggs, and whole wheat bread crumbs add body and a pleasing sweetness.

If you have a julienne blade or shredding blade for your food processor, you can make fast work of the shredding chore.

¾ pound zucchini, coarsely grated
¾ pound yellow summer squash
   (crookneck), coarsely grated
1 medium onion (8 ounces),
   chopped
1 tablespoon olive oil
2 tablespoons chopped parsley
1 tablespoon chopped fresh oregano
   or 1 teaspoon dried oregano

Salt and freshly ground black pepper
   to taste
1 whole egg
3 egg whites
⅓ cup low-fat or nonfat buttermilk
1 cup shredded sharp white Cheddar
   cheese
⅓ cup whole wheat bread crumbs
   (optional)

1. Place the grated squash in a kitchen towel and twist the towel to squeeze out the liquid. You will have to do this in batches.

2. Sauté the onion in hot oil in a nonstick pan until it is soft and beginning to brown. In a large bowl, combine the onion with the parsley, oregano, salt, pepper, and the squash. Slightly beat the egg and whites and stir in. Stir in the buttermilk and cheese, and the bread crumbs if using. Spoon the mixture into a buttered 1½-quart casserole, cover, and refrigerate.

3. To serve, remove the casserole from the refrigerator and let sit at room temperature about 30 minutes. Preheat the oven to 350 degrees. Bake the casserole for about 45 minutes, or until the mixture is bubbly. Serve hot.

yield: 4 to 6 servings

summer squash pudding

What is so appealing about this dish is its simple sweetness. It makes a nice accompaniment to a well-seasoned main dish, such as Breezy Barbecued Chicken (page 91).

The sugar, butter, and buttered bread crumbs that were in the original recipe have been removed.

2 pounds yellow or summer squash
3 tablespoons regular or light sour
  cream

2 eggs, beaten
Salt and freshly ground black pepper
  to taste

1. Scrub, trim, and cut the squash into ½-inch-thick slices and steam over boiling water for 7 to 10 minutes, until the squash is tender. Drain thoroughly. Purée the squash in a food processor and drain again, pressing to get as much moisture out as possible. Add the sour cream, eggs, and salt and pepper and process until the mixture is smooth. Spoon into a shallow baking dish and refrigerate.

2. To serve, remove the squash from the refrigerator and let it sit at room temperature for 30 minutes. Preheat the oven to 350 degrees. Bake the squash about 30 minutes, until the center is firm.

yield: 4 to 6 servings

squash with raisins and pine nuts

Put raisins and pine nuts together with some savory ingredients and you have a dish with Sicilian roots. This simple recipe is delicious either warm or at room temperature.

1 pound onions, chopped (3½ cups)
2 tablespoons extra-virgin olive oil
1½ pounds mixed zucchini and yellow squash, cut in julienne strips about ⅛ inch thick

1 tablespoon balsamic vinegar
¼ cup pine nuts
¼ cup raisins
Salt and freshly ground black pepper to taste

1. Sauté the onions in hot oil in a nonstick pan until they are soft and beginning to brown.

2. Add the squash to the onions and cook until they are tender but firm, just a few minutes.

3. Stir in the vinegar, pine nuts, and raisins, season with salt and pepper, and cook a few minutes longer to blend the flavors. Cover and refrigerate, if desired.

4. To serve, reheat slowly in a covered pan and serve warm or at room temperature.

yield: 4 to 6 servings

acorn squash stuffed with applesauce

Much of the sweetness in this dish comes from the dried cranberries or cherries, two items not available when we wrote the first *Elegant but Easy*. They are a grand addition to the culinary cupboard.

2 large acorn squash
¾ cup toasted slivered almonds
¼ cup dried currants, dried cranberries, or dried cherries (see Note)

2 cups unsweetened applesauce
1 teaspoon ground ginger
½ teaspoon ground nutmeg
2 to 3 tablespoons brown sugar

1. Preheat the oven to 375 degrees. Wash the squash and halve. Cover the bottom of a shallow baking dish with a little water. Place the squash halves in the baking dish, cut side up, cover, and bake the squash about 1 hour, or until tender. Remove from the oven and scoop out the seeds and fiber from the center of each half; discard. Scoop out the flesh carefully so that the skin is not torn. Set the shells aside and purée the flesh in a food processor or with a potato masher.

2. Mix the almonds, dried fruit, applesauce, ginger, nutmeg, and brown sugar with the squash pulp and spoon back into the shells. Cover and refrigerate.

3. To serve, remove the squash halves from the refrigerator and allow them to sit at room temperature for 30 minutes on a cookie sheet. Preheat the oven to 375 degrees. Bake for about 15 to 20 minutes, or until heated through, and serve.

yield: 4 servings

note: Many of the dried berries are now being processed with oil, an absolutely unessential ingredient for dried fruits. Check the ingredient statement.

spicy indian vegetables

2 large eggplants (about 2 pounds)
1 large Spanish onion (12 ounces), chopped
2 tablespoons olive oil
2 large red and/or yellow bell peppers (about 1 pound), cored, seeded, and chopped
1 large clove garlic, minced

2 tablespoons coarsely grated ginger
½ teaspoon hot red pepper flakes, or more
2 large ripe tomatoes (2 pounds), chopped
Salt and freshly ground black pepper to taste
¼ cup chopped cilantro

1. Preheat the oven to 500 degrees. Prick the eggplants all over with a fork and place on a cookie sheet. Roast the eggplants for 20 to 25 minutes, until they are tender.

2. Meanwhile, sauté the onion in hot oil in a large nonstick pan until it is soft and golden. Add the peppers, garlic, ginger, and red pepper flakes and cook until the peppers are soft. Add the tomatoes and cook until they are soft.

3. When the eggplants are cooked, run them under cold water and cut them up into small pieces. Do not peel. Add to the other vegetables and cook for a couple of minutes to blend. Season with salt and pepper. Refrigerate, if desired.

4. To serve, reheat slowly in a pot and serve sprinkled with the cilantro.

yield: 10 to 12 servings

sautéed peppers, onions, and rosemary

Onion lovers will be delighted with the meltingly sweet results of this sauté. It can also be used as a topping for polenta. This recipe makes enough to top 2 cups of polenta cooked in 8 cups of liquid. See the recipe for Polenta with Wild Mushrooms (page 172) for directions.

3 pounds onions, thinly sliced (6 medium)
3 tablespoons olive oil
3 pounds red and yellow peppers (or your choice of colors: brown, purple, orange), cored, seeded, and thinly sliced

2 tablespoons chopped fresh rosemary leaves
4 teaspoons balsamic vinegar
Salt and freshly ground black pepper to taste

1. Sauté the onions in hot oil in a very large nonstick pan over medium-high heat until they are soft and golden, about 10 to 15 minutes. Add the peppers and rosemary and continue cooking until the peppers soften and start to brown, 15 to 20 minutes.

2. Add the vinegar; season with salt and pepper; reduce the heat to low and cover the pan. Continue cooking until the vegetables are very soft, about 10 minutes longer. Refrigerate, if desired.

3. To serve, reheat over very low heat or in a microwave oven.

yield: 8 servings

ratatouille

This may not be the simplest way to make ratatouille, but it is the one that brings out the most flavor in all the vegetables. It can be made long before you want to serve it.

1 pound eggplant, washed, trimmed, and sliced ½ inch thick (do not peel)

4½ tablespoons fragrant extra-virgin olive oil

2 pounds onions (4 medium), coarsely chopped

6 cloves garlic, chopped

2 to 3 sprigs thyme, chopped

2 bay leaves

1 pound red peppers, seeded and coarsely chopped

1 pound green peppers, seeded and coarsely chopped

1 pound zucchini, cut into bite-size chunks

4 pounds ripe tomatoes, coarsely chopped

⅓ cup tightly packed fresh basil leaves

Salt and freshly ground black pepper to taste

1. Preheat the broiler. Spray the eggplant slices on both sides with pan spray and place on cookie sheets in a single layer. Broil the slices until they are brown, about 10 minutes, turn, and continue broiling until brown on the second side. Remove and coarsely chop, peel and all; set aside.

2. Heat 2 tablespoons of the oil in a very large nonstick pan and sauté the onions and garlic with the thyme and bay leaves over low heat until the onions are very, very soft, 15 to 20 minutes. Then raise the heat and cook the onions until they take on a little color. Set aside.

3. In 1½ tablespoons of the oil, sauté the peppers until they are tender, about 10 minutes; set aside. In the remaining 1 tablespoon oil, sauté the zucchini until they are beginning to brown. Add the tomatoes and basil and cook until the liquid has almost evaporated. Combine all of the ingredients and season with salt and pepper. Cook on the top of the stove very slowly until the liquid has evaporated, 15 to 30 minutes, depending on the amount of liquid. Refrigerate or freeze.

4. To serve, let the ratatouille defrost if frozen; remove the bay leaves, let the ratatouille return to room temperature, and serve.

yield: 12 to 14 servings

grains

marian's noodle pudding

In the original *Elegant but Easy*, I wrote: "Even Lois admits this one is great!"

The truth of the matter is that this is basically my mother's recipe, revised using light sour cream, 2 percent milk, much less salt and sugar, and much less butter. The crushed cornflakes that used to go on the top are gone and so is the direction to "dot the top with lots of butter."

The results are still awfully good, and the baking time has been reduced considerably. (I don't always use the sugar.)

1 pound broad egg noodles, cooked, drained, and rinsed in cold water	1 cup 2 percent milk
1 pint light sour cream	2 tablespoons sugar (optional)
1 pound 4 percent cottage cheese	3 tablespoons butter, melted
	Salt to taste

1. Mix the cooked noodles with the sour cream, cottage cheese, milk, sugar if using, melted butter, and salt. Spoon into a shallow greased 9x13-inch casserole and refrigerate or freeze, if desired.

2. To serve, let the noodle pudding defrost if frozen. Let it come to room temperature. Preheat the oven to 350 degrees. Bake for 30 to 45 minutes, until it is hot and bubbling.

yield: 8 servings

curried couscous

There is no curry powder in India; it was an invention of the English, and some is good. The premixed spices are a shortcut that provides the flavors with which Indian food is associated, but there are dozens of combinations of spices that provide that wonderful, complex taste. The cumin, coriander, cayenne, and turmeric give this recipe its "curry" flavor.

Look for instant whole wheat couscous instead of instant regular couscous. It tastes better and provides more fiber.

1 ½ cups low-sodium chicken stock or broth
¼ cup lemon juice
2 tablespoons minced crystallized ginger
1 tablespoon unsalted butter
¼ teaspoon ground cumin
⅛ teaspoon ground coriander

⅛ teaspoon turmeric
Few shakes cayenne
1 cup instant whole wheat couscous
¼ cup thinly sliced green onions
2 tablespoons chopped parsley
⅓ cup toasted pistachios, slivered almonds, or pine nuts

1. In a saucepan over high heat, bring the stock to a boil. Stir in the lemon juice, ginger, butter, cumin, coriander, turmeric, cayenne, and couscous. Cover the pan and remove from the heat; let stand for 5 minutes, or until the liquid has been absorbed. Stir with a fork. Refrigerate if desired.

2. To serve, mix in the green onions, parsley, and nuts and either let warm to room temperature or reheat in a microwave to room temperature before serving.

yield: 4 servings

polenta with wild mushrooms

2 cups fine-grained or quick-cooking polenta
8 cups low-sodium chicken stock or broth
2 cups grated Parmigiano-Reggiano
Salt and freshly ground black pepper to taste

2 tablespoons olive oil
2 pounds assorted cultivated wild mushrooms (portobello, cremini, shiitake, chanterelle, or others), washed, trimmed, dried and sliced
2 tablespoons chopped fresh thyme or 2 teaspoons dried thyme

1. To make the polenta: Stir the polenta thoroughly into 2 cups of the stock. Bring the remaining 6 cups of stock to a boil; reduce the heat to a simmer and slowly add the polenta, stirring. Cook until the mixture thickens, a couple of minutes. Stir in the cheese. Season with salt and pepper. Spoon into a shallow baking dish and refrigerate.

2. To make the mushrooms: Heat the oil in a large nonstick pan until it is very hot. Reduce the heat to medium-high and sauté the mushrooms with the thyme until the mushrooms release their juices and the juices begin to evaporate. Season with salt and pepper. Refrigerate.

3. To serve, remove the polenta and mushrooms from the refrigerator and allow to sit at room temperature for 30 minutes. Preheat the oven to 350 degrees. Reheat the polenta in the oven for about 30 minutes, until heated through. Reheat the mushrooms in a covered pan over very low heat. When the polenta is ready, spoon the mushrooms over the top.

yield: 10 to 12 servings

variation

❄ 🄱2 polenta with sautéed peppers, onions, and rosemary

- Prepare the polenta as in Step 1 of the recipe, eliminating the Parmigiano-Reggiano.

- Spread one prepared recipe of Sautéed Peppers, Onions, and Rosemary (page 167) evenly over the top and refrigerate or freeze.

- To serve, defrost if frozen, and allow to come to room temperature. Preheat the oven to 350 degrees. Bake, covered, for 20 to 30 minutes, until the mixture is heated through. Cut into serving rectangles and top each piece with a pitted black Greek, Italian, French, or Moroccan olive.

polenta with italian peppers and mushrooms

❄ ▢2

Italian peppers are light green and elongated. In some places they are called frying peppers.

¾ pound onion (1 large), chopped
2 tablespoons olive oil
¾ pound Italian peppers, seeded and thinly sliced
½ pound portobello mushrooms or assorted wild mushrooms, washed, dried, trimmed, and sliced
1 large clove garlic, minced
1 tablespoon chopped fresh thyme or 1 teaspoon dried thyme

Salt and freshly ground black pepper to taste
1 cup fine-grained or instant polenta
4 cups low-sodium chicken stock or vegetable stock
2 cups finely grated Parmigiano-Reggiano

1. Sauté the onion in hot oil in a large nonstick pan until it begins to soften and brown. Add the peppers and continue cooking until they begin to soften. Add the mushrooms, garlic, and thyme and continue cooking until all of the ingredients are soft and well blended, 5 to 7 minutes longer. Season with salt and pepper. Set aside.

2. Stir the polenta into 1 cup of the stock. Bring the remaining 3 cups of stock to a boil and slowly trickle in the polenta, stirring constantly so that lumps do not form. (If they do, mash with a spoon.) Reduce the heat and simmer a couple of minutes, until the mixture has thickened but still drops from a spoon. Season with salt and spoon half of the mixture into the bottom of a shallow baking dish about 9x13 inches. Top with half of the vegetables and half of the cheese. Spoon the remaining polenta on top of the vegetables; top with the remaining vegetables and sprinkle with the remaining cheese. Refrigerate or freeze.

3. To serve, let the polenta defrost if frozen. Let the polenta come to room temperature. Preheat the oven to 350 degrees. Bake the polenta for about 20 to 30 minutes, or until it is heated through and the cheese has melted.

yield: 8 servings

curried rice

A combination of nonfat yogurt and low-fat mayonnaise provides all the creaminess you could want, with very little fat.

3 cups cooked, hot long-grain rice
  (1 cup raw rice)
2 tablespoons balsamic vinegar
2 teaspoons lemon juice
2 tablespoons olive oil
½ cup raisins
½ teaspoon ground cumin
½ teaspoon ground coriander
½ teaspoon ground ginger
1 medium-large green pepper (8 to
  10 ounces), seeded and chopped
½ jalapeño, trimmed, seeded, and
  finely chopped
⅓ cup nonfat yogurt
3 tablespoons light mayonnaise
Salt to taste

1. In a large bowl, combine the hot rice with the vinegar, lemon juice, oil, raisins, cumin, coriander, ginger, green pepper, jalapeño, yogurt, mayonnaise, and salt. Mix well. Refrigerate, if desired.

2. To serve, let return to room temperature.

yield: 4 servings

wild rice with mushrooms, almonds, and sherry

There is more onion and mushroom and far less butter in this revisited recipe. The thyme is a new addition and adds a wonderful accent.

The best wild rice has been harvested by Native Americans. It is wild, not cultivated, and it has better texture and flavor.

1 ½ cups wild rice
3 tablespoons unsalted butter
1 ½ cups chopped onion (7 to 8 ounces)
¾ pound fresh mushrooms, washed, dried, trimmed, and sliced

1 ½ tablespoons fresh thyme or 1 ½ teaspoons dried thyme
3 tablespoons dry sherry
Salt and freshly ground black pepper to taste
½ cup toasted slivered almonds

1. Bring enough water to a boil to cover the rice generously. Rinse the rice and add to the boiling water; reduce the heat to a simmer and cook the rice about 20 minutes, until it is tender but still firm.

2. Meanwhile, heat the butter in a large nonstick skillet and sauté the onion until it begins to soften and brown. Add the mushrooms and thyme and cook until the mushrooms begin to soften and release their juice. Stir in the sherry, and when the rice is cooked, drain it well and stir it into the mushroom mixture. Season with salt and pepper. Refrigerate or freeze.

3. To serve, let the dish defrost if frozen. Reheat in a microwave oven in a deep casserole dish, lightly covered with plastic, for 5 to 7 minutes on high, or reheat very slowly in a pot on top of the stove, stirring often. Stir in the almonds and serve.

yield: 5 or 6 servings

pine nut and mushroom bulgur

Bulgur, or cracked wheat, makes a delightfully nutty and sweet addition to a main dish of strong flavors, particularly those with tomato.

¼ pound onion, chopped (1 cup)
1 tablespoon unsalted butter
1 large clove garlic, minced
½ pound mushrooms, washed, dried, and coarsely chopped
1 cup medium or fine bulgur
1 tablespoon fresh oregano or 1 teaspoon dried

2 cups low-sodium chicken or vegetable stock or broth
Salt and freshly ground black pepper to taste
5 tablespoons toasted sesame seeds
About 6 tablespoons lemon juice
½ cup toasted pine nuts
2 tablespoons minced parsley

1. In a large nonstick pan, sauté the onion in the butter over medium heat. When the onion has begun to brown, add the garlic and sauté for 30 seconds. Stir in the mushrooms and sauté until they give up their liquid and start to dry out.

2. Stir in the bulgur and sauté it over medium-low heat for about 5 minutes, stirring occasionally. Add the oregano, stock, salt, and pepper and remove from the heat. Allow the bulgur to absorb most of the liquid, about 20 minutes. Then refrigerate or freeze.

3. To serve, let the bulgur mixture return to room temperature, stir in the sesame seeds and lemon juice to your taste, and preheat the oven to 350 degrees. Spoon the bulgur into a baking dish and bake for about 20 minutes, until it is heated through. Stir in the pine nuts and parsley, reserving some of each for the top, and serve.

yield: 6 servings

salads

greens with pears and gorgonzola vinaigrette

Most of the preparation can be done the morning of the day you will be serving the salad. It can be served as a first course or as a combination salad/cheese course after the entrée.

9 ounces mixed salad greens like
   mesclun
2 tablespoons extra-virgin olive oil
2 tablespoons balsamic vinegar
1 tablespoon Gorgonzola or other blue
   cheese, separated into little pieces

2 ripe pears
Salt and freshly ground black pepper
   to taste
¼ cup pine nuts

1. Wash and dry the greens; wrap in paper towels, place in a plastic bag, and refrigerate. This can be done the day before.

2. Whisk together the oil, vinegar, and Gorgonzola. Peel, halve, and core the pears, cut into ¼-inch pieces, and stir into the dressing. Season with salt and pepper. This can be done in the morning and refrigerated. Let return to room temperature before tossing with the greens.

3. Just before serving, toss the greens, dressing, and pine nuts.

yield: 6 servings

arugula with raspberry vinaigrette and cheese in phyllo

□1

Like the Greens with Pears and Gorgonzola Vinaigrette, this salad is quite versatile. For a simpler salad, eliminate the phyllo-wrapped goat cheese. In its place put a wedge of cheese on the side of each salad plate: Parmigiano-Reggiano, dry aged Monterey Jack, taleggio, and goat cheese are all good choices. Accompany with bread.

1 pound 2 ounces arugula
Raspberry-Walnut Vinaigrette (recipe follows)

Phyllo-Wrapped Goat Cheese (recipe follows)

1. Trim the tough stems from the arugula and discard. Wash the leaves thoroughly and dry. Wrap in paper towels, place in a plastic bag, and refrigerate.

2. To serve, mix the greens with dressing; arrange on plates with 1 piece of phyllo-wrapped goat cheese on the side of each serving.

yield: 12 servings

raspberry-walnut vinaigrette

□1

There is no similar recipe in the old *Elegant but Easy*. Who had ever heard of walnut oil or raspberry vinegar in the 1950s or '60s?

And who had ever heard of such a ratio for oil and vinegar. The standard was 3 parts oil to 1 part vinegar. Be a miser with the vinegar and a spendthrift with the oil, an old cooking proverb said. That much oil makes the greens slip off the plate.

½ cup raspberry vinegar
1 cup plus 2 tablespoons walnut or hazelnut oil

2 teaspoons Dijon mustard

Whisk the vinegar, oil, and mustard together and refrigerate. To serve, return to room temperature.

yield: 12 servings

* 🄱2 phyllo-wrapped goat cheese

See page 36 for the handling of phyllo.

1 (12-ounce) log fresh goat cheese
1 heaping tablespoon fresh thyme or
oregano leaves

3 sheets phyllo
Olive oil

1. Roll the goat cheese log in the herbs. Place the 3 phyllo sheets on top of each other. Place the log at a short end of the sheets. Roll the phyllo over once, then tuck in the sides and continue to roll up to make a tight package. Place seam side down and brush with olive oil. Wrap in foil and refrigerate for up to 2 days, or freeze.

2. To serve, let the log defrost if frozen. Allow to sit at room temperature for 15 minutes. Preheat the oven to 425 degrees. Place the phyllo-wrapped log on a cookie sheet and bake in the middle of the oven for 10 to 15 minutes, until the phyllo is golden brown. Remove from the oven and allow to cool. Slice into ½-inch-thick slices.

3. The phyllo roll may be baked early in the afternoon and allowed to sit, covered, at room temperature. Slice an hour or so before serving. Arrange the slices on the sides of the salad plates. If you prefer, you can double the recipe and serve 2 slices per person.

yield: 12 slices

mesclun with chinese vinaigrette

81

Mesclun is a relatively new addition to the salad lexicon. It is supposed to be a mixture of baby and wild greens, but most mesclun sold in supermarkets is torn-up leaves of mature greens. This dumbed-down mixture has none of the delicacy of true mesclun, but frankly, it beats iceberg lettuce anytime.

½ pound mesclun
2 tablespoons extra-virgin olive oil
2 tablespoons balsamic vinegar

1 tablespoon reduced-sodium soy sauce

1. Wash and thoroughly dry the greens, wrap in paper towels, and place in a plastic bag. Refrigerate.

2. Whisk together the oil, vinegar, and soy sauce. Refrigerate.

3. To serve, mix the dressing again and stir in the greens, coating well.

yield: 4 servings

oriental dressing

82

This dressing has a distinct Asian accent. Excellent with all but the most tender lettuces like Bibb, it is marvelous over steamed or roasted vegetables.

¼ cup rice vinegar
2 tablespoons canola oil
1 teaspoon toasted sesame oil
2 tablespoons reduced-sodium soy sauce
2 teaspoons hoisin sauce

1 teaspoon dry mustard
1 teaspoon sugar
1 small clove garlic, minced
Salt and freshly ground black pepper to taste

Combine the vinegar, canola oil, sesame oil, soy sauce, hoisin, mustard, sugar, garlic, salt, and pepper and 1 tablespoon water or more, to taste. Whisk well. Refrigerate for at least ½ hour or up to 2 days.

yield: ½ cup, enough for 4 to 6 servings

tomato, mozzarella, and basil salad

There hardly seems a need for a recipe for this salad, but balance and proportion make a real difference in the flavor. This salad only tastes good when tomatoes are in season and local, if possible, and the mozzarella is fresh.

You can slice the mozzarella in advance and wash, dry, and strip the basil leaves from the stems ahead of time. But you can't cut up the tomatoes until just before serving, because they lose flavor and take on an unpleasant off-taste.

You can substitute thin slices of Parmigiano-Reggiano for the mozzarella. Two dozen pitted, halved black French, Greek, Italian, or Moroccan olives would make an interesting addition, too.

6 ripe medium tomatoes	2 tablespoons extra-virgin olive oil
1 bunch fresh basil, washed and dried	Freshly ground black pepper to
1 pound fresh mozzarella, thinly sliced	taste

1. Wash and dry the tomatoes and set aside at room temperature.

2. Remove 24 large leaves from the basil and place in a plastic bag in the refrigerator. (If the leaves are not large, use more.)

3. At serving time, slice the tops and bottoms from the tomatoes; slice each tomato in half and arrange 2 slices on each of 6 salad plates, or on a serving plate. Top each slice with a slice of mozzarella and two basil leaves. Drizzle on the olive oil and season with pepper.

yield: 6 servings

armenian vegetable salad

We didn't know what made this salad Armenian in the first book and still don't know, but it is delicious, especially made with fresh vegetables instead of the canned and frozen ingredients that were used in the original recipe. The exception is the roasted red peppers, which can be purchased or roasted at home (procedure follows). If buying roasted red peppers, drain and rinse them before using.

1 pound white mushrooms
2 pounds green beans, trimmed
5 tablespoons extra-virgin olive oil
7 tablespoons balsamic vinegar
1 tablespoon Dijon mustard
4 large roasted red peppers, julienned

2 bunches green onions, white and
   most of the green part, finely sliced
20 large or 30 small Italian, Greek, or
   French olives, pitted
Salt and freshly ground black pepper
   to taste

1. Wash and trim the mushrooms. Depending on their size, leave whole, halve, or quarter. Steam over hot water for about 5 minutes, until they are tender. Set aside. Steam the green beans about 7 minutes, depending on size. Drain and halve or cut in thirds, depending on size. Cover and refrigerate.

2. Whisk the oil, vinegar, and mustard together and pour over the mushrooms, peppers, green onions, and olives; cover and refrigerate.

3. To serve, stir the green beans into the rest of the salad. Season with salt and pepper. Do not stir the green beans into the dressing more than 30 minutes in advance because the acid will turn them gray green.

yield: 12 servings

note: To roast peppers: Preheat the broiler. Wash the peppers, place them on a cookie sheet, and broil about 2 or 3 inches from the source of heat, turning with tongs until the skins blister and char all over, 15 to 20 minutes. As each pepper is ready, place it in a large plastic bag and keep the bag closed for about 10 minutes; steaming will facilitate removal of the skin. Remove the peppers; the skins should peel off easily. After peeling, cut the peppers in half, remove the seeds, and julienne. Refrigerate.

a salad of fennel and
parmigiano-reggiano

One of the many variations on a salad often served in Italian restaurants, this could not be simpler. It depends on having the very best Parmigiano-Reggiano and a top-quality extra-virgin olive oil.

To get long, very thin slices of the Parmigiano-Reggiano, you can use a cheese slicer or a swivel-blade vegetable peeler.

6 small or 4 large bulbs fresh fennel
3 tablespoons extra-virgin olive
 oil
2 tablespoons fresh lemon juice

Salt and freshly ground black pepper
 to taste
6 very thin large slices of Parmigiano-
 Reggiano

1. Trim the bottoms and the top stems and leaves from the fennel. You can reserve a few feathery leaves for garnish, if desired. Slice off the bottom and discard the tough outer pieces. Slice the fennel bulbs very, very thin. You can use a mandoline, the very thin slicing disk of a food processor, the slicing side of a four-sided grater, or a very sharp knife.

2. Whisk together the oil and lemon juice and season with salt and pepper.

3. Wrap the fennel slices in plastic wrap; wrap the cheese slices in plastic wrap. Cover the dressing and refrigerate these three components overnight, if desired.

4. To serve, divide the fennel among 6 salad plates in a single layer. Break up the cheese slices and arrange over the fennel. Drizzle dressing over each portion and serve.

yield: 6 servings

fennel, red pepper, and corn salad

The anise flavor of the fennel and the sweetness of the corn combined with fresh herbs are an unusually refreshing combination.

1 large fennel bulb, thinly sliced
1 medium red pepper (5 or 6 ounces), seeded and julienned
Corn kernels from 1 fresh ear
1 small red onion (4 ounces), thinly sliced
1 teaspoon pink peppercorns
12 fresh basil leaves

12 cilantro sprigs, chopped, plus 4 whole sprigs
1 tablespoon lemon juice
3 tablespoons rice vinegar
3 tablespoons extra-virgin olive oil
Salt and freshly ground black pepper to taste

1. Combine the fennel, red pepper, corn, onion, peppercorns, basil, 12 chopped cilantro sprigs, lemon juice, rice vinegar, and olive oil in a large mixing bowl. Season with salt and pepper. Refrigerate.

2. To serve, arrange on 4 salad plates and top with the 4 whole sprigs of cilantro.

yield: 4 servings

raita

The combination of yogurt and cucumbers in a salad or condiment occurs in many culinary cultures, including those of India (from which this version comes), the Middle East, Greece, and the Republic of Georgia. You can also add ¼ cup chopped walnuts, or chop 2 sprigs of cilantro and use them in place of the mint.

1 pound Kirby cucumbers
½ teaspoon toasted cumin seeds
2 tablespoons chopped mint
½ to 1 whole serrano chile, finely minced (or ¼ to ½ jalapeño)

1 large clove garlic, minced
¼ cup raisins (optional)
2 cups plain nonfat or low-fat yogurt
Salt and white pepper to taste

1. Peel the cucumbers, seed, and coarsely grate. Place the grated cucumber in a towel and twist to squeeze out the liquid.

2. Stir the cucumber, cumin, mint, chile, garlic, and raisins, if using, into the yogurt. Season with salt and pepper and refrigerate at least several hours but preferably overnight.

3. To serve, stir.

yield: 2 cups, or about 6 servings

green bean and potato salad

If you can find haricots verts—the tiny French green beans—use them instead of regular green beans: their flavor and texture are better. They are, however, much more expensive.

2 pounds tiny new potatoes, scrubbed but not peeled
1 pound haricots verts (French green beans) or regular green beans, washed and trimmed
3 tablespoons olive oil
¼ cup white wine vinegar
2 tablespoons lemon juice
2 teaspoons Dijon mustard
4 teaspoons chopped fresh thyme
½ cup finely chopped red onion
Salt and freshly ground black pepper to taste

1. Cook the potatoes in water to cover for 10 to 20 minutes, depending on their size, until they are tender but firm; drain and cut in quarters or halves, again depending on size. Meanwhile, steam the green beans 5 to 7 minutes, depending on the thickness of the beans; drain and rinse under cold water to stop the cooking. Cut in quarters or thirds, depending on size.

2. Whisk together in a large nonreactive bowl the oil, vinegar, lemon juice, and mustard; stir in the thyme and onion. When the potatoes are cooked, stir them into the dressing. If the salad is not going to be served immediately, do not add the green beans: the acid in the dressing will turn them gray green. Cover the beans well; cover the dressed potatoes; refrigerate separately.

3. To serve, let the vegetables return to room temperature. Stir the green beans into the potatoes, season with salt and pepper, and serve.

yield: 6 to 8 servings

creamy potato and broccoli salad

The idea for this salad comes from my column in the *New York Times* for quick low-fat meals. Forget I ever said it was low in fat if that turns you off. Just remember that it is delicious.

2 pounds tiny new potatoes, scrubbed but not peeled
2 pounds broccoli
1 cup low-fat or nonfat plain yogurt
⅔ cup regular, low-fat, or nonfat buttermilk

¼ cup chopped dill, plus additional dill for garnish
30 oil-cured olives, such as Italian or Moroccan, chopped
Salt and freshly ground black pepper to taste

1. Boil the potatoes in water to cover for 10 to 20 minutes, depending on their size, or until just tender. Drain and let cool.

2. Trim the tough stems from the broccoli and reserve for another use. Cut the broccoli florets into bite-size pieces and steam until they are tender but still firm, 5 to 7 minutes. Drain. Meanwhile, cut the cooked potatoes into halves or quarters, depending on their size.

3. Mix together in a large bowl the yogurt, buttermilk, the ¼ cup dill, and the olives and stir in the broccoli and potatoes. Season with salt and pepper. Refrigerate, if desired.

4. To serve, sprinkle with additional dill.

yield: 6 to 8 servings

tabbouleh

As recently as fifteen years ago, very few people would have known what you were talking about if you suggested some tabbouleh for dinner. Today every carryout shop offers tabbouleh. There is one serious problem with those offerings: cut tomatoes cannot sit around all day in such a salad and taste good at dinnertime. Add the tomatoes to your tabbouleh at the last minute.

Cracked wheat, or bulgur, comes in three grinds: coarse-grain, medium-grain, and fine-grain, and for this salad you want fine-grain.

1 cup fine-grain bulgur, rinsed and drained
½ cup lemon juice
5 tablespoons olive oil
1 bunch green onions (6 to 8), green and white parts minced

2 cups finely chopped parsley
¼ teaspoon cinnamon
Salt and freshly ground black pepper
¼ cup finely chopped fresh mint (optional)
2 large ripe tomatoes

1. Mix the rinsed bulgur with the lemon juice and just enough hot water to cover. Allow the mixture to stand for about 30 minutes, until the bulgur has become light and fluffy and the liquid has been absorbed. Drain if there is liquid left.

2. Combine the bulgur with the olive oil, green onions, parsley, cinnamon, salt, pepper, and mint if using, and mix well; refrigerate for at least 1 hour or overnight.

3. To serve, cut the tomatoes into small dice and stir into the bulgur.

yield: 4 to 6 servings

asparagus rice salad

1½ cups long-grain rice
3 cups low-sodium chicken stock or
   broth
2 pounds asparagus
5 teaspoons toasted sesame oil

3 tablespoons rice vinegar
Salt and freshly ground black pepper
½ pound ripe tomato, seeded and
   finely chopped
2 tablespoons toasted sesame seeds

1. Combine the rice and stock and bring to a boil. Reduce the heat to a simmer and cover. Cook the rice for a total of 17 minutes, until the liquid has been absorbed. Set aside.

2. Break the asparagus stalks at the point where the woody part of the stalk and the tender part meet. Steam over hot water for 5 to 7 minutes, depending on the thickness of the asparagus. Drain, cut the asparagus into 1-inch lengths, and refrigerate, if desired.

3. Whisk together the oil and vinegar and mix in the rice; season with salt and pepper. Refrigerate, if desired.

4. To serve, stir the tomato into the rice, along with the asparagus. Sprinkle with the sesame seeds.

yield: 6 servings

desserts

fruit

blueberry kir sauce

What is particularly appealing about this recipe is that it can be served in the dead of winter as well as in blueberry season. Frozen berries work very well. It can be served cold, at room temperature, or slightly heated, over ice cream, sorbet, frozen yogurt, or a plain cake, such as angel food or pound cake.

1½ teaspoons unsalted butter
1 tablespoon cornstarch
¼ cup crème de cassis

¼ cup dry white wine
1 tablespoon lemon juice
1½ cups fresh or frozen blueberries

1. Melt the butter in a small saucepan. In a small bowl, combine the cornstarch and cassis to make a smooth mixture. Gradually stir the cassis mixture into the melted butter. Add the wine and lemon juice and cook over medium heat, stirring, until the mixture is thick. Stir in the berries and cook over medium-low heat just until they begin to burst. Refrigerate, if desired.

2. Serve warm or chilled.

yield: 1¼ cups; five ¼-cup servings

poached dried berries

There are so many wonderful dried fruits available today—far beyond the range of raisins and pears. They make a luscious, rich compote that has a lovely edge of tartness.

You can use any combination of dried fruits you prefer, and you can use almost any white wine from a Chardonnay to a late-harvest Riesling (which I prefer). It doesn't have to be one of the expensive ones, since you are not drinking it!

2 cups white wine—late-harvest Riesling or Chardonnay—plus additional if needed
¼ cup sugar, or to taste
1 to 2 teaspoons aniseed
Zest of 1 lemon, cut into ½-inch strips, white pith removed

½ pound dried strawberries
½ pound mixed dried cranberries and apples, in any proportion you prefer
¼ pound dried cherries

1. Combine the wine, sugar, aniseed, and lemon zest in a pot large enough to hold all the fruit and bring to a simmer.

2. Add the fruit and simmer, covered, for 10 to 15 minutes, stirring often.

3. Remove the zest and add more sugar if needed, and more wine if the mixture is too thick. Refrigerate.

4. Serve warm or cold over vanilla ice cream or frozen vanilla yogurt, or with a plain cake or butter cookies.

yield: 12 servings

zabaglione for berries

Whether you call this luscious but airy sauce zabaglione or sabayon depends on whether you are an Italophile or a Francophile.

One day I found myself without marsala in the house and the stores were closed; I took a chance and used Madeira. When I finally had an opportunity to buy marsala and compared it to the Madeira, I was amazed at the similarity in their tastes. Moral: For a dish like this they can be used interchangeably. And you can also use a sweet wine like a Sauternes or a late-harvest Riesling, or a Moscato or other Italian unfortified sweet wine.

8 egg yolks
¼ cup sugar
1 cup marsala

2 tablespoons brandy
1 tablespoon water

1. Beat the yolks with the sugar to mix well. Then beat with a wire whisk or rotary beater until lemon-colored. Add the marsala, brandy, and water and beat well.

2. Place the mixing bowl over a pan of hot water and continue beating until the mixture is very thick and has tripled in volume. Remove from the heat and chill.

3. To serve over assorted berries, allow 1½ cups of prepared berries per serving. Use a combination of fresh strawberries, raspberries, blueberries, blackberries—whatever you can find. Or serve over poached pears.

yield: 8 servings

mango cream

This has the consistency of a sauce or pudding but it is neither, though it would be superb on slices of angel food cake. The cream is served like a mousse, though it does not firm up like one.

3 pounds ripe mangoes
4 to 5 tablespoons fresh lime juice, depending on sweetness of mangoes
2 egg whites

3 to 4 tablespoons sugar, depending on ripeness of mangoes
1 cup heavy cream

1. Peel the mangoes; remove the flesh from the pits and purée in a food processor. Stir in the lime juice.

2. Beat the egg whites until frothy; gradually beat in the sugar until the egg whites are stiff.

3. Whip the cream until stiff and fold it into the mango purée; then fold in the beaten whites until the mixture is smooth. Spoon into 6 or 7 glass compotes or balloon wine glasses. Refrigerate for several hours or overnight. Serve cold.

yield: 6 or 7 servings

note: See pages 19–20 for pasteurized egg whites.

baked peaches and almonds

The original recipe from *The Summertime Cookbook* called for something called peach nectar. If it is still available, I couldn't find it, but I did find frozen concentrated peach and mango juice and used it, undiluted. It is delicious.

Look for any kind of frozen peach-something concentrate. Just be sure it is all fruit juice.

16 fresh, ripe peaches, halved and pitted
1 cup slivered almonds
½ cup orange liqueur, like Grand Marnier, Cointreau, or orange triple sec

½ cup frozen, defrosted, undiluted peach-mango concentrate or peach nectar
Whipped cream or vanilla ice cream (optional)

1. Place the peach halves, cut sides up, in a greased 9x13-inch baking dish and fill the cavities with the almonds.

2. Mix together the liqueur and peach-mango concentrate and spoon over the peaches. Refrigerate, if desired.

3. To serve, preheat the oven to 250 degrees and bake the peaches for 1 hour to 1 hour and 15 minutes, until they are soft. Spoon the pan liquid over the peaches several times as they bake.

4. Serve warm or chilled, topped with whipped cream or ice cream, if desired.

yield: 8 servings

jeremiah tower's poached pears in wine with basil

Jeremiah Tower is a talented chef who owns Stars restaurant and Stars Café in San Francisco. He provided me with this recipe in 1982 for a story in the *New York Times* and it was memorable. He kindly consented to its use in this book, somewhat adapted. It is a gorgeous dessert, suffused with flavor. Serve with a simple butter cookie or shortbread.

6 cups (almost two 750-ml bottles) dry red wine, like Cabernet Sauvignon
Zest of ⅓ lemon, white pith removed
½ to 1 cup sugar
6 ripe pears, with stems if possible, peeled

20 large basil leaves
½ tablespoon unsalted butter
Basil leaves and basil flowers for garnish (optional)

1. In a large pot, bring the wine, lemon zest, and sugar to a boil; add the pears; reduce the heat and simmer until the pears are tender-firm, from 20 to 45 minutes depending on the ripeness of the pears. Turn the pears frequently as they simmer. When the pears are cooked, remove them to a bowl and boil the liquid to syruplike consistency, about 15 minutes.

2. Turn off the heat. Swirl in the butter and quickly submerge the 20 basil leaves in the syrup; let steep for 1 hour.

3. Strain the syrup, pour it over the pears, and refrigerate until serving time. Serve decorated with a garnish of basil leaves and basil flowers if you wish.

yield: 6 servings

pears stuffed with
gorgonzola two ways

Here are two versions of this simple but luxurious recipe. The original recipe couldn't be easier; the second is the result of a request by a magazine to create a really low-fat version. It is just as good, though quite different. Here's the first, earliest version. Simple and quick.

3 large, ripe, firm pears with stems	5 ounces Gorgonzola cheese, softened

1. Wash the pears, halve, and remove the cores with a teaspoon. Leave the stems intact, if possible. Spoon the cheese into the cavities and refrigerate.

2. To serve, remove the pears from the refrigerator. Let sit half an hour before serving for the most intense flavor.

yield: 6 servings

Second, low-fat version:

3 large, ripe pears with stems	1 tablespoon medium-dry or sweet
2 ounces Gorgonzola cheese, softened	sherry
1 tablespoon reduced-fat ricotta cheese	

1. Wash the pears, halve, and remove the cores with a teaspoon. Leave the stems intact, if possible.

2. Place the Gorgonzola, ricotta, and sherry in a food processor and process to blend completely; then stuff the mixture into the cavities. Refrigerate.

3. To serve, remove the pears from the refrigerator. Let sit half an hour before serving for the most intense flavor.

yield: 6 servings

poached pears with apricot sauce

1¼ cups sugar
1 teaspoon pure vanilla extract
Strips of zest from ½ orange
Strips of zest from ½ lemon
2 thin slices fresh ginger, 2 inches long
4 cups water

6 ripe pears, peeled, halved, and cored
1 cup dried apricots
2 tablespoons lemon juice
⅓ cup fresh orange juice
3 tablespoons orange liqueur

1. In a large saucepan, combine 1 cup of the sugar, the vanilla, the orange and lemon zests, the ginger, and the water. Bring to a boil and add the pears; reduce the heat and simmer until the fruit is tender, about 15 minutes, depending on the ripeness of the pears. Let the pears cool in the syrup, then chill.

2. In a small saucepan, combine the apricots with 2 cups water; bring to a boil and simmer about 20 minutes, until the fruit is tender. Purée the apricots and their cooking liquid in a food processor or blender until smooth. Stir in the lemon juice, orange juice, orange liqueur, and remaining ¼ cup sugar. Chill.

3. To serve, drain the pears, reserving a little of the syrup. Garnish with the apricot sauce and a little of the pear syrup.

yield: 6 servings

pineapple surprise

This has always been a family favorite, and even though some last-minute work is required for this recipe, it could not be left out of *The New Elegant but Easy*. Some new techniques make it possible to make the meringue in advance.

I used to make this with vanilla ice cream, but more recently have tried it with pineapple sorbet, and it was almost as spectacular. Either way, if you want a delicious dessert, here is your ticket to fame.

3 small, ripe, whole pineapples
6 large scoops vanilla ice cream,
   raspberry sorbet, or pineapple sorbet

6 egg whites
9 tablespoons superfine sugar
¾ teaspoon cream of tartar

1. Cut the pineapples in half lengthwise, preserving the leaves. Using a small sharp knife, scoop out the pineapple centers. Remove the tough core and discard; cut the remaining pineapple into small pieces, and put most of the flesh back into the cavities. Cover the leaves with aluminum foil; cover the pineapple with plastic wrap and refrigerate.

2. Using an ice cream scoop, scoop 6 large or 12 small scoops of ice cream or sorbet onto a cookie sheet, cover, and freeze. They should be rock-hard. The recipe can be prepared a day ahead up to this point.

3. Several hours before finishing the dessert, let the egg whites come to room temperature. Place the whites in a bowl with the sugar and set over a pot of gently simmering water. Stir constantly until the sugar is completely dissolved; it will take only a few minutes. Remove the mixing bowl from the top of the pot and wipe the bottom dry.

4. Beat the whites on medium-low speed until frothy. Add the cream of tartar, increase the speed to high, and beat until stiff peaks form and the meringue looks glossy. Cover the mixer bowl tightly with plastic wrap and set aside until just before serving dessert. (Meringue made in this manner will weep and collapse like others after an hour or so, but *this* meringue will come back and fluff up beautifully after it is rebeaten for a minute or so.)

5. To serve, preheat the oven to 400 degrees. Rewhip the meringue. Remove the scoops of ice cream from the freezer and place them in the pineapple halves. Coat the ice cream and pineapples with the meringue, covering well to protect the ice cream so it won't melt. Place the prepared pineapples on a cookie sheet and bake 5 or 6 minutes, until the meringue begins to brown. Serve immediately.

yield: 6 servings

plum compote

¾ cup sugar
1 cup dry white wine
1 cup water
4 whole cloves

3-inch stick cinnamon
Zest of ½ lemon
16 large, firm, ripe red or black
  plums, stemmed

1. Combine the sugar, wine, water, cloves, cinnamon, and lemon zest in a saucepan large enough to hold the plums. Bring the ingredients to a boil and cook, uncovered, for 5 minutes.

2. Add the plums and bring the mixture back to a boil; lower the heat and simmer the plums for 10 to 20 minutes, depending on their ripeness, until they are tender but still hold their shape. Some plums will be ready before others. Remove them as they are. Then when they are all cooked, return the plums to the syrup and let cool.

3. Chill the plums in the syrup.

4. Serve plain or over vanilla ice cream or frozen yogurt, with some of the syrup, or serve with their syrup topped with whipped cream or Crème Fraîche (page 223).

yield: 6 servings

strawberry-rhubarb cream

This creamy tart-sweet dessert can be served over slices of angel food cake or with the cake broken up into small pieces and stirred into the strawberry-rhubarb mixture.

2 cups finely diced fresh rhubarb
1 pint strawberries plus 5 or 6 good-
  looking large strawberries for garnish
⅓ cup crème de cassis or framboise
¼ cup strawberry preserves made
  only with fruit

1 cup plain low-fat or nonfat yogurt
3 tablespoon thinly sliced crystallized
  ginger
½ cup heavy cream

1. Combine the rhubarb, 1 pint of strawberries, the crème de cassis, and preserves in a nonreactive pot and bring to a boil. Reduce the heat and simmer until the mixture is reduced and thickened, about 10 minutes. Remove and cool in the freezer for 30 minutes, or refrigerate and cool for several hours.

2. When the mixture is cool, beat in the yogurt and stir in the ginger. Refrigerate, if desired.

3. A few hours before serving, whip the cream and fold it into the strawberry-rhubarb mixture; refrigerate.

4. To serve, spoon into individual glass bowls or stemware and decorate each with a strawberry.

yield: 5 or 6 servings

gingered strawberry-rhubarb compote

1½ to 1¾ pounds rhubarb, diced (4 cups)
2 cups hulled, halved strawberries
½ cup sugar
½ cup fresh orange juice

Grated zest of 1 orange and 1 lemon
2 tablespoons chopped candied ginger
Pinch salt

1. Combine the rhubarb, berries, sugar, orange juice, zests, ginger, and salt in a heavy nonreactive saucepan and stir well. Bring to a boil. Reduce the heat and cover. Simmer, stirring occasionally, until the rhubarb is tender, 10 to 15 minutes.

2. Cover and refrigerate until serving.

3. To serve warm, reheat slowly. If desired, serve over ice cream, frozen yogurt, or plain cake.

yield: 8 servings

refrigerator desserts

Many desserts in this section call for uncooked eggs. Please read *carefully* the information on pages 19–20 before proceeding with any of these recipes.

prepare-ahead chocolate soufflé

Shortly after Le Cirque 2000 opened in New York City, I was assigned to write a story about the restaurant. Standing in the kitchen watching the action, I noticed the pastry chef, Jacques Torres, scoop up some ready-made soufflé batter, put it into a dish, and prepare to bake it. Jacques said he was able to make the batter several hours in advance and hold it. I told him that the only kind I had been able to fashion had to be frozen. Was it possible, I wondered, to make a soufflé batter in the morning and use it at night?

He said he was going to try, and a few weeks later he had come up with a soufflé batter that would hold for 12 hours in the refrigerator. The secret? An Italian meringue—one that is slightly cooked, giving the whites more stability.

Here is the recipe, with many thanks to Jacques.

You will need a scale to measure the chocolate and a candy thermometer to make the meringue.

1¾ ounces bittersweet chocolate, finely chopped
1½ ounces unsweetened chocolate, finely chopped
⅓ cup half-and-half
⅓ cup plus 1½ tablespoons unsweetened cocoa powder

Scant ½ cup water
8 egg whites
½ cup sugar
½ pint heavy cream, sweetened (optional)

1. Place the chopped chocolate in a mixing bowl. Bring the half-and-half almost to a boil and pour over the chocolate immediately. Allow to stand for 30 seconds, then stir until the chocolate has melted.

2. Bring an inch or two of water to a boil in a small pot with a diameter smaller than the bottom of the bowl in which the chocolate was melted.

3. Mix the cocoa with the scant ½ cup water; the mixture will not be smooth. Stir the paste into the melted chocolate and place the bowl over the boiling water. Whisk briskly until the chocolate mixture is smooth and very hot. Remove from the heat and set aside.

4. Place the egg whites in the bowl of an electric mixer.

5. Combine the sugar and ¼ cup of water in a small saucepan and stir to dissolve. Place over medium-high heat with a candy thermometer in the pan and cook the mixture to 250 degrees. Watch carefully; when the sugar-water mixture reaches 250 degrees, *immediately* remove it from the heat. Beat the egg whites for 5 seconds on high speed and then slowly pour the hot sugar down the side of the bowl, continuing to beat the whites. (Be careful not to pour the hot sugar onto the beaters because it will splatter.) Continue beating the meringue until the outside of the bowl is warm, not hot.

6. Fold one-third of the meringue into the chocolate. Then fold the remaining meringue into the meringue-chocolate mixture.

7. Butter and sugar the inside of a 7-inch-diameter soufflé dish. Make a collar of wax paper for the dish by folding a length of wax paper in half and in half again. Then butter it and attach it to the soufflé dish using tape or a rubber band, leaving an inch or so above the edge of the dish. Spoon the soufflé into the dish; cover lightly with foil and refrigerate for up to 12 hours.

8. To serve, preheat the oven to 375 degrees and place an oven rack in the middle of the oven. Thirty minutes before baking, remove the soufflé from the refrigerator and remove foil. Bake the soufflé 15 to 20 minutes, or until a straw or cake tester inserted in the center comes out almost clean. Remove wax paper.

9. Meanwhile, whip cream and sweeten, if using. Serve immediately, plain or with sweetened whipped cream.

yield: 4 servings

mousse au chocolat

others has been changed. The classic recipe remains. What is different is the availability of superb chocolate, so go for something imported like Valrhona (see page 23). The difference is amazing. If you can't get the best imported, use Nestlé.

½ pound bittersweet chocolate	4 eggs, separated
¼ cup sugar	1 inch of vanilla bean
3 tablespoons water	1 cup heavy cream

1. In the top of a double boiler heat the chocolate, the sugar, and the 3 tablespoons water over hot water until the chocolate is melted; mix well and let cool. Add the egg yolks one at a time, mixing well after each addition. Slit the piece of vanilla bean in half lengthwise, scrape out the seeds, and add them to the mixture.

2. Beat the egg whites until they are stiff but not dry. Fold into the chocolate mixture. Spoon the mixture into 6 or 8 individual pots or stemmed compote glasses. Refrigerate.

3. To serve, whip the cream and dollop it on the mousse.

yield: 6 to 8 servings

note: To pasteurize the egg yolks for the mousse au chocolat, use the following ingredients list instead of the one above:

6 ounces bittersweet chocolate	1 teaspoon butter
1 ounce unsweetened chocolate	4 eggs, separated
½ cup sugar	1 inch of vanilla bean
3 tablespoons plus 1 teaspoon water	1 cup heavy cream

As directed in Step 1, heat the chocolate, ¼ cup of the sugar, and 3 tablespoons water, adding 1 teaspoon of butter, until the chocolate is melted. Pasteurize the yolks using 2 tablespoons of the remaining sugar and the 1 teaspoon of water, following the directions on page 20, and add one-quarter of the yolks at a time, mixing well after each addition. Then continue with the directions in Step 1. Beat the remaining 2 tablespoons sugar with the egg whites as directed in Step 2.

note: See pages 19–20 for pasteurized egg whites.

double chocolate threat

This was designed for chocoholics, for whom there is no such thing as too rich. A few small changes to the original recipe have been made, including the addition of some orange liqueur to the whipped cream topping.

Brownie crust
⅔ stick unsalted butter
2 squares (2 ounces) unsweetened chocolate, plus 1 additional square (1 ounce) for decoration
1 cup sugar

2 eggs, well beaten
⅔ cup unbleached flour
½ teaspoon baking powder
⅛ teaspoon salt
1 teaspoon pure vanilla extract or 1 inch of vanilla bean, slit

Filling
1½ pounds semisweet chocolate
½ cup very strong coffee (like espresso)

3 eggs, separated
½ cup coffee liqueur
½ cup heavy cream

Topping
1½ cups heavy cream
3 tablespoon orange liqueur, such as Grand Marnier

Semisweet chocolate

1. Preheat the oven to 350 degrees. Adjust a rack to the lower middle third of the oven.

2. Melt the butter and chocolate over low heat or in the top of a double boiler over hot water. Remove from the heat; add the sugar and eggs, and mix well.

3. Sift together the flour, baking powder, and salt and stir into the chocolate mixture. Stir in the vanilla extract or scrape in the seeds from the slit vanilla bean. Pour the batter into a greased and floured 8- or 9-inch-square baking pan, and bake 20 to 25 minutes, until the brownies are baked but not dry; the batter will have pulled away from the sides of the pan slightly. Let cool.

4. Remove from the pan and cut into strips wide enough to come most of the way up the sides of a 2-quart soufflé dish or charlotte mold. Cut each strip laterally through the center to make two thinner pieces. Line the bottom and sides of the dish with the brownie strips. Don't worry about piecing; it won't show.

5. While the brownie crust is baking, make the filling: Heat the chocolate and coffee over low heat or in the top of a double boiler over hot water until the chocolate is melted. Remove from the heat.

6. Beat the egg yolks until they are pale in color; stir them into the chocolate. Stir in the coffee liqueur; let cool.

7. Beat the egg whites until stiff but not dry. In a separate bowl, whip the ½ cup cream until stiff. Fold the whites and cream into the chocolate mixture and spoon into the brownie-lined dish. Wrap well and chill overnight in the refrigerator, or freeze.

8. To serve, let the dish return to room temperature. To remove from the pan, loosen the sides with a knife, then quickly dip the pan into hot water to loosen further. Turn out onto a serving plate.

9. A few hours before serving, whip the 1½ cups heavy cream until fairly thick. Add the orange liqueur and continue beating until the cream is stiff. Cover the top and sides with the cream. Using a vegetable peeler, scrape bits of semisweet chocolate over the whipped cream.

yield: 12 servings

note: To pasteurize the egg yolks for the filling, use the following ingredients list instead of the list for the filling on page 207:

18 ounces semisweet chocolate	3 eggs, separated
3 ounces unsweetened chocolate	6 tablespoons sugar
½ cup very strong coffee (like espresso)	½ cup coffee liqueur
	½ cup heavy cream
1 tablespoon unsalted butter	

As directed in Step 5, heat the chocolate and the ½ cup coffee, adding the 1 tablespoon butter, until the chocolate is melted. Remove from the heat. Pasteurize the yolks using 3 tablespoons of the sugar, following the directions on page 20, and continue with Step 6. When the mixture is cool, beat the remaining 3 tablespoons sugar with the egg whites as directed in Step 7.

note: See pages 19–20 for pasteurized egg whites.

dione lucas' chocolate roll

Dione Lucas was a cooking teacher, one of the first on television, in the 1950s. I learned this incredible dessert in classes I took with her.

Described in the original *Elegant but Easy* as "Marian's favorite dessert," it is certainly as good today as it was when the book was first published in 1960. Not a thing has been changed, but today it is possible to buy much better chocolate (see page 23).

This is a very delicate cake; the directions *must* be followed to the letter or the cake won't roll properly. I know; here's my disaster story: I had made the cake base the morning of a party, and when I started to roll it up it collapsed into a dozen sections, the whipped cream oozing. I spooned it into a pretty glass bowl and served it as chocolate whipped cream pudding. The taste was great; the appearance left something to be desired. My guests inhaled it.

7 eggs, separated	Pinch salt
1 cup sugar	2 cups heavy cream
½ pound bittersweet chocolate	2 tablespoons rum
7 tablespoons coffee	Unsweetened cocoa powder

1. Adjust a rack to the lower middle third of the oven. Preheat the oven to 350 degrees. Oil a 10x15-inch jelly-roll pan. Line the pan with buttered wax paper.

2. In a small mixing bowl, beat the egg yolks and sugar until the mixture is light, fluffy, and creamy. Heat the chocolate and coffee over very low heat until the chocolate is melted; allow to cool slightly. Meanwhile, beat the egg whites with the salt until stiff but not dry. Mix the yolks with the chocolate and then fold in the whites.

3. Spoon the mixture into the pan and spread to level the top. Bake 15 to 20 minutes in a gas oven or 12 minutes in an electric oven, or until the cake is firm and pulling away from the sides of the pan. Remove from the oven and let cool for 5 minutes. Cover with a slightly damp cloth and let cool completely to room temperature.

4. Refrigerate for 1 hour. Whip the cream until almost stiff; add the rum and continue beating until stiff. Remove the cloth carefully from the roll and sprinkle the cake top generously with cocoa. Arrange two sheets of wax paper overlapping. Invert the cake onto the wax paper and carefully remove the pan and the wax paper that lined the pan. Spread the

whipped cream over the cake and carefully roll up from the long side, using the wax paper to help with the rolling. Roll the cake directly onto a long flat serving plate or chocolate roll board, if you have one. This cake cracks as it rolls: it should resemble the bark of a tree. Refrigerate. To serve, slice.

yield: 8 to 10 servings

mike's triple chocolate mocha madness cake

⊟1

This fabulous cake comes to you courtesy of Mustards, a marvelous restaurant in the Napa Valley. It is a big production, so save it for very special occasions, like a grown-up birthday party, when you are responsible only for the cake.

The saving grace is that every component of the cake can be made at least 24 hours in advance.

The Chocolate Cornflake Crunchies are definitely optional. They make the cake look nicer, but it will taste just as good without them.

❄ ⊟3   **Devil's Food Cake**

1 ounce unsweetened chocolate	3 eggs
1⅓ cups hot coffee	1½ teaspoons pure vanilla extract
⅔ cup Dutch-process cocoa powder	2 cups sifted cake flour
12 tablespoons (1½ sticks) unsalted butter, softened	½ teaspoon salt
	⅜ teaspoon baking powder
1¾ cups packed dark brown sugar	1½ teaspoons baking soda

❄ ⊟3   **Bittersweet Chocolate Marquise**

5 ounces bittersweet chocolate	4 eggs, separated
5 ounces semisweet chocolate	½ teaspoon cream of tartar
¼ pound (1 stick) unsalted butter	2 tablespoons superfine sugar
1½ teaspoons coffee extract	

⊟3   **Coffee Crème Anglaise**

2 cups half-and-half	5 egg yolks
2 tablespoons French roast coffee beans	1½ teaspoons coffee extract
½ cup superfine sugar	Pinch of salt

⊟1   **Coffee Cream Topping**

2 cups (1 pint) heavy cream, preferably not ultrapasteurized	3 tablespoons sugar
	1½ teaspoons coffee extract

⊟7   **Chocolate Cornflake Crunchies** (optional)

6 ounces semisweet chocolate morsels (1 cup)	1 tablespoon solid shortening
	2 cups cornflakes

To make the Devil's Food Cake:

1. Adjust a rack to the lower third of the oven. Preheat the oven to 350 degrees. Butter and flour the bottom and sides of a 10-inch springform pan, line the bottom with wax paper or baking parchment, and butter and flour the paper.

2. Combine the chocolate, hot coffee, and cocoa powder. Whisk until the chocolate is melted and reserve.

3. Beat the butter until pale yellow. Add the sugar and beat several minutes until very light and fluffy. Add the eggs, one at a time, beating well after each addition. Add the vanilla and beat to mix in.

4. Sift the flour, salt, baking powder, and baking soda together and add to the butter mixture, alternating with the cooled coffee mixture. Pour into the prepared springform pan. Bake 35 to 45 minutes or until a cake tester inserted near the center comes out clean. Let cool slightly on a wire rack, invert, remove the pan and paper, and allow to cool completely. The cake should be about 1½ inches high. Slice the cake laterally into three ½-inch layers and set aside.

To make the Bittersweet Chocolate Marquise:

5. Melt the chocolate and butter in the top of a double boiler over barely simmering water. Whisk until smooth. Whisk the coffee extract and the egg yolks into the chocolate mixture and reserve.

6. In a clean bowl, beat the egg whites at medium-low speed until frothy. Add the cream of tartar, increase the speed to high, and beat until soft peaks form. Add the sugar gradually, continuing to beat until stiff but not dry.

7. Fold one-quarter of the whites into the chocolate mixture, then gently fold in the remaining whites. Divide in half and spread the filling between the cake layers. (You will have a 3-layer cake with 2 layers of chocolate filling.)

8. Wrap tightly and refrigerate for a few days, or freeze for longer storage. To defrost, remove from the freezer and place, fully wrapped, in the refrigerator overnight.

To make the Coffee Crème Anglaise:

9. Bring the half-and-half and coffee beans to a boil in a heavy-bottomed saucepan. Turn off the heat and let steep for 10 minutes.

10. Meanwhile, in a medium bowl, whisk the sugar and egg yolks together until blended. Place the bowl on top of the saucepan with the hot half-and-half mixture and whisk the egg mixture until the sugar dissolves. (The slight heat from the saucepan below will make the sugar dissolve more quickly and will create a more stable egg mixture.)

11. When the 10 minutes are up, pour a small amount of the coffee mixture into the egg mixture, whisking constantly. Gradually pour all the coffee mixture into the egg mixture. Then return to the saucepan and cook, stirring constantly, over medium-high heat until the cream thickens. This should take less than a minute. Do not allow the mixture to boil. Strain, cover, and cool quickly in the refrigerator.

12. When the crème anglaise is cool, stir in the coffee extract and the salt. Return it to the refrigerator to chill until serving time. The crème will keep several days.

To make the Coffee Cream Topping:

13. Whip the heavy cream, sugar, and coffee extract until fluffy and thick. Generously frost the sides and the top of the cake. At this point the frosted cake may be refrigerated again and held up to 24 hours before serving, preferably covered (if you have a box or plastic container large enough). Garnish with the Chocolate Cornflake Crunchies, if using, just before serving.

To make the Chocolate Cornflake Crunchies:

14. In a 4-cup glass measure, combine the chocolate morsels and shortening. Pour warm water (100 to 110 degrees) into a mixing bowl and set the glass measure in the bowl. The water should come up to the 2-cup mark. Stir the chocolate almost constantly with a rubber spatula until it melts. This could take 15 to 20 minutes. (Do not splash any water into the chocolate or it will seize and become grainy.) As the water in the bowl becomes cool, replace it with more very warm water. When the chocolate is completely melted, it is ready to use. Remove the chocolate from the bowl of water and carefully wipe the measuring cup dry with a towel.

15. Gently stir in the cornflakes. Keep stirring and folding until they're evenly covered with chocolate.

16. Spread out in nice bite-size chunks on a cookie sheet lined with wax paper. Refrigerate until hard.

17. Place the crunchies in a tightly covered container in the refrigerator. Don't put them on the finished cake until just before serving, because they will become soggy after a few hours. Crunchies will keep about a week.

To assemble and serve:

17. Spoon some of the crème anglaise on each dessert plate and place a slice of cake on top, or spoon the crème anglaise around each slice.

yield: 12 to 16 servings

note: To pasteurize the egg yolks for the Bittersweet Chocolate Marquise, use the following ingredients list instead of the one for the marquise on page 211:

3 ounces bittersweet chocolate	4 eggs, separated
1 ounce unsweetened chocolate	6 tablespoons superfine sugar
5 ounces semisweet chocolate	1 teaspoon water
¼ pound (1 stick) plus 1 tablespoon unsalted butter	1½ teaspoons coffee extract
	½ teaspoon cream of tartar

As directed in Step 5, melt the chocolate and the ¼ pound butter together, adding the 1 tablespoon butter. Pasteurize the yolks using 2 tablespoons of the sugar and the 1 teaspoon water, following the directions on page 20, and continue with the directions in Step 5. Beat the whites with the remaining 4 tablespoons sugar and the cream of tartar as directed in Step 6.

note: See pages 19–20 for pasteurized egg whites.

lemon angel trifle

Almost no changes here, just a little less sugar.

1 angel food cake about 8 or 10 inches in diameter or a 10- to 14-ounce angel food cake (page 239), omitting the gingers
1 envelope unflavored gelatin
¾ cup fresh lemon juice

1¼ cups sugar
3 tablespoons grated lemon zest
6 eggs, separated
1 cup heavy cream
A few strawberries for garnish

1. Break the cake up into walnut-size pieces.

2. Sprinkle the gelatin over ½ cup cold water and set aside.

3. Combine the lemon juice, ¾ cup of the sugar, 2 tablespoons of the lemon zest, and the egg yolks in the top of a double boiler and cook over hot water, stirring, until the mixture coats the back of a spoon. Stir in the gelatin mixture and set aside to cool.

4. Beat the egg whites until they are foamy. Gradually beat in the remaining ½ cup of sugar until the mixture is stiff. Fold into the cooled yolk mixture along with the angel food cake pieces. Spoon the mixture into a 9-inch springform pan and refrigerate at least overnight. To serve, whip the heavy cream. Remove the ring from the springform. Top the cake with whipped cream and sprinkle with the remaining tablespoon of grated lemon zest and a few strawberries.

yield: 10 servings

note: See pages 19–20 for pasteurized egg whites.

cold lemon soufflé

This dish is both light and refreshingly tart. Perfect for warm weather, but delicious anytime.

You do not have to have a soufflé dish to make a dessert like this, but it looks very pretty when the collar is removed and the dessert rises above the top of the dish. It would also look attractive in a glass bowl.

6 eggs, separated, plus 2 additional egg whites
2 envelopes unflavored gelatin
½ cup cold water
1 cup freshly squeezed lemon juice
2 cups superfine sugar
1 tablespoon finely grated lemon zest
2 cups heavy cream
Strawberries, raspberries, and/or toasted slivered almonds (optional)

1. Let the 8 egg whites come to room temperature.

2. To make a collar for the soufflé dish, fold a 30-inch length of foil, 12 inches wide, in half lengthwise. Lightly butter the inside of the foil collar and wrap it around the outside of a 2-quart soufflé dish so the collar stands above the rim by 3 inches. Fasten with tape or a rubber band.

3. Sprinkle the gelatin over the cold water to soften.

4. In the top of a double boiler, combine the egg yolks, lemon juice, and 1 cup of the sugar. Cook over boiling water, stirring, until the mixture coats the back of a spoon. Stir in the softened gelatin and lemon zest; turn into a large bowl and refrigerate until the mixture is slightly thickened, stirring occasionally.

5. Beat the egg whites at medium-low speed until frothy, then increase the speed to high and beat until the whites form soft peaks. Add the remaining 1 cup of sugar, 1 tablespoon at a time, and beat until the mixture is glossy and holds stiff peaks.

6. Whip the cream until stiff. Fold the cream and whites gently into the slightly thickened lemon mixture.

7. Pour into the prepared soufflé dish and refrigerate until firm, at least 3 hours. (The finished soufflé may be refrigerated in a tightly sealed covered container or carefully wrapped in foil for up to 2 days.) To serve, remove the collar and top the soufflé with berries and/or almonds, if desired.

yield: 10 to 12 servings

note: To pasteurize egg yolks, you will need the:

    6 tablespoons sugar

Pasteurize the yolks using 3 tablespoons of the sugar, following the directions on page 20, and continue with Step 4. Beat the whites with the remaining 3 tablespoons sugar as directed in Step 5.

note: See pages 19–20 for pasteurized egg whites.

espresso mousse

1 envelope unflavored gelatin
¼ cup cold water
1 cup brewed extra-strength espresso
¾ cup granulated sugar
2 cups heavy cream
3 tablespoons brandy or coffee-
  flavored liqueur
1 teaspoon grated lemon zest

½ cup chopped toasted almonds or
  chopped walnuts
3 egg whites
¼ cup superfine sugar
24 chocolate-covered espresso beans,
  or grated lemon zest and grated
  chocolate, for garnish

1. Sprinkle the gelatin over the cold water to soften.

2. Heat the espresso and granulated sugar in a saucepan until the sugar dissolves. Add the gelatin to the hot mixture and stir to dissolve the gelatin. Let cool and then chill until the mixture begins to thicken.

3. Whip the cream until soft peaks form. Fold into the coffee mixture along with the brandy, lemon zest, and nuts.

4. Beat the egg whites at medium-low speed until frothy. Increase the speed to high and beat until soft peaks form. Gradually beat in the superfine sugar, beating until stiff peaks form. Fold into the coffee mixture.

5. Spoon into a 2- or 2½-quart soufflé dish (or into individual ramekins) and refrigerate for several hours, until firm, or up to 3 days in a tightly sealed container.

6. Decorate with chocolate-covered espresso beans, or with grated lemon and grated chocolate.

yield: 8 to 12 servings

note: See pages 19–20 for pasteurized egg whites.

tiramisù

Well, of course, there had to be a recipe for this Italian dessert. It swept the country in the eighties and has become so much a part of the culture that a nice, bland, boring version of it can now be found in the frozen prepared food section of some supermarkets.

There are dozens of recipes, but this version is one of the most delicious. It is certainly the lightest, since there are beaten egg whites in it.

Italian ladyfingers, *savoiardi*, are much larger and drier than American ladyfingers, and I prefer them in this recipe. If they are not available at your local Italian-American market, use the American ladyfingers, adding about 6 to 8 more to the recipe and toasting them at 375 degrees for about 15 minutes to dry them out. Or see the mail-order listing, page 24, for a source for the *savoiardi*.

24 to 28 ladyfingers—Italian (savoiardi), if possible
2 to 2½ cups strong espresso, cooled
6 eggs, separated
3 tablespoons sugar
1 pound mascarpone

1 tablespoon each marsala (or Madeira), triple sec, and brandy or to taste
1 teaspoon orange extract
8 ounces bittersweet chocolate, coarsely grated

1. Dip half the ladyfingers very quickly into the cooled espresso and arrange on a flat serving platter in a single layer (the length and width depend on the size of the plate).

2. Beat the egg yolks and sugar until pale. Beat in the mascarpone, marsala, triple sec, brandy, and orange extract. Beat the whites until stiff but not dry. Fold the whites into the mascarpone mixture.

3. Spread half the mascarpone mixture on top of the ladyfingers. Sprinkle with half of the grated chocolate.

4. Dip the remaining ladyfingers quickly in the remaining espresso. Arrange the ladyfingers on top of the mascarpone mixture and spoon the remaining mascarpone over that. Cover lightly with foil and refrigerate at least six hours or as long as overnight.

5. To serve, sprinkle the remaining chocolate over the top.

yield: 12 servings

note: To pasteurize the yolks, you will need:

6 tablespoons sugar

Pasteurize the yolks using 3 tablespoons of the sugar, following the directions on page 20, then continue with the directions in Step 2. Beat the whites with the remaining 3 tablespoons sugar.

note: See pages 19–20 for pasteurized egg whites.

strawberry "icebox" cake

Despite the fact that this is called an icebox cake, the recipe does not go back to the early part of this century. Very few Americans even knew what mascarpone was until the 1980s. But what a find! Mascarpone is an exceedingly rich triple cream with a mild taste and a texture like firm, heavy whipped cream.

The similarities between the recipe for tiramisù and this are obvious, including the richness. If you cannot find Italian ladyfingers, use American ladyfingers, adding another 6. See the mail-order section (page 24) for *savoiardi*.

A raspberry version would be equally wonderful; simply substitute an equal amount of raspberries for the strawberries.

Filling
6 egg yolks
3 tablespoons sugar
2 tablespoons orange liqueur

1 pound mascarpone
2 cups heavy cream

Soaking mixture
3 pints strawberries of any size, plus 2 pints medium strawberries for garnish
3 tablespoons orange liqueur

1 tablespoon sugar
2 dozen ladyfingers—Italian (*savoiardi*), if possible

1. Beat the yolks with the sugar and whisk in the orange liqueur. Beat in the mascarpone. Whip the cream until stiff and fold in.

2. Wash and stem the 3 pints of strawberries and purée in a food processor with the liqueur and sugar. Dip the ladyfingers quickly in the strawberry purée and place half of them in a single layer on the bottom of a large, flat serving plate with sides. The length and width depend on the size of the plate. Cover with half the filling mixture. Top with the remaining ladyfingers and spread on the remaining filling mixture. Cover and refrigerate.

3. To serve, stem the 2 pints medium berries and arrange on top of the cake.

yield: 12 to 14 servings

note: Pasteurize the yolks using the 3 tablespoons sugar, following the directions on page 20, and continue with the directions in Step 1.

ginger crème brûlée

No fat has been removed from this recipe. None. It has been updated by the addition of ginger and a little sugar in the crème.

Susan Simon, who helped with the testing, figured out how to caramelize the sugar topping without the use of a salamander or blow torch, à la Julia Child, and without burning your fingers.

8 egg yolks
½ cup superfine sugar
½ cup coarsely grated fresh ginger
4 cups heavy cream (1 quart)

1 teaspoon pure vanilla extract
½ cup light brown sugar
½ cup granulated sugar

1. Combine the egg yolks with the superfine sugar and beat well, until lemon-colored.

2. Place the ginger and cream in a saucepan and bring to the boiling point, stirring constantly. Boil exactly 1 minute. Remove from the heat. Strain out the ginger, then whisk the cream into the yolk mixture. Cook over low heat, stirring constantly, until the mixture thickens. (You'll know it's ready when the mixture adheres to your finger without dripping.) *Do not let it come to a boil or it will curdle.* Remove from the heat and add the vanilla.

3. Pour into 8 to 10 individual ovenproof ramekins or cups arranged on a cookie sheet, and refrigerate. When the custard has firmed up, cover the ramekins. Let chill at least 2 hours, or overnight if desired.

4. Set the broiler pan 3 or 4 inches from the heat source. Preheat the broiler. Combine the light brown and granulated sugars. Remove the ramekins on the cookie sheet from the refrigerator. Cover the tops evenly with about ⅛ inch of the sugar mixture (about 3 to 4 teaspoons per ramekin). Be sure the sugar touches the edges of the ramekins or it will shrink.

5. Place the ramekins (on the cookie sheet) under the broiler. Leave the broiler door open and broil the sugar until it melts, turning the cookie sheet as necessary to ensure even melting. Depending on the broiler, this will take anywhere from 1 minute to 4 minutes. Watch *very, very* carefully, since the sugar will burn almost as soon as it melts. Refrigerate the ramekins a few hours but no longer than about 24 hours or the crunchy sugar will liquefy.

yield: 8 to 10 servings

note: Because broiling the sugar can be tricky, you might try doing one or two at a time to make it easier.

crème fraîche

This is so easy to make, it's a wonder anyone bothers to buy it. If you have crème fraîche on hand, you always have the makings of a dessert as long as there is a little chocolate around. See below for some quick ways to satisfy your sweet tooth after dinner.

> 2 cups heavy cream
> 2 tablespoons buttermilk

Pour the cream into a container with a top. Stir in the buttermilk. Cover loosely and leave in a warm place, such as the back of the stove, until the cream thickens to the consistency of whole-milk yogurt. This can take as little as overnight or as long as a day. Store in the refrigerator for up to 2 weeks. If the mixture separates a little, stir to make smooth.

> *yield: 1 pint*

note: Do not use ultrapasteurized cream. In fact, the better the cream, the better the crème fraîche. Some organic creams are so rich in butterfat, the cream practically whips by itself.

Some quick suggestions for using crème fraîche

Start with a touch of the tartness of crème fraîche and add the sweetness of chocolate and liqueur:

Mix as much grated bittersweet chocolate as you like with a little crème fraîche and add a little orange liqueur.

Or mix the crème fraîche with chocolate and a little extra-strong hot coffee or espresso, with or without orange liqueur.

Of course, any liquid will thin it.

Make up your own combinations! Serve in small dessert dishes or over plain cake.

quick caramel sauce

This is easy to double or triple. It is an all-purpose sauce.

1 cup superfine sugar
½ cup water

1 cup heavy cream
1 teaspoon pure vanilla extract

1. Combine the sugar and water in a heavy-bottomed 1-quart saucepan. Bring to a boil, stirring constantly. Continue to boil gently, without stirring, until caramel in color, brushing down the crystals on the sides of the pan with a pastry brush dipped in water, if necessary. Remove from the heat.

2. Gradually whisk in the heavy cream. The hot sauce will bubble up. If the sauce is not quite smooth, return the pan to the heat, bring back to a gentle boil, and cook, whisking constantly, for 1 to 3 minutes. Remove from the heat. Stir in the vanilla.

3. Serve warm or at room temperature. This will keep a week or so in the refrigerator and can be frozen.

4. To serve, let the sauce defrost if frozen, and return to room temperature, or heat it gently. Serve over vanilla ice cream, frozen yogurt, pound cake, or angel food cake.

yield: about 1½ to 2 cups

frozen desserts

frozen grand marnier soufflé

When I tasted this for the first time in many years, it seemed a little too gelatinous, so some revisions were made: more water, more Grand Marnier, more sugar, some orange juice, no egg whites. Oh yes. And the ladyfingers have been retired.

Okay. So it isn't the same as the version in *Elegant but Easy*. But you'll love it anyway.

Praline
½ cup sugar
2 tablespoons water

½ cup toasted slivered almonds

Soufflé
2 envelopes unflavored gelatin
¼ cup cold water
½ cup boiling water
6 egg yolks
1⅓ cups fresh orange juice

2 cups sugar
⅔ cup Grand Marnier
2 cups (1 pint) heavy cream

To make the praline:

1. In heavy-bottomed saucepan, combine the ½ cup sugar and the 2 tablespoons water. Bring to a boil, stirring constantly. Then stop stirring and cook until caramel in color. (If sugar crystals form on the pan sides, brush them down using a pastry brush dipped in water.) Stir in the almonds and pour onto a greased cookie sheet. Allow to harden.

2. When the praline is cold and crisp, grind or pound into crumbs. The praline will keep indefinitely in a tightly covered jar in the refrigerator.

To make the soufflé:

3. To make a collar for the soufflé dish, fold a 30-inch length of wax paper in half lengthwise and then in half again. Lightly butter the inside of the wax paper and wrap it around the outside of a soufflé dish 7 inches in diameter so the collar stands above the rim by 3 inches. Fasten with tape or a rubber band.

4. Sprinkle the gelatin over the ¼ cup cold water to soften. Let stand for 10 minutes. Dissolve the softened gelatin in the ½ cup boiling water.

5. In a separate bowl, beat the yolks until light. Add the orange juice, sugar, Grand Marnier, and dissolved gelatin. Refrigerate, stirring occasionally, until the mixture starts to thicken.

6. Whip the cream until stiff. Fold into the slightly thickened egg mixture. Pour into the soufflé dish with its wax paper collar. Wrap well and freeze at least 4 hours. (The soufflé will keep at least 2 weeks in the freezer.)

7. A half hour before serving, remove from the freezer. Remove the collar. Roll the edge in the ground praline and sprinkle some of the praline on top. If there is some praline left over, it can be sprinkled on individual slices as well.

yield: 10 to 12 servings

note: Pasteurize the egg yolks using ¼ cup of the sugar, following the directions on page 20, and continue with the directions in Step 5. Add the remaining 1¾ cups sugar with the orange juice as directed in Step 5.

frozen plum soufflé

❄

I hadn't made this in a long time, but when I went prowling through my recipe files for the revision of this book, I found this in a 1980 article I had written for *Family Circle*. It has stood the test of time. Very few changes were made here: a little less sugar, a few more plums.

2½ pounds ripe red or purple plums, halved, pitted, and sliced
½ to ¾ cup sugar
2 teaspoons grated lemon zest, plus 1 teaspoon for garnish (optional)
4 egg yolks

½ cup confectioners' sugar
½ cup orange liqueur
2 cups (1 pint) heavy cream, plus ½ cup heavy cream for garnish (optional)

1. Prepare a 5-cup soufflé or other straight-sided dish. Fold in half a strip of wax paper long enough to encircle the dish, then fold in half again. Butter the wax paper and wrap around the dish, securing with tape or a rubber band to form a collar that extends 2½ inches above the rim of the dish.

2. Combine the plums and sugar in a large pot for a few minutes, until plums yield some of their juices and the sugar is partly dissolved. Bring to a boil, lower the heat, and simmer until the plums are tender, about 15 minutes. Purée mixture in a food processor, food mill, or blender; let cool; stir in the 2 teaspoons lemon zest.

3. Beat the egg yolks with the confectioners' sugar until very thick and pale yellow in color. Add the orange liqueur in a slow, steady stream while continuing to beat. Beat 5 minutes longer. Stir into the plum mixture.

4. Whip the 2 cups cream until stiff; fold into the plum mixture. Pour into the prepared soufflé dish and freeze until firm. This will keep for 1 week.

5. About 30 minutes before you are ready to serve, remove the soufflé from the freezer to the refrigerator to allow it to soften a little. Whip the ½ cup cream. Garnish the soufflé with the additional whipped cream and the 1 teaspoon grated lemon zest, if desired.

yield: 8 to 10 servings

note: Pasteurize the egg yolks, using the ½ cup confectioners' sugar, following the directions on page 20, and continue with Step 3.

lemons stuffed with lemon-raspberry sorbet

There will be more sorbet than needed for the lemons, but you will probably want it to serve your guests seconds. I did.

10 large lemons
Sugar to sprinkle lightly inside of
    lemons
2 pints lemon sorbet

1 to 2 teaspoons finely grated orange
    zest
3 tablespoons raspberry liqueur, such
    as framboise or Chambord

1. Cut about 2 inches off the top of each lemon, if they are large. Using a serrated grapefruit-sectioning knife, remove as much of the lemon pulp as possible from the lemons, then carefully squeeze the lemons with a hand juicer to remove additional pulp. Be careful not to split the skin. Save the juice for other uses. Remove a very thin slice from the bottom of each lemon so that they will stand up straight. Sprinkle the inside of each shell lightly with sugar.

2. Let the sorbet soften to room temperature.

3. Mix the softened sorbet with the orange zest and raspberry liqueur until well blended. Spoon the sorbet into the prepared lemons and freeze until the sorbet is firm, or overnight. Serve directly from the freezer. These will keep for a week.

yield: 10 servings

strawberry sorbet with berry topping

Y ou can buy strawberry sorbet everywhere, but this homemade version is special because of its intense fruit flavor.

1¼ cups sugar
1 cup water
3 cups puréed strawberries (2½ pints whole)
1 tablespoon lemon juice

2 pints blackberries or strawberries, washed and trimmed
Juice of ½ lime
2 tablespoons orange liqueur (optional)

1. Bring 1 cup of the sugar and the water to a boil to dissolve the sugar. Let cool completely. Whisk in the puréed strawberries and the lemon juice. Freeze in an ice cream freezer according to the manufacturer's directions. (If you do not have an ice cream maker, freeze the mixture in a metal pan, and when it is partially frozen, beat it with an electric beater; refreeze and cover well. This is not as smooth as sorbet made in an ice cream maker, but the flavor is just as rich and deep.) The sorbet will keep a few days.

2. In a food processor or blender process half the whole berries with the remaining ¼ cup sugar, the lime juice, and the orange liqueur if using; slice the remaining berries and stir into the puréed fruit. Refrigerate overnight at most.

3. To serve, spoon the berry mixture over individual portions of the sorbet.

yield: 6 servings

red wine sabayon ice cream

❄

While traveling through South Africa with friends, we were served a version of this incredibly rich, special-occasion ice cream at the Fancourt, a hotel in the town of George. It took many tries to get it right, but those who like wine with or in their dessert cannot do better.

¾ cup (12 tablespoons) superfine
    sugar
6 egg yolks
1 cup heavy cream
1½ cups (½ of a 750-ml bottle) good-
    quality red wine, merlot or cabernet

Fresh raspberries and/or blackberries,
    and fresh mint leaves, for garnish
    (optional)
½ cup heavy cream, whipped with 2
    tablespoons granulated sugar (op-
    tional, see Note)

1. Combine 6 tablespoons of the superfine sugar with the egg yolks in a large mixer bowl. Set aside.

2. Place 1 cup heavy cream and the remaining 6 tablespoons superfine sugar in a heavy-bottomed saucepan. Bring to a boil. Turn off the heat and set a timer for 10 minutes. Immediately place the bowl containing the egg yolk mixture on top of the pot with the cream mixture to cover. Whisk the yolk mixture until the sugar dissolves, and then remove the mixing bowl from over the pot. Cover the pot with a lid for the remainder of the 10 minutes. With an electric mixer, beat the yolk mixture until it is pale and thick and forms a ribbon when it drops from the beaters.

3. While the egg yolks are beating, heat the wine until hot (ideally, if you have a candy thermometer, to 140 degrees). Remove from the heat and set aside.

4. Bring the cream mixture back to a boil, stirring constantly. Remove from the heat and pour a small amount of the cream into the bowl with the egg yolk mixture, whisking constantly as the hot liquid is added. Gradually pour in the rest of the cream mixture and the wine, whisking until well blended.

5. Pour the entire mixture back into the saucepan, place over medium-low heat, and cook, stirring constantly with a wooden spoon, until the mixture thickens. *Do not let the mixture come to a boil or it will curdle.* (If you have a thermometer, cook the cream until it registers 180 to 185 degrees, no more.) Immediately remove from the heat and continue stirring for a minute or two. Pour this ice cream base into a bowl and chill for at least an hour and preferably overnight, stirring occasionally.

6. When the cream mixture is thoroughly chilled, pour it into an ice cream maker and proceed according to the manufacturer's instructions. If you do not have an ice cream maker, follow the directions below (see Note).

7. Serve immediately, garnished with berries and mint leaves, if desired. Or transfer from the ice cream maker to a freezer container. Although the ice cream will keep a month or so, the flavors diminish slightly. It is better to serve it within 2 to 3 days if it's for a special occasion.

yield: about 1 quart, or eight ½-cup servings

note: This ice cream can be made without an ice cream maker. Simply chill, then pour into a freezer-safe bowl. Cover and freeze, whisking every hour or so to prevent large ice crystals from forming, until it is frozen.

If you prefer a richer, more custardlike ice cream with a less pronounced wine flavor, add the sweetened whipped cream about halfway through the freezing process. If you are a merlot or cabernet fan, you'll probably prefer to leave out the whipped cream.

cakes

original plum torte

❄ ⊟2

Because of reader demand, this recipe has been published in one form or another in the *New York Times* almost every year since I went to work there in 1981. Lois brought this recipe, originally called Fruit Torte, to *Elegant but Easy*, and its appeal comes from its lovely old-fashioned flavor and its speed of preparation.

When I had been married just a couple of years, I had worked out an assembly-line process for making many tortes and putting them in the freezer. A friend who loved the tortes said that in exchange for two she would let me store as many as I wanted in her freezer. A week later she went on vacation for two weeks and her mother stayed with her children. When she returned, my friend called and asked:

"How many of those tortes did you leave in my freezer?"

"Twenty-four, but two of those were for you."

There was a long pause. "Well, I guess my mother either ate twelve of them or gave them away." Her mother must have liked them as much as I do. And the children. And possibly the neighbors.

¼ pound (1 stick) unsalted butter, softened	2 eggs
¾ cup plus 1 or 2 tablespoons sugar	Pinch salt
1 cup unbleached flour, sifted	24 halves pitted Italian (prune or purple) plums
1 teaspoon baking powder	1 teaspoon cinnamon or more, to taste

1. Arrange a rack in the lower third of the oven. Preheat the oven to 350 degrees.

2. Cream the butter and the ¾ cup of sugar. Add the flour, baking powder, eggs, and salt and beat to mix well. Spoon the batter into an ungreased 9- or 10-inch springform pan. Cover the top with the plums, skin sides down. Mix the cinnamon with the remaining 1 or 2 tablespoons of sugar and sprinkle over the top.

3. Bake for 40 to 50 minutes, until a cake tester inserted in the center comes out clean. Remove from the oven and let cool; refrigerate or freeze if desired.

4. To serve, let the torte return to room temperature and reheat at 300 degrees until warm, if desired. Serve plain or with vanilla ice cream.

yield: 8 servings

note: I've tried this with other plums, too. It's great.

new age plum torte

After I started writing the "Eating Well" column in the *Times*, I created a version of plum torte that was lower in fat (by about half) and calories (by a few). If you don't sample the tortes side by side—the old and the new age—you will love the lower-fat one as much as the full-fat one. It's the only excuse I can offer for using an egg substitute. As with the original recipe, other varieties of plums work well, too.

¼ cup (½ stick) unsalted butter, softened
¾ cup plus 1 or 2 tablespoons sugar
1½ ripe medium bananas, cut into large chunks
½ cup unsweetened applesauce
1 cup unbleached flour, sifted
1 teaspoon baking powder
½ cup egg substitute
Pinch salt
24 halves ripe pitted Italian plums
1 teaspoon cinnamon or more, to taste

1. Adjust a rack to the lower third of the oven. Preheat the oven to 350 degrees.

2. Beat the butter and the ¾ cup sugar until light and fluffy. Beat in the bananas and applesauce. Add the flour, baking powder, egg substitute, and salt and beat until well blended. Spoon the batter into an ungreased 9- or 10-inch springform pan and arrange the plums, skin sides down, on top. Mix the remaining 1 or 2 tablespoons of sugar with the cinnamon and sprinkle over the top of the plums.

3. Bake for 40 to 50 minutes, until a cake tester inserted in the center comes out clean. Remove from the oven and set on a wire rack to cool. Refrigerate or freeze.

4. To serve, let the torte return to room temperature. Reheat at 300 degrees until warm .

yield: 8 servings

apple-cranberry torte

When it's winter and there are no plums, make this version of the torte instead.

½ cup dried cranberries
3 large, tart, firm apples
½ lemon
½ cup (1 stick) unsalted butter, softened
¾ cup plus 2 to 3 tablespoons sugar

2 eggs
1 cup unbleached flour, sifted
1 teaspoon baking powder
1 to 2 teaspoons cinnamon, or to taste
¼ cup currant jelly

1. Adjust a rack to the bottom third of the oven. Preheat the oven to 350 degrees. Butter a 10-inch springform pan.

2. Bring 1½ cups water to a simmer; remove from the heat and add the dried cranberries. Soak the berries until they are plump, about 15 to 20 minutes. Drain well. Peel, core, and slice the apples into ½-inch-thick wedges. Squeeze the ½ lemon over the apples. Toss to coat and set aside.

3. Cream the butter and the ¾ cup sugar until light and fluffy. Add the eggs, flour, and baking powder and mix until well blended. Stir in the cranberries, reserving a handful to sprinkle on the top later. Spread the batter evenly in the prepared pan.

4. Combine the cinnamon with the 2 to 3 tablespoons of sugar; add more cinnamon, if desired.

5. Arrange the apple slices in concentric circles, pointed edges toward the center of the pan and the slices slightly overlapping one another. Work toward the center. Sprinkle with the cinnamon mixture and then with the reserved handful of cranberries.

6. Bake about 40 to 50 minutes, or until the cake is golden brown, the apples are tender but not mushy, and a cake tester inserted in the center of the exposed cake comes out clean. Remove from the oven and set on a wire rack. Let cool, then refrigerate or freeze.

7. To serve, defrost if frozen. Preheat the oven to 300 degrees and warm the torte briefly, or serve it at room temperature. Before serving, melt the jelly and with a pastry brush glaze the cake.

yield: 8 servings

❄ ❄₂ *new age apple-cranberry torte*

Here's a lower-fat version of the Apple-Cranberry Torte. Like the New Age Plum Torte, it, too, calls for an egg substitute. The excuse is the same.

1½ cups water	1½ ripe medium bananas, broken into
½ cup dried cranberries	large chunks
3 large, tart, firm apples	½ cup unsweetened applesauce
½ lemon	½ cup egg substitute
4 tablespoons (½ stick) unsalted butter,	1 cup unbleached flour, sifted
softened	1 teaspoon baking powder
¾ cup plus 2 to 3 tablespoons	1 or 2 teaspoons cinnamon, or to taste
sugar	¼ cup currant jelly

1. Adjust a rack to the bottom third of the oven. Preheat the oven to 350 degrees. Coat a 10-inch springform pan with nonstick pan spray.

2. Bring water to a simmer; remove from the heat and add the dried cranberries. Soak the berries until plump, about 15 to 20 minutes. Drain well; discard the water.

3. Peel, core, and slice the apples into ½-inch-thick wedges. Squeeze the ½ lemon over the apples and toss to coat; set aside.

4. Cream the butter and the ¾ cup sugar until light and fluffy. Beat in the bananas and applesauce. Add the egg substitute, flour, and baking powder and mix until well blended. Stir in the cranberries, reserving a handful to sprinkle on the top later. Spread the batter evenly in the prepared pan.

5. Combine the cinnamon with the 2 to 3 tablespoons of sugar; add more cinnamon, if desired.

6. Arrange the apple slices in concentric circles, pointed edges toward the center of the pan and slightly overlapping one another. Work toward the center. Sprinkle with the cinnamon mixture and then with the reserved handful of cranberries.

7. Bake about 40 to 50 minutes, or until the cake is golden brown, the apples are tender but not mushy, and a cake tester inserted in the center of the exposed cake comes out clean. Remove from the oven and set on a wire rack. Let cool, then refrigerate or freeze.

8. To serve, defrost if frozen. Preheat the oven to 300 degrees and warm the torte briefly, or serve it at room temperature. Before serving, melt the jelly and with a pastry brush glaze the cake.

yield: 8 servings

judy's lemon poppy seed cake

Cake

½ pound (2 sticks) unsalted butter, softened
1½ cups sugar
4 eggs, separated
1 cup sour cream
1 teaspoon baking soda

2 cups unbleached flour
Finely grated zest of 2 large lemons
2 ounces (6 tablespoons) poppy seeds
1 tablespoon pure vanilla extract

Glaze

½ cup sugar

Scant ¼ cup freshly squeezed lemon
  juice

1. Adjust an oven rack to the lower third of the oven. Preheat the oven to 350 degrees. Grease and flour a bundt pan.

2. Cream the butter. Add the 1½ cups sugar and beat until very light and fluffy, about 2 to 3 minutes. Add the egg yolks, one at a time, mixing well after each addition.

3. Combine the sour cream and baking soda. On lowest speed, add the flour and the sour cream mixture to the butter, followed by the lemon zest, poppy seeds, and vanilla. Mix well.

4. Beat the egg whites until stiff but not dry and then fold them into the batter. Pour into the bundt pan. Bake for 1 hour. Let cool for 5 minutes; while the cake cools, make the glaze by combining the ½ cup sugar and lemon juice and mixing well. The glaze must be used immediately after mixing. Invert the cake onto a wire rack placed over a jelly-roll pan and remove the cake from the bundt pan. While the cake is still hot, cover the entire surface of the cake with the glaze, using a pastry brush. Let cool completely and serve. The cake will keep a few days, tightly wrapped, at room temperature, or 5 days if refrigerated. Bring to room temperature to serve.

yield: 10 to 12 servings

pumpkin cheesecake in nut crust

If you can find plain canned pumpkin at other times, this Thanksgiving treat can be enjoyed all year long. The pumpkin keeps the cheesecake from being achingly sweet, and for those who say they don't like pumpkin, don't tell them.

Nut crust
2 cups ground toasted pecans
 (see Note)
2 tablespoons brown sugar

1 teaspoon ground ginger
1 teaspoon finely grated lemon zest
3 tablespoons unsalted butter, melted

Filling
2½ pounds cream cheese, softened
1 cup firmly packed dark brown sugar
½ cup granulated sugar
1 cup heavy cream
4 eggs
3 egg yolks
2 teaspoons cinnamon
1 teaspoon nutmeg

1 teaspoon ginger
¼ teaspoon allspice
2½ teaspoons grated lemon zest, plus
 coarsely grated lemon zest for garnish
3 tablespoons flour
1 tablespoon pure vanilla extract
1 (16-ounce) can pumpkin purée
 (about 1¾ cups)

1. To make the crust: Generously butter the bottom, sides, and top rim of a 10-inch springform pan. Mix the pecans with the brown sugar, ginger, and lemon zest; stir in the butter and mix well. Press into the bottom and a little way up the sides of the prepared springform. Set aside.

2. Adjust a rack to the lower third of the oven. Preheat the oven to 400 degrees. Place a pan of hot water in the bottom of the oven to keep the cake from cracking.

3. To make the filling: Beat the softened cream cheese until it is fluffy and completely smooth. Gradually add the brown and granulated sugars and beat well. Beat in the cream. Add the eggs and egg yolks, one at a time, beating well after each addition. Beat in the cinnamon, nutmeg, ginger, allspice, 2½ teaspoons lemon zest, and flour. Then add the vanilla and pumpkin.

4. Pour the filling into the nut crust and rotate briskly back and forth to help eliminate air bubbles. Bake for 20 minutes. Reduce the heat to 275 degrees and bake 45 to 55 minutes

longer. When done, the top of the cake should be golden brown and feel dry to the touch, but the cake will still be soft inside. Turn off the heat and allow the cake to cool in the oven for 2 hours. Then cover and chill.

5. To serve, remove the sides of the springform; decorate with coarsely grated lemon zest.

yield: 12 to 16 servings

note: For ground toasted pecans, toast and then grind.

ginger angel food cake

It's so nice that angel food cakes have been rescued from the obscurity to which they were relegated a few years ago. I love the texture, and the added ginger perks up the flavor immeasurably. If you prefer your angel food cake plain, simply omit the crystallized and ground ginger.

1 cup sifted cake flour
1½ cups sifted confectioners' sugar
¼ teaspoon salt
1½ cups egg whites (approximately 12), at room temperature
1½ teaspoons cream of tartar

1 cup superfine sugar
1 teaspoon pure vanilla extract
1 tablespoon finely chopped crystallized ginger
½ teaspoon ground ginger

1. Adjust an oven rack to the lower third of the oven and preheat the oven to 350 degrees.

2. Combine the cake flour, confectioners' sugar, and salt in a triple sifter, or sift three times. Sift onto wax paper and set aside.

3. Whip the egg whites until frothy. Add the cream of tartar. At medium speed, continue to beat the egg whites until soft peaks form. Gradually add the superfine sugar, 1 tablespoon at a time, and beat at high speed until glossy and stiff but not dry. Fold in the vanilla, crystallized ginger, and ground ginger. Sprinkle a quarter of the flour mixture over the beaten whites and gently fold in. Repeat with the remaining mixture, a quarter at a time, folding quickly but thoroughly.

4. Gently pour the batter into a dry, ungreased 10-inch tube pan. Bake 40 to 45 minutes, or until the top of the cake is light golden, the cake feels spongy, and a cake tester inserted in the center of the cake comes out dry.

5. Invert the cake pan onto the neck of a bottle or funnel and let cool completely before removing the cake from the pan. (Run a metal spatula around the sides and center core to help loosen.) Angel food cake will keep for a day at room temperature, tightly wrapped, or a week in the refrigerator.

6. Serve with fresh berries, Blueberry Kir Sauce (page 192), Strawberry Sorbet with Berry Topping (page 229), ice cream, or frozen yogurt.

yield: 10 to 12 servings

chocolate angel food cake

Another variation on the plain angel food cake.

¼ cup Dutch-process cocoa powder
¼ cup boiling water
2 teaspoons pure vanilla extract
1 cup sifted cake flour
1½ cups sifted confectioners' sugar

¼ teaspoon salt
1½ cups egg whites (approximately 12), at room temperature
1½ teaspoons cream of tartar
1 cup superfine sugar

1. Adjust an oven rack to the lower third of the oven and preheat the oven to 350 degrees.

2. Combine the cocoa with the boiling water and add the vanilla.

3. Combine the cake flour, confectioners' sugar, and salt in a triple sifter or sift three times. Sift onto wax paper and set aside.

4. Whip the egg whites until frothy. Add the cream of tartar. At medium speed, continue to beat the egg whites until soft peaks form. Gradually add the superfine sugar, 1 tablespoon at a time, and beat at high speed until glossy and stiff but not dry.

5. Fold the cocoa mixture into 1 cup of the beaten egg white mixture until well incorporated. Set aside.

6. Sprinkle a quarter of the flour mixture over the remaining beaten whites and gently fold in. Repeat with the remaining flour mixture, a quarter at a time, folding quickly but thoroughly. Fold the cocoa–egg white mixture into the flour–egg white mixture.

7. Gently pour the batter into a dry, ungreased 10-inch tube pan. Bake 40 to 45 minutes, or until the cake feels spongy and a cake tester inserted in the center of the cake comes out dry.

8. Invert the cake pan onto the neck of a bottle or funnel and let cool completely before removing it from the pan. (Run a metal spatula around the sides and center core to help loosen.) Angel food cake will keep for a day at room temperature, or tightly wrapped for a week in the refrigerator. Serve with vanilla frozen yogurt, ice cream, or whipped cream.

yield: 10 to 12 servings

cherry wine sauce for angel food cake

Whether you make the low- or full-fat version is your choice. Both versions are delicious in their own way.

1½ cups dried tart cherries
1½ cups dessert wine such as late-harvest Riesling
¾ cup sugar

3½ cups heavy cream or plain nonfat yogurt
10-inch angel food cake, plain (see page 239)

1. Combine the cherries, wine, and sugar and cook over medium heat just until the cherries are plump and soft. Purée with 1½ cups of the cream or 1½ cups of yogurt until smooth. Refrigerate until serving time.

2. To serve, return the sauce to room temperature. Whip the remaining 2 cups heavy cream, if using.

3. Serve plain angel food cake slices topped with the cherry sauce and either the whipped cream or the remaining yogurt.

yield: 10 to 12 servings

pear cake with sweet wine and olive oil

This cake has a distinctive but subtle, sophisticated flavor; it may not be for everyone. It is not a sweet cake and is best served with a glass of the same late-harvest Riesling used in the batter.

Cake

5 eggs, separated, plus 2 additional egg whites
¾ cup superfine sugar
1 tablespoon finely grated lemon zest

1 cup sifted unbleached flour
Generous pinch of salt
½ cup late-harvest Riesling
½ cup extra-virgin olive oil

Pear Topping

4 very ripe Bartlett, Anjou, or Comice pears
1 teaspoon freshly squeezed lemon juice, or to taste

1 tablespoon unsalted butter
2 tablespoons brown sugar
¼ to ½ cup late-harvest Riesling

1. Adjust a rack to the bottom third of the oven. Preheat the oven to 375 degrees.

2. Generously butter an 8-inch springform pan; line the bottom with a wax or parchment paper circle and butter the top of the paper.

3. Whisk together the egg yolks and superfine sugar in a large mixing bowl placed over a pot of gently simmering water. Keep whisking until the sugar is dissolved.

4. Remove the bowl from the heat and with an electric mixer beat the yolk mixture until it is pale and thick and forms a ribbon as it drops from the beaters, about 3 to 4 minutes. Add the lemon zest.

5. Gradually add the flour and salt to the egg yolk mixture, beating constantly. Slowly add the Riesling, still beating. Then, in a slow, steady stream, add the olive oil, beating constantly until well incorporated. Set aside.

6. Beat the 7 egg whites until stiff but not dry. Gently but thoroughly fold the egg whites into the batter.

7. Pour the batter into the prepared springform and bake for 20 minutes. Reduce the oven temperature to 325 degrees and bake for 20 minutes more. Turn off the oven, but leave the cake inside 10 additional minutes before removing it from the oven. At this

point, the cake will fall and look like a collapsed soufflé. Let cool completely, invert the cake, remove the springform and parchment, and invert again onto a serving plate.

8. For the topping, peel, core, and slice the pears into ½-inch-thick wedges. Toss with the lemon juice.

9. Melt the butter in a large skillet. Stir in the brown sugar. Add the pear wedges and sauté until the pears just begin to soften. Pour in ¼ cup Riesling and cook till the pears are tender, adding additional Riesling if necessary, and reducing the sauce to a slightly syrupy consistency. Spoon over the cake. Refrigerate, if desired.

10. To serve, let return to room temperature.

yield: 8 servings

flourless chocolate cake

❄ 🝖1

Chocolate and coffee: is there any finer combination? This flourless cake gets all of its height from the egg whites. (You can sift confectioners' sugar over a paper doily to make a design on the top of the cake.)

14 ounces bittersweet chocolate, broken into small pieces
1¾ sticks unsalted butter, at room temperature
1½ cups superfine sugar

10 eggs, separated
2½ tablespoons instant coffee powder
2 tablespoons coffee liqueur
1 teaspoon pure vanilla extract
Confectioners' sugar for decoration

1. Adjust the oven rack to the middle of the oven. Preheat the oven to 250 degrees. Grease and flour a 12-inch springform pan; line the bottom with a wax or parchment paper circle and then grease and flour the paper.

2. Melt the chocolate and the butter in the top of a double boiler over hot, not boiling, water. Add 1¼ cups of the superfine sugar and stir until the sugar is almost dissolved.

3. In a mixing bowl, beat the egg yolks until smooth. Gradually beat in half of the hot chocolate mixture, a little at a time, beating constantly. Add the mixture in the mixing bowl to the remaining hot chocolate mixture and continue cooking until the mixture thickens slightly. Stir constantly. Add the instant coffee powder, coffee liqueur, and vanilla. Remove from the heat, transfer to a large bowl, and let cool slightly.

4. In a clean bowl, beat the egg whites on medium-low speed until frothy. Increase to high speed and continue beating until soft peaks form. Add the remaining ¼ cup superfine sugar, 1 tablespoon at a time, beating until the peaks are stiff but not dry. Gently fold the whites into the chocolate mixture. Pour the batter into the prepared springform.

5. Bake for 3 hours. The cake will rise to the top of the pan but then will deflate as it cools.

6. Let the cake cool to room temperature in the pan. Then cover it (still in the pan) tightly with plastic wrap and chill overnight.

7. To serve, run a knife around the sides of the pan and remove the sides. Invert the cake onto a serving plate. Remove the pan bottom and the paper. The cake may be frozen at this point, wrapped tightly in plastic wrap and then overwrapped in foil. Before serving, let the cake defrost, fully wrapped. Sift confectioners' sugar over the top, or spread with whipped cream or crème fraîche.

yield: 12 to 14 servings

cookies

❋ ▢7 william greenberg's sand tarts

William Greenberg Desserts is an institution in New York City, an institution that deserves its enviable reputation for the highest-quality sweets. They have very kindly allowed us to reprint the recipe for one of their most popular cookies.

1 pound (4 sticks) unsalted butter, softened
1 cup sugar, plus additional sugar for dipping
1 egg

1½ teaspoons pure vanilla extract
4½ cups sifted unbleached flour
6 ounces (about 1½ cups) ground toasted pecans

1. Adjust oven racks to the middle of the oven. Preheat the oven to 350 degrees.

2. Beat the softened butter until light. Gradually add 1 cup sugar and the egg and beat several minutes, until pale and very fluffy. Beat in the vanilla. Gradually stir in the flour and nuts, blending well to make a stiff dough. Gather the dough into a ball. There is no need to refrigerate.

3. Divide the dough in quarters and roll each quarter separately to a thickness slightly more than ¼ inch on a lightly floured surface with a lightly floured rolling pin. Cut into rounds with a 1½-inch cookie cutter. Place the rounds on ungreased cookie sheets, ¼ inch apart. Reroll and cut out all the trimmings.

4. Bake for 15 minutes, or until the bottoms of the cookies are lightly browned and the edges just begin to brown. Dip the warm cookies on both sides in additional sugar. Place the cookies on wire racks to cool thoroughly. Store in tightly covered containers for up to a week at room temperature, or freeze. If frozen, let them defrost and return to room temperature before serving. (Though we do know some people who eat these directly out of the freezer . . . while they are still frozen.)

yield: 100 cookies

"icebox" ginger cookies

I cebox. That's how old this recipe is.
   We've added a little more spice and used blackstrap molasses instead of the more readily available unsulfured molasses. You can use whichever is easier to find.

   To achieve a lace effect, do not slice the dough any thicker than ⅛ inch.

   For a change, use an equal amount of rum extract instead of vanilla.

½ pound (2 sticks) butter, melted	2 teaspoons ground ginger
1 cup sugar	½ teaspoon ground cinnamon
½ cup blackstrap molasses	1 teaspoon pure vanilla extract
1 teaspoon baking soda	2½ cups sifted unbleached flour

1. Pour the warm melted butter over the sugar and mix well. Heat the molasses separately and stir into the butter-sugar mixture.

2. Add the baking soda, ginger, cinnamon, vanilla, and flour and mix well. Chill at least ½ hour or overnight to harden the mixture enough so you can work with it. Shape the dough into two rolls. Wrap in wax paper or plastic wrap. Chill again until the rolls are very firm, several hours or overnight.

3. Preheat the oven to 400 degrees. Slice the dough ⅛ inch thick and arrange the slices about 2 inches apart on well-greased cookie sheets. Bake for 6 to 8 minutes, until the cookies have spread and look like lace. Watch carefully so they don't burn. Remove from the oven and allow to cool slightly, then lift from the cookie sheets so they don't stick. Let cool further and remove from the cookie sheets. Wrap well and keep dry. Store at room temperature for up to a week, or freeze. If they are frozen, let them return to room temperature before serving.

   yield: 6 dozen cookies

molasses butter rum balls

For years, when anyone asked me for a cookie recipe for a book or article, this is the one I submitted.

½ pound (2 sticks) unsalted butter, softened
¼ cup unsulfured molasses
2 tablespoons granulated sugar
2 cups unbleached flour
¼ teaspoon salt
1 cup finely chopped walnuts or pecans

1 cup chopped or shredded unsweetened coconut
1 tablespoon dark rum
1 teaspoon pure vanilla extract
Confectioners' sugar

1. Adjust the oven racks to the middle of the oven. Preheat the oven to 350 degrees.

2. Cream the butter with the molasses and granulated sugar until light and fluffy.

3. Sift together the flour and salt. Stir in the nuts and coconut. Combine the flour mixture with the butter mixture and mix thoroughly. Blend in the rum and vanilla.

4. Shape the dough into small balls about the size of a large grape. Place on ungreased cookie sheets about 1 inch apart. Bake 15 to 18 minutes, or until lightly browned on the bottom and firm enough to handle.

5. Roll in confectioners' sugar while still warm. These will keep 2 weeks in a tightly covered container at room temperature. They freeze beautifully and, in fact, taste even better after being frozen. Defrost to serve.

yield: about 7 dozen cookies

michael's anise cookies

In 1997, my son Michael, a superb cook, opened a restaurant in Santiago de Compostela, Spain, called O Cabaliño do Demo (literally, The Devil's Horse), which is Dragonfly in Galegan.

He sent me this recipe, which I have adapted to make it easier for the home cook. If you love licorice, you will love these simple butter cookies.

¼ pound (1 stick) unsalted butter, at
   room temperature
⅔ cup sugar
2 eggs
1 tablespoon aniseed, crushed

Finely grated zest of 1 lemon
1 teaspoon pure vanilla extract
2 cups unbleached flour
¼ teaspoon salt

1. Beat the butter and sugar until smooth. Add the eggs, aniseed, lemon zest, and vanilla extract and mix well.

2. Add the flour and salt, mixing by hand. Do not overmix. Shape the dough into a ball and wrap in plastic wrap. Chill for 1 hour.

3. Preheat the oven to 350 degrees. Break off about 2 teaspoons of dough for each cookie, roll each into a ball, and place on cookie sheets about ½ inch apart.

4. Bake in the middle of the oven 10 to 15 minutes, or until the bottoms are golden and the tops begin to take on color. Let cool. Place in a tightly covered container and store at room temperature or wrap well and freeze.

5. To serve, let the cookies defrost if frozen.

yield: 3½ dozen cookies

russian tea cookies

These are a very buttery, melt-in-your-mouth kind of cookie. I've cut the amount of sugar, and I've added 1 egg yolk for richness. They are quite similar to the cookie that follows, which is the Greek version of the ultimate butter cookie.

½ pound (2 sticks) unsalted butter, softened

½ cup plus ¾ cup confectioners' sugar

1 egg yolk

1 teaspoon pure vanilla extract, or 1 inch of vanilla bean

2¼ cups sifted unbleached flour

⅛ teaspoon salt

¾ cup finely chopped walnuts

1. Adjust racks to the middle of the oven.

2. Cream the butter and ½ cup of the confectioners' sugar until well blended. Beat in the egg yolk. Add the vanilla extract, or slit the vanilla bean and scrape the seeds into the mixture.

3. With the mixer on low to medium-low speed, beat in the flour and salt until the mixture is thoroughly blended. Then add the walnuts and if necessary, do the final mixing with your hands.

4. Chill the dough in the freezer for 30 minutes so it will be manageable. Meanwhile, preheat the oven to 400 degrees. Shape the dough into 1-inch balls and place them 2 inches apart on ungreased cookie sheets. Bake only until set, 9 to 10 minutes. Do not let the cookies brown.

5. While they are still warm, roll the cookies in the remaining ¾ cup confectioners' sugar. Let cool and roll again. Package well and store in the refrigerator or freezer. To serve, let return to room temperature.

yield: 3 dozen cookies

kourambiedes

The Greeks have given us many good things, including what we consider the ultimate butter cookie. It is a close cousin to the preceding cookie, but calls for almonds instead of walnuts, and some brandy. Do not overbake these. In this case, browner is not better.

½ pound (2 sticks) unsalted butter
2 tablespoons confectioners' sugar,
 plus additional for rolling
½ egg yolk

1 to 2 tablespoons Cognac or brandy
3 cups unbleached flour
6 tablespoons finely chopped
 blanched almonds

1. Adjust racks to the middle of the oven. Preheat the oven to 375 degrees.

2. Melt the butter and bring to a boil, stirring occasionally. Remove from the heat and pour slowly into a mixing bowl. Add the 2 tablespoons confectioners' sugar and the ½ egg yolk and beat for 2 minutes. Beat in the Cognac.

3. Add the flour gradually, mixing constantly. Knead vigorously for 3 to 5 minutes by hand. At this point, the dough will be crumbly but smooth. Add the almonds and mix thoroughly.

4. Pinch off small amounts of dough and form into balls about the size of cherries (¾ to 1 inch in diameter). Place on cookie sheets about 1 inch apart. Bake about 20 to 30 minutes, or until the cookies are firm to the touch and pale golden in color. Let cool on wire racks.

5. Sift some confectioners' sugar into a large bowl and roll the cookies in it. The cookies will keep for 2 weeks in a tightly covered container at room temperature. They can also be frozen. Defrost to serve.

yield: about 3 to 4 dozen cookies, depending on size

erna's lace cookies

Years ago a friend, Erna Miller, served these cookies and graciously gave the recipe to me with permission to use it in *Pure and Simple*.

⅔ cup (scant 3 ounces) blanched almonds
¼ pound (1 stick) unsalted butter
Pinch of salt

½ cup sugar
4 teaspoons unbleached flour
4 teaspoons milk

1. Adjust the oven racks to the middle of the oven. Preheat the oven to 350 degrees.

2. In a food processor or blender, grind the almonds until they resemble coarse cornmeal. Do not overprocess or you will wind up with almond butter. Melt the butter in a small skillet. Add the salt, sugar, and flour and stir very briefly over low heat until the sugar becomes completely incorporated. Add the almonds and milk. Blend well, stirring until the mixture thickens a little. Let cool about 1 minute.

3. Drop the batter from a teaspoon onto greased and floured cookie sheets, leaving plenty of room between the cookies because they really spread. You can get only about 6 to 8 cookies per sheet.

4. Bake for 6 to 8 minutes, or until golden brown. Allow to cool only long enough for the cookies to firm up so they can be removed from the cookie sheet with a knife or metal spatula. If they set too hard, return to the oven briefly to soften. Let cool completely on wire racks. These cookies freeze beautifully if wrapped tightly, with wax paper or parchment between each cookie, and stored in an airtight container. They will keep a couple of days at room temperature if stored in an airtight container and kept dry.

yield: about 30 cookies

peanut meringues

If there is an easier cookie recipe than this one of Lois's, we haven't seen it. These will last quite a while if kept in a tightly covered container at room temperature.

1 egg white
½ cup sugar

¾ cup whole salted peanuts

1. Preheat the oven to 250 degrees.

2. Beat the egg white until stiff. Slowly beat in the sugar to make a meringue and then fold in the peanuts.

3. Line a cookie sheet with brown paper or wax paper. Drop meringues by the teaspoonful onto the paper. Bake for 45 minutes. Leave in the oven with the heat off for 15 minutes.

yield: 2 dozen-plus cookies

chocolate chip cookies

These cookies were first introduced when I was working for WRC-TV, the NBC television station in Washington, D.C., as a consumer reporter. The response was amazing: we received between 1,500 and 2,000 requests for the recipe, which is based on the original Toll House cookie recipe. This recipe is especially appealing because the mix can be made ahead and the cookies can be made as quickly as those that come from a box. Unlike those from the box, these are homemade good.

The recipe for the mix can also be made with butter instead of shortening: in that case the mix must be kept in the refrigerator or freezer.

1 teaspoon pure vanilla extract	7 cups Chocolate Chip Cookie Mix
2 eggs, slightly beaten	(recipe follows)

1. Preheat the oven to 375 degrees. Mix the vanilla with the 2 eggs. Combine with the cookie mix. This batter is heavy.

2. For larger cookies, drop batter by heaping tablespoonsful on greased cookie sheets. For smaller cookies, drop by heaping teaspoonsful. Bake 10 to 12 minutes for large cookies, 8 to 10 minutes for smaller cookies. Let cool slightly on the cookie sheets, then remove to racks.

For flatter cookies, pat down with the back of a spoon before baking.

yield: about 2½ dozen large cookies

chocolate chip cookie mix

9 cups unbleached flour	4 cups vegetable shortening
4 teaspoons baking powder	4 cups chopped pecans
2 teaspoons salt	4 (12-ounce) packages semisweet real
3 cups firmly packed dark brown sugar	chocolate chips
3 cups granulated sugar	

Combine the flour, baking powder, salt, brown sugar, and granulated sugar in a large bowl. Using your fingers, mix in the shortening. Stir in the nuts and chocolate chips. Store in an airtight container in a cool, dry place.

yield: about 28 cups

kate's lemon squares

❄ 83

The amount of sugar is cut considerably in this recipe. The result is a luscious lemony bar that tastes great directly from the freezer, so there's no point in hiding them there!

Crust
½ pound (2 sticks) unsalted butter, softened
½ cup confectioners' sugar

2 cups unbleached flour
Pinch of salt

Topping
4 eggs
1½ cups granulated sugar
6 tablespoons unbleached flour
6 tablespoons freshly squeezed lemon juice

6 tablespoons finely grated lemon zest
Confectioners' sugar for topping

To make the crust:

1. Adjust the oven rack to the middle shelf. Preheat the oven to 350 degrees.

2. Combine the butter, confectioners' sugar, flour, and salt; blend with your fingers or a pastry blender. Pat evenly into a 10x15-inch jelly-roll pan. Bake for 15 to 18 minutes, until firm.

To make the topping:

3. Meanwhile, beat the eggs slightly; stir in the sugar, flour, lemon juice, and zest. Mix well and spread over the baked crust. Bake for 20 to 25 minutes more, until the topping is firm.

4. Let cool. Cut into 2x1-inch rectangles, or 1¼-inch squares for petits fours. The lemon squares can be refrigerated or frozen, tightly wrapped, at this point.

5. To serve, let the cookies defrost in the refrigerator if frozen (although these are delicious straight out of the freezer). Sprinkle the tops with confectioners' sugar.

yield: about seventy-five 2x1-inch bars, or one hundred 1¼-inch squares for petits fours

millionaire's shortbread

Appropriately named, these extremely rich, extremely delicious bars were served at Londolozi, a luxurious, private wild game reserve in the Eastern Transvaal in South Africa. They're unquestionably worth the work.

Base
½ pound (2 sticks) unsalted butter, softened
½ cup superfine sugar

2¾ cups cake flour, sifted
⅔ cup lightly toasted pecan halves, finely chopped

Filling
½ pound (2 sticks) unsalted butter
½ cup superfine sugar

1 (14-ounce) can sweetened condensed milk
¼ cup Lyle's Golden syrup (see Note)

Topping
8 ounces bittersweet chocolate
¼ pound (1 stick) unsalted butter
4 teaspoons water

1 tablespoon light corn syrup
½ cup toasted pecans, very finely chopped

To make the base:

1. Adjust a rack to the lower third of the oven. Preheat the oven to 325 degrees.

2. Cream the softened butter with the sugar until light and fluffy. Gradually mix in the flour and pecans. Knead until smooth. Press evenly into the bottom of a 9x13-inch metal baking pan. Bake for 20 to 25 minutes, until light golden. Remove from the oven and let cool on a wire rack in the pan.

To make the filling:

3. Combine the butter, sugar, condensed milk, and syrup in a small, heavy-bottomed saucepan. Cook over low heat, stirring, until the butter is melted and smooth. Bring to a boil and cook 3 to 5 minutes, stirring constantly. The mixture should be the color of caramel. Have a whisk and a small amount of cold water ready. If the mixture shows signs of separating, you can save it by removing the pan from the heat and immediately whisking in a few teaspoons of water.

4. Pour the hot filling over the cooled base, tilting the pan to make sure the surface is entirely covered, and let cool completely.

To make the topping:

5. Combine the chocolate, butter, water, and the corn syrup in the top of a double boiler over gently simmering water. Stir constantly until the chocolate mixture melts and becomes smooth and shiny. Pour quickly over the cooled filling and tilt the pan to get an even layer of chocolate over the entire surface. Sprinkle with the pecans. Refrigerate at least several hours or a couple of days. Freeze, if desired.

6. To serve, let defrost if frozen. Cut into 1½-inch squares for serving.

yield: 48 squares

note: Lyle's Golden syrup, a product of England, does not seem to have a generic counterpart. It is a form of cane syrup and comes in a green and gold can or jar. Believe it or not, I have seen it in many, many supermarkets near the corn syrup. But if you cannot find it, you can substitute 8 teaspoons of light corn syrup mixed with 4 teaspoons dark corn syrup.

orange mocha brownies

These started life in *Elegant but Easy* as "Barbara's Brownies," but we have become so spoiled about brownies that if they are not knockouts, we aren't interested. So with a nip here and a tuck there, the new version qualifies as a knockout.

½ pound (2 sticks) unsalted butter
4 ounces unsweetened chocolate
4 ounces semisweet or bittersweet
  chocolate
2 cups sugar
5 eggs

1½ cups unbleached flour
2 tablespoons Grand Marnier
1 tablespoon coffee extract
1 tablespoon grated orange zest
Dash salt
1½ cups chopped pecans (optional)

1. Preheat the oven to 350 degrees.

2. Melt the butter and chocolates over hot water or in the microwave. Set aside.

3. Cream the sugar and eggs thoroughly and then stir in the cooled chocolate mixture. Thoroughly stir in the flour, Grand Marnier, coffee extract, orange zest, salt, and pecans, if using. Spoon the batter into a greased and floured 9x13-inch baking pan and bake for 20 to 25 minutes. The brownies should be quite moist when tested with a cake tester inserted in the center. Let cool and refrigerate or freeze.

4. To serve, defrost if frozen, or remove the brownies from the refrigerator. Let them return to room temperature and cut into squares or rectangles.

yield: 24 to 30 brownies

chocolate mint sticks

Is there anything more appealing than chocolate and mint? This is one of Lois's specialties.

Brownie layer
2 ounces unsweetened chocolate
¼ pound (1 stick) unsalted butter
2 large eggs
1 teaspoon pure vanilla extract

1 cup sugar
½ cup unbleached flour
1 cup chopped walnuts
⅛ teaspoon salt

Filling layer
4 tablespoons (½ stick) unsalted butter, softened
2 cups sifted confectioners' sugar

2 tablespoons milk
2 ½ teaspoons crème de menthe or ½ teaspoon mint extract

Glaze
3 ounces semisweet chocolate

3 tablespoons unsalted butter

For decoration
Confectioners' sugar or cocoa powder

1. To make the brownies: Adjust an oven rack to the lower third of the oven. Preheat the oven to 350 degrees. Slowly melt the chocolate and butter together in a double boiler over low heat, stirring constantly; remove from the heat. Beat the eggs and add to the chocolate mixture along with the vanilla, sugar, flour, walnuts, and salt. Spread into a greased and floured 9x13-inch pan and bake for 20 to 30 minutes, or until a cake tester inserted in the center comes out fairly clean. Allow to cool in the pan on a wire rack.

2. To make the filling: With a wire whisk, blend the butter, sugar, milk, and crème de menthe or mint extract until smooth. Spread on the cooled brownie layer. Refrigerate at least 30 minutes before glazing.

3. To make the glaze: Melt the chocolate and butter together in a double boiler over low heat, stirring constantly. Pour over the filling, tilting the pan quickly so the glaze completely covers the surface. Refrigerate to harden.

4. Cut into 3x¾-inch sticks. Refrigerate or freeze. If frozen, let them thaw in the refrigerator before proceeding.

5. Just before serving, sift confectioners' sugar or cocoa powder very lightly over the chocolate sticks.

yield: 48 sticks

mock strudel

Ann Amernick, Washington, D.C.'s premier wedding cake maker and one of the finest bakers in the country, was, at one time, assistant to the White House pastry chef, Roland Mesnier, an acknowledged master of the art.

When I heard that she uses this recipe for mock strudel from *Elegant but Easy*, I called her up to check it out. Sure enough, she does, with some minor changes. (See page 261 for her variation.) How flattering!

½ pound (2 sticks) unsalted butter, melted and cooled slightly
1 tablespoon granulated sugar
½ teaspoon salt
1 cup regular sour cream, at room temperature
2¼ cups unbleached flour

6 ounces bitter orange marmalade
6 ounces apricot preserves
6 tablespoons dark brown sugar
1 tablespoon cinnamon
½ cup golden raisins
1 cup chopped walnuts
Confectioners' sugar

1. Combine the butter, granulated sugar, salt, sour cream, and flour in a bowl. Stir lightly with a fork just until the mixture can be formed into a ball. Divide the dough into quarters; shape each piece into a rough log shape and roll up each piece in wax paper. Refrigerate for 1 hour.

2. Meanwhile, combine the marmalade and apricot preserves in a small bowl. In another bowl, combine the brown sugar, cinnamon, raisins, and walnuts. Set both bowls aside while you roll out the dough.

3. Adjust a rack to the lower third of the oven. Preheat the oven to 325 degrees. Grease and flour a 10x15-inch jelly-roll pan or a large cookie sheet.

4. Roll out each piece of dough on floured wax paper to form a 6x10-inch rectangle. Spread the marmalade mixture equally over each dough rectangle, leaving the last inch of one long side of each rectangle plain. Sprinkle the raisin-nut mixture equally over the marmalade mixture. Tightly roll up each rectangle jelly-roll style, beginning at the long end and rolling the uncovered part last. Pinch the edges to seal. Place the strudels on the prepared jelly-roll pan, seam side down, and tuck both pinched ends under.

5. Bake for 35 to 45 minutes, or until the strudels are golden brown. Allow to cool slightly, then remove to a wire rack with a long metal spatula. (The strudels may be refrigerated or frozen when thoroughly cooled, individually wrapped in foil.)

6. To serve, let the rolls defrost, if frozen, fully wrapped. Warm refrigerated or defrosted rolls in a 300-degree oven (still wrapped in foil) for 10 to 15 minutes. Remove the foil and bake a few minutes more to crisp up the pastry.

7. Slice each strudel into 10 pieces, sift confectioners' sugar over, and serve.

yield: 40 slices

ann amernick's variation:

Eliminate the marmalade and double the amount of apricot jam. Eliminate the brown sugar and add *a lot* of cinnamon, chopped walnuts, raisins, and currants. Do not sprinkle the top with confectioners' sugar. When the rolls come out of the oven, immediately cut off the ends with a serrated knife. While the strudels are still hot, cut the slices with a serrated knife three-quarters of the way through with a sawing motion, finishing at the bottom with a sharp knife. Ann prefers the strudel after it has had a chance to age a little rather than being served immediately. So freezing or refrigerating is in order.

pies, tarts, crisps, and cobblers

apple-cranberry crisp

W hen food writers start to wax poetic about old-fashioned goodness, this is what they are talking about. But *this* old-fashioned goodness has some new-fashioned touches like dried cranberries and candied ginger. It's better than old-fashioned.

2 pounds apples (about 5 or 6), peeled, cored, quartered, and sliced ¼ inch thick	6 tablespoons dark brown sugar
½ cup dried cranberries	2 cups chopped pecans
2 tablespoons flour, plus 1 cup	Few shakes salt
¼ cup finely cut candied ginger	½ teaspoon cinnamon
6 tablespoons granulated sugar	2 teaspoons grated lemon zest
	2 teaspoons lemon juice
	½ cup chilled unsalted butter

1. Preheat the oven to 375 degrees.

2. Mix the apples and cranberries with the 2 tablespoons flour and spoon into a 9-inch square baking dish.

3. Using your fingers or a pastry blender, thoroughly combine the remaining 1 cup of flour with the ginger, granulated sugar, brown sugar, pecans, salt, cinnamon, lemon zest, juice, and butter. Sprinkle this topping evenly over the apple-cranberry mixture. Cover with foil and bake for 20 minutes. Remove the foil and bake another 20 minutes, or until the topping is browned and the filling is bubbling.

4. Let cool, cover, and refrigerate.

5. To serve, preheat the oven to 350 degrees and let the crisp come to room temperature. Bake for about 15 minutes, until the crisp is warmed through. Serve plain, or with Crème Fraîche (page 223) if desired.

serves 6

variations:
In place of the apples and cranberries, you can use 6 ripe pears, peeled, cored, and sliced, OR 1 pound rhubarb, cut into 1-inch pieces and mixed with 1 quart stemmed strawberries OR 5 peaches, pitted and sliced, mixed with 1 cup blueberries.

sour cream apple pie in pâte brisée

Wh. hat is so terrific about this pie—in addition to the fabulous taste, of course—
is that the reason most people are afraid of making pie crusts has been eliminated. This crust does not have to be rolled out (the bugaboo for nonbakers): it can be
patted into the pie plate with your hands.

The recipe for the pastry comes from my friend Marion Cunningham, *the* expert
on baking and author of *The Fannie Farmer Baking Book.*

3 tablespoons unsalted butter, softened
6 tablespoons sugar, plus ⅔ cup
   sugar
1 teaspoon cinnamon
5 tablespoons flour
1⅓ cups regular or light sour cream
¼ teaspoon salt

2 teaspoons pure vanilla extract
1 large egg and 2 egg whites
2 to 2½ cups, peeled, cored and
   thinly sliced Granny Smith apples
   (about 5 large)
1 (11-inch) pie crust (pâte brisée)
   (recipe follows)

1. To make the topping, blend the butter, 6 tablespoons of the sugar, the cinnamon, and 2
tablespoons of the flour and mix together with a fork until well blended; chill.

2. Adjust a rack to the middle of the oven. Preheat the oven to 350 degrees.

3. Meanwhile, in a large bowl, whisk together the sour cream, the ⅔ cup sugar, the salt,
vanilla, egg and egg whites, and the remaining 3 tablespoons of flour. Stir in the apples,
spoon the filling into the unbaked pie shell, and crumble the topping over the apples
evenly. Bake the pie for 1 to 1¼ hours, or until the pie is golden and the apples are tender.
Let the pie cool on a rack and when it is completely cooled, cover and refrigerate.

4. To serve, let the pie come to room temperature, or preheat the oven to 350 degrees
and warm the pie for about 15 minutes.

yield: 8 servings

marion cunningham's pâte brisée

2 cups unbleached flour
2 tablespoons sugar
½ teaspoon salt

½ pound (2 sticks) chilled unsalted
  butter
2 tablespoons ice water

1. Blend the flour, sugar, salt, and butter, using a pastry blender or your fingers. Add the water and shape the dough into a ball.

2. Flatten the ball and take small pieces of it and press them into the bottom and sides of the pie plate, making sure the dough is not too thick at the bottom edge. Use the palm of your hand to flatten the dough. The pie shell is ready to fill.

yield: enough dough to fill an 11-inch pie plate

strawberry-rhubarb pie

New touches to an old favorite: candied ginger, Grand Marnier, orange zest.

Filling

3 cups fresh rhubarb, cut into ½-inch slices (preferred) or 3 cups thawed frozen rhubarb

2 pints sliced fresh strawberries

¾ cup granulated sugar

¼ cup firmly packed light brown sugar

6 tablespoons unbleached flour

1½ tablespoons finely minced candied ginger

1 tablespoon Grand Marnier (optional, but delicious)

1 teaspoon finely grated orange zest

½ teaspoon freshly squeezed lemon juice

¼ teaspoon grated nutmeg

1 recipe Marion Cunningham's Pâte Brisée (page 264), chilled

Crème Fraîche (page 223) for garnish, if desired

1. Adjust the oven racks to the bottom and top positions in the oven. Preheat the oven to 425 degrees.

2. In a large bowl, combine the rhubarb, strawberries, granulated sugar, brown sugar, flour, ginger, Grand Marnier if using, orange zest, lemon juice, and nutmeg. Pour into the chilled crust and bake on the bottom rack of the oven at 425 degrees for 10 to 15 minutes, or until lightly browned. Reduce the temperature to 350 degrees and bake for 35 to 45 minutes more, moving the pie from the bottom rack to the top rack for the final 10 minutes of cooking. The crust should be nicely browned and the filling somewhat thickened.

3. Remove the pie from the oven and place on a wire rack to cool. Using a pastry brush dipped in the pie juices, gently glaze the top of the pie. Serve warm or at room temperature. Or you may refrigerate, if desired. Let the pie return to room temperature before serving. This pie would be particularly nice with Crème Fraîche.

yield: 8 to 10 servings

chocolate pecan pie

If you're tired of regular pecan pie, try this chocolate version made with dark corn syrup, dark brown sugar, and rum.

Crust
1½ cups unbleached flour
⅛ teaspoon salt
¼ pound (1 stick) unsalted butter

1 egg
2 tablespoons ice water

Filling
2 ounces unsweetened chocolate
3 tablespoons unsalted butter
¾ cup firmly packed dark brown
  sugar
1 cup dark corn syrup

3 eggs, beaten
1 tablespoon dark rum
1 cup coarsely chopped pecans
Pinch salt
1 cup (½ pint) heavy cream, for garnish

To make the crust:

1. Blend the flour, salt, and butter, using a pastry blender or your fingers to make a crumbly mixture. Whisk the egg and ice water together and add to the flour mixture, blending until the pastry is smooth and holds together in a ball.

2. Pull pieces of dough from the ball and press them evenly over the bottom and sides of a buttered 9-inch pie plate, using the heel of your hand. Be sure the dough is not too thick around the bottom edge. Don't worry about the patches—they won't show when the pie is baked.

3. Preheat the oven to 350 degrees.

4. Melt the chocolate and butter over very low heat. Boil the sugar and corn syrup for 2 minutes to melt completely. Let cool slightly; blend the chocolate and sugar mixtures together and whisk into the beaten eggs, whisking constantly to prevent the eggs from cooking. Stir in the rum, pecans, and salt.

5. Pour the filling into the pie crust. Bake for 40 to 50 minutes, until the filling is slightly firm. Remove and let cool. Refrigerate or freeze.

6. To serve, let the pie defrost if frozen, and allow it to return to room temperature. Whip the cream and top the pie with the whipped cream.

yield: 8 servings

french apple tart à la suechef ❄ 🄱

If apples are in season, almost any cooking apple will do nicely; if not, Granny Smiths rarely let you down.

Crust
12 tablespoons (1½ sticks) chilled unsalted butter, cut into ½-inch pieces
1½ cups unbleached flour
3 tablespoons sugar
⅛ teaspoon salt
1½ to 2 tablespoons cider vinegar

Filling
5 firm, tart, unblemished cooking apples, such as Granny Smiths
2 or 3 teaspoons freshly squeezed lemon juice
¼ cup granulated sugar
2 tablespoons packed light brown sugar
2 tablespoons unsalted butter, cut into ¼-inch pieces

Glaze
⅓ cup clear apple jelly

To make the crust:

1. Combine the butter, flour, sugar, and salt in a food processor fitted with the metal blade. Pulse on and off until the mixture resembles coarse meal. Turn on the motor and pour 1½ tablespoons cider vinegar through the feed tube in a steady stream. Add more vinegar, ½ teaspoon at a time, until the crust mixture barely holds together when pressed between your thumb and forefinger.

2. With lightly floured hands, press the crust mixture into a buttered 11x1-inch fluted tart pan with a removable bottom. The sides of the crust should be about ¼ inch thick. Freeze at least 1 hour, or for a couple of days.

3. Adjust the racks to the bottom third and middle of the oven. Preheat the oven to 400 degrees.

To make the filling:

4. Peel, core, and slice the apples into ⅜-inch-thick slices. Sprinkle with the lemon juice to taste. Toss to coat evenly. Arrange the apple slices in the pie crust in concentric circles, pointed edges toward the center of the pan and slightly overlapping one another. Work toward the center. Sprinkle with both sugars. Dot with the butter.

5. Bake for 15 minutes at 400 degrees in the bottom third of the oven; reduce the oven temperature to 375 degrees. Move the tart to the middle of the oven and bake about 20 to 30 minutes more, until the crust is golden and the apples are slightly browned and tender, but not mushy. Remove from the oven and place on a wire rack.

To make the glaze:

6. Melt the apple jelly over low heat in a heavy-bottomed saucepan. With a pastry brush glaze the entire surface of the tart with the melted jelly. Let cool 10 minutes and then re-move the fluted rim of the pan. (If you place the tart pan on top of a coffee can or the like, the rim will almost fall off by itself.) Carefully lift the tart, holding it by the pan bottom, and return it to the cooling rack. Serve warm or at room temperature.

7. The tart may be frozen before glazing. Wrap the cooled tart tightly.

8. The night before you plan to serve the tart, let it defrost in its original wrapping overnight in the refrigerator. Unwrap and reheat for a few minutes at 300 degrees, or until warm. Glaze as above.

yield: 8 to 10 servings

note: This is wonderful as is, or for a more extravagant presentation, serve each slice on a pool of Quick Caramel Sauce (page 224) or topped with vanilla or butter pecan ice cream.

suechef's very blueberry blueberry tart

Sue Simon's home state of New Jersey is well known for its blueberries, and when they are in season, she goes blueberry picking and freezes some for use when they are out of season.

Of all her blueberry dishes, this, she says, is the most popular.

Filling
2 pints fresh blueberries
¾ cup sugar
2 tablespoons plus 2 teaspoons unbleached flour

Topping
2 pints fresh blueberries, the biggest,
   most beautiful you can find

¼ teaspoon ground cinnamon
1 recipe crust for French Apple Tart
   (page 267), substituting distilled
   white vinegar for the apple cider
   vinegar, frozen

1. Adjust a rack to the lowest position in the oven. Preheat the oven to 400 degrees. Wash and drain the blueberries.

2. Combine the sugar, flour, and cinnamon. Sprinkle about one-quarter of the mixture evenly on the bottom of the frozen crust. Add 2 cups of the blueberries and sprinkle with more sugar mixture. Add 2 more cups of blueberries and top with the rest of the sugar mixture. Do not overfill the tart; the blueberries should be level. (Snack on any leftovers.)

3. Bake the tart 50 to 60 minutes, or until the crust is well browned and the filling is bubbling. Remove it from the oven and place on a wire rack. Let cool 10 minutes and then remove the sides of the pan. (If you place the tart pan on top of a coffee can or the like, the sides will almost fall off by themselves.) Carefully lift the tart, holding only the pan bottom, and return it to the cooling rack. Refrigerate or freeze, if desired, wrapped tightly.

4. To serve, defrost if frozen. Let the tart return to room temperature. Arrange the topping blueberries on top in concentric circles, covering the tart. If the tart is refrigerated only, the blueberries can be placed on top before refrigerating.

yield: 8 to 10 servings

note: If fresh blueberries are out of season, you can substitute frozen for the filling but not for the topping. Instead, top the tart with a layer of crème fraîche, swirled in soft peaks.

suechef's cranberry walnut tart

✲ ⊟1

Great for the holiday season.

1 recipe crust for French Apple Tart à la SueChef (page 267), substituting 1 egg yolk mixed with 1½ tablespoons of ice water for the vinegar, frozen

Filling
3 large eggs, at room temperature
⅔ cup packed dark brown sugar

⅔ cup light corn syrup
4 tablespoons (½ stick) butter, melted and cooled slightly
¼ teaspoon salt
1 tablespoon pure vanilla extract
1 cup plus 2 tablespoons whole raw cranberries
1 cup coarsely chopped walnuts or toasted pecans

1. Adjust the racks to the bottom third and the middle of the oven. Preheat the oven to 400 degrees.

2. Whisk together the eggs, brown sugar, corn syrup, melted butter, salt, and vanilla. Stir in the cranberries and the nuts. Pour into the frozen crust and bake for 30 minutes on the lower rack, checking to make sure that the crust is not getting too brown. If so, cover the edges with foil and continue. Move the tart to the middle rack of the oven and bake an additional 10 to 20 minutes, checking every 5 minutes, or until the filling is puffed and the crust is golden brown.

3. Remove the tart from the oven and place on a wire rack. Let cool 10 minutes and then remove the sides of the pan. (If you place the tart pan on top of a coffee can or the like, the sides will almost fall off by themselves.) Carefully lift the tart, holding only the pan bottom, and return it to the cooling rack. Serve warm or at room temperature, or refrigerate or freeze, tightly wrapped.

4. If the tart is frozen, the night before you plan to serve it let it defrost in the original wrapping overnight in the refrigerator. Unwrap the defrosted or refrigerated tart and serve at room temperature, or reheat for a few minutes at 300 degrees. As for gilding the lily, try some Grand Marnier–flavored whipped cream.

yield: 8 to 10 servings

raspberry peach crumb cobbler

SueChef keeps a few of these in her freezer: the rest of us will be lucky to get out one at a time.

Fruit filling
4 to 5 medium peaches (about 1½ pounds)
2 cups (1 pint) raspberries
A few squeezes of fresh lemon juice

1 tablespoon granulated sugar
2 tablespoons packed light brown sugar
2 tablespoons unbleached flour
1 teaspoon pure vanilla extract

Batter
1 cup sifted unbleached flour
¼ cup granulated sugar
1¼ teaspoons baking powder
⅛ teaspoon salt

½ cup whole or 2 percent milk, at room temperature
¼ teaspoon pure vanilla extract
2½ tablespoons unsalted butter, melted and slightly cooled

Crumb topping
1¼ cups flour
7 tablespoons granulated sugar
⅓ cup packed dark brown sugar
2 teaspoons ground cinnamon

10 tablespoons (1¼ sticks) chilled unsalted butter, cut into ¼-inch pieces
Sifted confectioners' sugar to sprinkle over finished cobbler

1. Adjust a rack to the middle of the oven. Preheat the oven to 400 degrees. Butter a 9-inch square pan (preferably ovenproof glass).

To make the fruit filling:

2. Bring a pot of water to a boil. Drop in the peaches and blanch 10 to 15 seconds, drain, and run under cold water to refresh. Remove the skins and pits, cut into ½-inch slices, and place in a large bowl. Add the raspberries, lemon juice, granulated sugar, brown sugar, flour, and vanilla. Mix well and pour into the prepared pan.

To make the batter:

3. In a mixing bowl, combine the flour, sugar, baking powder, and salt. Add the milk, vanilla, and melted and cooled butter. Stir just until the dry ingredients are moistened. Do not overmix.

4. Spread the batter over the fruit filling with a small metal spatula. It's okay if there are some bare spots.

To make the crumb topping:

5. In a large bowl combine the flour, granulated sugar, brown sugar, and cinnamon. Add the chilled butter. Dig in with both hands and squeeze until crumbly. Scatter the crumbs evenly over the batter.

6. Bake for 25 to 30 minutes, or until the crumbs are golden brown and the filling is bubbling. Remove from the oven to a wire rack to cool a bit.

7. When the cobbler is barely warm, sprinkle with confectioners' sugar and serve. (The finished cobbler will keep, refrigerated, for a day or two. Reheat briefly at 300 degrees before serving, sprinkling with more confectioners' sugar if necessary.)

8. To freeze, wrap in foil (before sprinkling with confectioners' sugar). To serve, put the frozen or defrosted cobbler, still wrapped in foil, into a 350-degree oven and reheat until warm (about 30 to 40 minutes frozen or 15 to 25 minutes defrosted). Remove the foil and bake 5 to 10 minutes more, or until the crumbs are browned and crisp. Sprinkle with confectioners' sugar.

yield: 9 servings

strawberry and raspberry shortcakes

The real "cake" for strawberry shortcake is a southern-style biscuit. My son Michael, a restaurateur in the city of Santiago in Galicia, Spain, created this superb biscuit for me, and then suggested a layer of lemon curd between the biscuit layers. To my mind the curd makes the best strawberry shortcake I have ever eaten.

The biscuits can be prepared in the morning and wrapped until serving time. The strawberries can be prepared the day before and marinated overnight in the refrigerator. The lemon curd can be prepared up to three days ahead. The cream can be whipped several hours ahead and refrigerated.

Biscuits
2 cups sifted unbleached white flour
3 tablespoons brown sugar
1 tablespoon baking powder
¼ teaspoon salt

¼ pound (1 stick) unsalted butter, cut into small pieces
1 teaspoon pure vanilla extract
1 cup heavy cream

Topping and filling
2 pints strawberries, washed, dried, trimmed, and sliced
2 tablespoons crème de cassis or orange liqueur

A little superfine sugar, as needed
½ pint raspberries, washed and dried

Lemon curd (optional)
2 eggs and 1 egg yolk
4 tablespoons (½ stick) unsalted butter, softened

1 cup sugar
Juice of 1½ lemons
Finely grated zest of 1 lemon

Whipped cream
1 cup (½ pint) heavy cream
1 or 2 tablespoons sugar

16 teaspoons unsalted butter (5 tablespoons plus 1 teaspoon), softened

To make the biscuits:

1. Place a rack in the middle of the oven. Preheat the oven to 425 degrees.

2. In a large bowl, combine the flour, sugar, baking powder, and salt. Add the ¼ pound of

butter and cut in with your fingers until the mixture resembles coarse crumbs. Add the vanilla and the cream and mix until the ingredients hold together.

3. Turn the dough out onto a lightly floured board and knead a few times. Press the dough into a rectangle ¾ inch thick. Cut into 8 equal pieces.

4. Place the pieces on a lightly greased cookie sheet and chill for 20 minutes. Bake for 15 to 20 minutes, until the bottoms of the biscuits are browned and the tops are golden. Remove the biscuits to a wire rack and let cool.

5. If you are not using the biscuits immediately, wrap them loosely in aluminum foil after they have cooled and leave at room temperature. The biscuits can be prepared the morning of the party.

To make the topping and filling:

6. Mix the sliced strawberries with the crème de cassis or orange liqueur and stir well. Add the sugar, if needed. Let stand at room temperature for several hours, or refrigerate overnight. Warm gently on the back of the stove or some warm place while dinner is cooking; the strawberries should be slightly warmer than room temperature.

To make the lemon curd:

7. In a medium, heatproof bowl, beat the eggs and yolk until light. Add the butter, sugar, lemon juice, and zest. Place over hot water, stirring occasionally, until the mixture begins to thicken or reaches 160 degrees on a candy thermometer. Remove the bowl from the heat and let cool slightly. Cover with plastic wrap to prevent a crust from forming, and refrigerate for up to 3 days. Leave at room temperature for at least 30 minutes before serving.

To whip the cream:

8. In a large bowl, whip the cream and sugar until soft peaks form. The whipped cream may be prepared several hours before serving and refrigerated, tightly covered.

To assemble:

9. Preheat the oven to 400 degrees. Cut the biscuits in half horizontally and spread the cut sides with the 16 teaspoons of softened butter. Place the biscuits on a cookie sheet, cut sides up, and heat for about 5 minutes.

10. Place each biscuit bottom on a serving plate. If you are using the lemon curd, generously spread each biscuit with the curd.

11. Spoon equal amounts of the warmed strawberries and their liquid over the biscuit bottoms. Add the top halves of the biscuits, spoon the raspberries over the top, and garnish with whipped cream. Serve at once.

yield: 8 servings

ten menus with countdown game plans

The hardest part of having company is planning the menu. If you follow these plans you can have guests for dinner without thinking.

These lists include all ingredients, even those you are likely to have in the house, so check before doing your shopping.

fancy dinner for 12

For a very special occasion, when you want to impress
but don't want to work too hard.

❄Toasted Mushroom Rolls   30

☐7 Olive Lover's Spread   50

☐4 Gravlax with Mustard Sauce   60

❄Baked Imperial Chicken with ☐7 Cumberland Sauce   101

❄Polenta with Sautéed Peppers, Onions, and Rosemary   172

☐1 Arugula with Raspberry Vinaigrette and Cheese in Phyllo   179

☐3 Espresso Mousse   218

Espresso, coffee, or tea

Double the Baked Imperial Chicken recipe and make 1½ times the Espresso
Mousse recipe. The salad recipe calls for phyllo-wrapped goat cheese. Eliminate
it and use just plain good cheese, your choice. Make 1½ polenta recipes.

purchases

Two Weeks Before

½ pound white mushrooms or exotic mushrooms

1 pound unsalted butter

Flour

½ pint light cream or half-and-half

1 bunch chives

3 lemons

Salt

Whole black pepper

21 slices very fresh thin-sliced white bread (1 or 2 loaves)

12 cups (3 quarts) low-sodium chicken stock or broth

3 cups fine-grained or quick-cooking polenta

3 pounds onions

Olive oil

3 pounds red and/or yellow peppers

1 or 2 bunches rosemary

Balsamic vinegar

½ pound Parmigiano-Reggiano

4 cups unseasoned bread crumbs

Dried basil

Dried thyme

Dried rosemary

½ cup sesame seeds

1 dozen eggs

6 pounds skinless bone-in chicken breasts or 24 small chicken breast
   halves

Nonstick pan spray

Currant jelly

One 12-ounce container orange juice concentrate

Dry sherry

Ground ginger

Dry mustard

Cayenne pepper

Unflavored gelatin

Sugar

Superfine sugar

Brandy or coffee-flavored liqueur

½ cup chopped almonds

Raspberry vinegar

Walnut or hazelnut oil

Dijon mustard

1 head garlic

Extra-virgin olive oil

3½ cups black and green Greek, Italian, French, or Moroccan olives (more than one kind); (1–1½ cups are for decorating polenta)

2 large roasted red peppers

White vinegar

Canola oil

Wines, sparkling water, other alcoholic beverages

Tea

Candles

Four Days Before

2½ pounds center-cut fresh salmon, skinned

2 bunches dill

2 lemons

Espresso coffee, regular or decaffeinated, for Espresso Mousse and for after dinner

3 cups heavy cream

½ dozen eggs

3 dozen chocolate-covered coffee beans or bittersweet chocolate to grate over mousse

1 bunch parsley (for garnishing platters)

¾ pound assorted good cheeses for salad, or just one—your choice—cow's milk, goat, or sheep milk

Package of black pumpernickel rounds

Two Days Before
18 ounces (1 pound, 2 ounces) arugula

Day of Party
Bread for main course and salad, and bread for olive spread if not using
    black pumpernickel rounds
Flowers for table

preparations
Two Weeks before the Party
Buy items in the shopping list for "two weeks before" and cook the dishes
    that can be frozen: mushroom rolls, chicken, polenta

One Week Before
Make sure the silver is polished and the table linens are clean
Make Cumberland Sauce and Olive Lover's Spread

Four Days Before
Buy ingredients in shopping list under "four days before"
Make gravlax and mustard sauce

Three Days Before
Make Espresso Mousse

Two Days Before
Buy ingredients under "two days before"
Start making ice

Day Before
Remove the frozen mushroom rolls, chicken, and polenta from the freezer
    and let them start to defrost in the refrigerator
Set the table and take out all serving pieces
Wash salad greens; make Raspberry Vinaigrette
Chill white wine and sodas

Day of Party (guests invited for 7:30 P.M.)

By midday buy bread and flowers. If frozen food is not completely thawed, remove from refrigerator and let thaw, but watch carefully so that the food does not warm up.

In the afternoon *take a nap!*

6:30 P.M. Take the mushroom rolls, chicken, Cumberland sauce, mustard sauce, gravlax, polenta, salad dressing, and Olive Lover's Spread from refrigerator; set up coffee maker

Preheat oven to 400 degrees for mushroom rolls

7:00 P.M. Bake mushroom rolls

Arrange gravlax on salad plates, drizzle with mustard sauce, garnish with dill

Slice bread and place in basket

Put out Olive Lover's Spread and bread

7:30 P.M. After taking mushroom rolls out of the oven, reduce oven to 350 degrees

7:45 P.M. If serving bone-in chicken breasts, bake

8:00 P.M. Bake polenta

8:05 P.M. If serving boneless chicken breasts, bake

Put gravlax on table

Reheat the Cumberland sauce over very low heat; fill wineglasses

8:15 P.M. Serve gravlax

8:30 P.M. Serve polenta and chicken with Cumberland sauce and bread

Later, after clearing the dishes, mix the salad dressing with the greens; place cheese wedge on each plate and serve

After clearing dishes, start coffee; top Espresso Mousse with chocolate-covered coffee beans and serve with coffee

accept kudos!

new year's eve dinner for 12

This is a dinner I do every year with my friend Sherley Koteen.
We share the labor and the party alternates houses.
This dinner was at Sherley's house. She is Host 1, and the food she made is
set in roman type; I am Host 2, and the food I made is set in italics.
The meal requires either two ovens or an oven and a toaster oven. You will
need to double or triple the recipe for the rack of lamb; double the corn
pudding, green beans, and the crabmeat canapés; and either double or
make 1½ times the recipe for the salmon. Serve the salmon on arugula.

⊟1 Sherley's Parmesan Puffs   26

❄*Crabmeat Canapés*   32

❄*Caponata*   51

⊟*1 Cold Poached Salmon with Green Coriander Mayonnaise
and Dill Mayonnaise on Arugula*   67

⊟1 Rack of Lamb   120

⊟1 Michele's Corn Pudding   154

⊟1 Green Beans Provençal   149

❄*Frozen Grand Marnier Soufflé*   225

Espresso, coffee, or tea

purchases, host 1

Two Weeks Before

Regular or light mayonnaise

Olive oil

1 tin anchovy fillets

1 jar capers

Garlic

Salt

Whole black pepper

6 cups frozen corn kernels

Baking powder

Flour

Sugar

¼ pound unsalted butter

Alcoholic and nonalcoholic beverages (Champagne as well as wine)

Tea

Candles

Three Days Before

Large wedge Parmigiano-Reggiano

1 onion

1½ quarts whole milk

2 dozen eggs

Espresso or coffee

Day Before

4 or 5 racks of lamb

2 loaves firm white bread

4 pounds green beans or haricots verts

2 bunches arugula

Day of Party

Bread

Flowers

preparations, host 1

Two Weeks Before
Buy ingredients listed under "two weeks before"

One Week Before
Make sure all silver is polished and table linens are clean

Three Days Before
Buy ingredients listed under "three days before"
Start making ice

Day Before
Buy ingredients listed under "day before"
Make and bake corn pudding
Make topping for Sherley's Parmesan Puffs
Prepare racks of lamb for roasting
Make dressing for green beans; wash and trim green beans and refrigerate
Set table
Chill white wines and nonalcoholic drinks
Wash all greens

purchases, host 2

Two Weeks Before
Garlic
12 ounces reduced-fat or full-fat cream cheese
3 onions
Worcestershire sauce
Cayenne pepper
3 lemons
1 pound fresh crabmeat
2 medium eggplants
Nonstick pan spray
1 bunch celery
Olive oil

2 large zucchini
1 large ripe tomato
Capers
Red wine vinegar
Sugar
Pine nuts
Dry white wine
Garlic
Ground coriander seeds
Light or regular mayonnaise
Salt
Unflavored gelatin
1 dozen eggs
1 quart fresh orange juice
Grand Marnier
4 to 6 cups fish stock or broth
1 pint heavy cream
Slivered almonds

Day Before
Rounds or squares of black bread
6 pounds salmon fillet
Bunch spinach
Bunch parsley
2 bunches cilantro
1 lemon
Nonfat plain yogurt
Large bunch dill (8 ounces)
Two bunches arugula

Day of Party
2 baguettes

preparations, host 2

Two Weeks Before

Buy ingredients listed under "two weeks before" and make crabmeat
  canapés, caponata, Grand Marnier soufflé

Day Before

Buy ingredients listed under "day before"

Defrost crabmeat canapés and caponata in the refrigerator

Poach salmon; make dill mayonnaise and green coriander mayonnaise

Rinse and trim arugula and refrigerate in plastic bag

Day of Party

Buy ingredients listed under "day of party"

If food isn't defrosted, defrost at room temperature; watch carefully so
  food does not become warm

both hosts

Day of Party (guests invited for 8:30 P.M.)

Buy ingredients listed under "day of party"

In the afternoon *take a nap!*

7:00 P.M. Put Sherley's Parmesan Puffs topping on bread rounds; get coffee ready

7:15 P.M. Take corn pudding out of refrigerator

7:30 P.M. Put crabmeat topping on bread

8:00 P.M. Put out caponata

8:10 P.M. Turn on broiler (toaster oven or second oven)

8:15 P.M. Heat another oven to 325 degrees

8:15 P.M. Take dressing for green beans from refrigerator

8:20 P.M. Slice bread

8:30 P.M. Broil Parmesan puffs and crabmeat canapés

8:50 P.M. If you have only one oven, bake corn pudding at 325 degrees*

If you have 2 ovens, preheat second oven to 450 degrees*

Fill wineglasses

*If you have two ovens, the corn pudding can go in at 9:20 in one; the racks of lamb at 9:15 in the other.

9:00 P.M. Arrange salmon on arugula; dress with sauces and place on table

9:10 P.M. Take out corn pudding, cover with aluminum foil, and keep in warm place

9:10 P.M. If you have only one oven, raise oven temperature to 450 degrees*

9:15 P.M. Roast racks of lamb at 450 degrees

9:20 P.M. Cook green beans

If you have two ovens, bake corn pudding at 325 degrees

9:30 P.M. Before sitting down, drain green beans and mix with dressing

9:30 P.M. Sit down for salmon

9:35 P.M. Check racks of lamb; if ready, remove from oven or continue to roast

9:45 P.M. Remove racks from oven

Remove first course

Slice racks and serve with corn pudding, green beans, and bread

Remove soufflé from freezer when main course is served; start coffee

Remove main course; make coffee; sprinkle praline on soufflé and serve

Serve Champagne at midnight

*If you have two ovens, the corn pudding can go in at 9:20 in one; the racks of lamb at 9:15 in the other.

happy new year!

old-fashioned casual dinner for 6

There is very little last-minute work for this dinner. It's quite simple.
You will need to make 1½ times the recipe for the salad and dressing and,
if you wish, for the squash.

❄Cheese Cigarettes   28

❄Coq au Vin   98

⊟1 Squash with Raisins and Pine Nuts   164

❄Layers of Potato and Smoked Mozzarella   160

⊟1 Mesclun Salad with ⊟2 Chinese Vinaigrette   181

⊟2 Apple-Cranberry Crisp   262

Espresso, coffee, or tea

purchases

Two Weeks Before

1 pound unsalted butter

Unbleached flour

1 pint milk, whole, 1 percent, or 2 percent

Salt

White pepper

Whole black pepper

½ pint heavy cream

¾ pound Parmigiano-Reggiano

½ dozen eggs

Cayenne pepper

48 slices (2 to 3 loaves) very fresh thinly sliced supermarket white bread

Rice vinegar

Canola oil

Toasted sesame oil

Hoisin sauce

Reduced-sodium soy sauce

Dry mustard

Sugar

Extra-virgin olive oil

2 heads garlic

5 pounds skinless, boneless chicken breasts and thighs

Cognac or brandy

Bunch fresh thyme or jar dried thyme

Bay leaves

1 bunch parsley

1 small can tomato paste

1 pound small whole mushrooms

24 pearl onions

1 bottle (750 milliliters) good red wine for cooking and 3 to 4 additional
   bottles for drinking

1 small bag or box of raisins

1 bag pine nuts

Balsamic vinegar

2 pounds Yukon gold or other potatoes

8 ounces smoked or fresh mozzarella

1 quart low-fat or nonfat buttermilk

1 bunch basil

Nonstick olive oil pan spray

1 box gelatin

Madeira or marsala

1 package dried cranberries

1 package candied ginger

Granulated sugar

Dark brown sugar

2 cups chopped pecans

Cinnamon

Alcoholic beverages, club soda, or soft drinks, as desired

Tea

Candles

Three Days Before

Espresso or regular coffee (decaffeinated perhaps?)

2 pounds Granny Smith apples

2 lemons for dessert plus additional lemons for drinks

1½ pounds onions

Two Days Before

12 ounces mesclun or other greens

1 bunch parsley

2¼ pounds mixed zucchini and yellow summer squash

Day of Party

Good-quality dense, crusty bread

Flowers or other decorations for table

preparations

Two Weeks before the Party

Buy items in the shopping list for "two weeks before," and cook dishes that can be frozen: Cheese Cigarettes, Coq au Vin, and Layers of Potatoes and Mozzarella

One Week Before

Make sure the silver is polished and the table linens are clean

Three Days Before

Buy ingredients in shopping list for "three days before"

Two Days Before

Buy ingredients in shopping list under "two days before"

Make Apple Cranberry Crisp

Make salad dressing

Start making ice

Day Before

Remove the frozen Cheese Cigarettes, Coq au Vin, and potato dish from the freezer and start to defrost in the refrigerator

Set the table and take out all serving pieces

Make the squash with raisins and pine nuts

Wash salad greens

Chill white wine if serving, and sodas

Day of Party (guests invited for 7:30 P.M.)

By midday, buy bread and flowers. If frozen food is not completely thawed, remove from refrigerator and thaw, but watch carefully so that the food does not warm up.

In the afternoon *take a nap!*

6:00 P.M. Remove squash dish from refrigerator

6:30 P.M. Take the Cheese Cigarettes, chicken, potatoes, salad dressing, and apple crisp from refrigerator; set up coffee maker

7:00 P.M. Preheat the oven to 400 degrees for the Cheese Cigarettes

7:15 P.M. Bake the Cheese Cigarettes

7:20 P.M. Slice the bread and place in bread basket

7:30 P.M. Set oven at 375 degrees

7:50 P.M. Bake potato dish

8:00 P.M. Reheat chicken very slowly, stirring occasionally

8:10 P.M. Check the chicken and fill the wineglasses; reheat the squash dish if you are not serving it at room temperature

8:15 P.M. Serve dinner with bread; reduce oven to 350 degrees

Later, after clearing the dishes, mix the salad dressing with the greens and serve with bread

Put the apple crisp in the oven; start coffee to serve with dessert

take a bow

red-checked tablecloth dinner for 6

You can plan this party way ahead or three days before. Or make it a cooperative dinner. The lasagna recipe serves 12; halve it or make it all and freeze in two separate containers. For dressing use 1½ recipes of Chinese vinaigrette, eliminating soy sauce and adding 1 teaspoon Dijon mustard.

⊟7 Tapenade   52

❄Lasagna   126

⊟1 Mesclun with Chinese Vinaigrette   181

Italian bread

⊟1 Poached Pears with Apricot Sauce   199

Espresso, coffee, or tea

purchases

Two Weeks Before

Olive oil

¾ pound hot or sweet turkey or chicken Italian-style sausages

¼ pound pork tenderloin

2 medium onions plus 1 medium-small onion

Garlic

28-ounce can low-sodium crushed tomatoes or tomato purée

28-ounce can low-sodium Italian plum tomatoes

1 bottle dry red wine

Fresh or dried basil

Fresh or dried oregano

Salt

Whole black pepper

Lasagna noodles

2 pounds eggplant

Nonstick olive oil–flavored pan spray

1 pound reduced-fat ricotta

1 pound part-skim mozzarella

2½ or 3 ounces Parmigiano-Reggiano

6½- or 7-ounce can white meat tuna packed in water

1 can sardines

Toasted sesame paste

Kalamata olives

Capers

Anchovy paste

Unsalted crackers for tapenade

Balsamic vinegar

Extra-virgin olive oil

Dijon mustard

Sugar

Pure vanilla extract

1 package dried apricots

1 small bottle orange liqueur

Alcoholic beverages, sodas, as desired
Tea

One Week Before
Bunch parsley
Lemon
Bunch fresh thyme or jar dried thyme

Two Days Before
1 orange
1 lemon
Knob fresh ginger
6 ripe pears (you may want to purchase these even sooner to let them ripen)
1 small container fresh orange juice
Espresso or regular coffee

One Day Before
12 ounces salad greens

Day of Party
Bread
Flowers or other table decorations

preparations
Two Weeks Before
Purchase nonperishables and ingredients for dish to be made and frozen
Make lasagna and freeze

One Week Before
Shop for ingredients listed under "one week before"
Make tapenade

Two Days Before
Shop for ingredients listed under "two days before"
Start making ice

One Day Before

Shop for ingredients listed under "one day before"

Make poached pears

Wash salad greens

Make salad dressing

Set table and put out serving pieces

Chill white wine if using, and soft drinks

Defrost lasagna in the refrigerator

Day of Party (Guests invited for 7:30 P.M.)

Buy bread and flowers

If lasagna is not defrosted yet, remove from refrigerator and defrost at
   room temperature. Watch carefully so that it does not get warm

7:00 P.M. Preheat oven to 375 degrees

Arrange tapenade and crackers on serving plate

Slice bread

7:15 P.M. Bake lasagna

7:50 P.M. Dress salad

Fill wineglasses

Remove dessert from refrigerator

8:00 P.M. Serve lasagna, salad, and bread

Make coffee

Clear plates

Serve dessert and coffee

elegant and simple dinner for 10

To honor a friend's promotion, arrival in town, marriage, or other occasion.
You will need to double the recipes for the pork tenderloin
and the arugula salad.

❄Phyllo with Seafood and Basil   37

▢1 Pork Tenderloin with Mustard and Thyme   123

▢1 Roasted Fennel, Potatoes, and Onions   157

▢1 Greens with Pears and Gorgonzola Vinaigrette   178

▢2 Cold Lemon Soufflé   216

Espresso, coffee, or tea

purchases

1 pound phyllo dough (fresh preferred)

1 pound unsalted butter

¼ pound cooked, peeled shrimp

¼ pound crabmeat

1 bunch fresh basil

6 ounces cream cheese

1 small wedge Parmigiano-Reggiano

Dry sherry

Ground nutmeg

Whole-grain mustard (1 cup)

Garlic

Dried thyme

Salt

Whole black pepper

Balsamic vinegar

Dry red wine

Olive oil

1 small package pine nuts

Unflavored gelatin

Slivered almonds (optional for lemon soufflé)

Superfine sugar

Alcoholic and nonalcoholic beverages

Tea

Candles

Three Days Before

1 dozen eggs

3 or 4 large lemons

2 cups heavy cream

2½ pounds red onions

3 pounds tiny new potatoes

4 pears

1 small wedge Gorgonzola
Espresso or regular coffee

Two Days Before
4 large fennel bulbs
Bunch fresh rosemary
4 pounds pork tenderloin (about 4 tenderloins)
18 ounces mixed salad greens like mesclun
½ pint strawberries or raspberries

Day of Party
Bread
Flowers or other decorations for table

preparations
Two Weeks before the Party
Buy items listed under "two weeks before" and prepare the phyllo

One Week Before
Make sure the silver is polished and the table linens are clean

Three Days Before
Buy ingredients listed under "three days before"

Two Days Before
Make lemon soufflé
Buy ingredients listed under "two days before"
Start making ice

Day Before
Marinate pork tenderloin
Prepare fennel, potatoes, and onions
Remove frozen phyllo from freezer and defrost in refrigerator
Wash and dry salad greens
Make salad dressing but do not add pears

Set the table and take out all the serving pieces
Chill wine and sodas

Day of Party (guests invited for 7:30 P.M.)
By midday buy bread and flowers. If frozen food is not completely thawed, remove from refrigerator and thaw, but watch carefully so that the food does not warm up
Wash and dry berries for dessert; toast almonds, if using for dessert
Cut up pears and add to salad dressing
In the afternoon *take a nap!*

6:30 P.M. Take the phyllo and the fennel-potato dish out of the refrigerator; set up coffee maker
6:45 P.M. Preheat oven for phyllo
7:10 P.M. Heat phyllo
7:20 P.M. Raise heat to 425 degrees for fennel-potato dish
7:30 P.M. Roast fennel-potato dish; take pork out of refrigerator
8:05 P.M. Cook pork; fill wineglasses
8:15 P.M. Serve pork, fennel-potato dish, and bread
        Later, after clearing dishes, mix the salad dressing with the greens and serve with bread
        After clearing dishes, start coffee; remove soufflé collar from dessert; decorate and serve with coffee

accept praise graciously

supper for 12 friends

With so little to prepare the day before the dinner, this is perfect for the working person. Double the recipes for the guacamole and the fennel and cheese salad.

⊟1 Molded Guacamole   46

❊Beef Stew with Burgundy (Boeuf Bourguignonne)   115

⊟1 A Salad of Fennel and Parmigiano-Reggiano   184

⊟5 Judy's Lemon Poppy Seed Cake   236

Espresso, coffee, or tea

purchases

Two Weeks Before

4 pounds extra-lean or lean beef round, cubed

Canola oil

Bunch carrots

4 onions

4 cups canned low-sodium Italian tomatoes

Bay leaves

Garlic

1 bottle good Burgundy, Cabernet, or Pinot Noir

2 cups low-sodium beef stock or broth

Salt

Whole black pepper

Egg noodles

Medium piece Parmigiano-Reggiano

Extra-virgin olive oil

Unflavored gelatin

Dry sherry

½ pound unsalted butter

Sugar

Baking soda

Unbleached flour

2 ounces poppy seeds

Pure vanilla extract

Alcoholic beverages and soda, as desired

Tea

Candles

One Week Before

½ dozen eggs

½ pint sour cream and ½ pint light sour cream

6 large lemons

Two Days Before
12 small or 8 large fennel bulbs
6 ripe medium avocados (you may need to buy them earlier to ripen them)
1 small onion
2 jalapeños
1 bunch cilantro
Tortilla chips or crackers or pita
1½ pounds mushrooms, white or exotic
Espresso or regular coffee

Day of Dinner
Bread
Flowers, if using

preparations
Two Weeks Before
Shop for ingredients listed under "two weeks before"
Make beef stew and freeze

One Week Before
Shop for ingredients listed under "one week before"

Five Days Before
Make cake

Two Days Before
Shop for ingredients listed under "two days before"
Start making ice

Day Before
Set table and get out serving pieces
Chill wine and soda
Defrost beef stew in refrigerator
Prepare salad components, including dressing
Make molded guacamole

Day of Party (guests invited for 7:30 P.M.)

Buy bread, and flowers for table, if using

If beef stew is not completely defrosted, allow to defrost at room temperature but watch carefully so that it doesn't get warm

Chill white wine, if using, and beverages

Take a nap!

5:00 P.M. Sauté mushrooms for beef stew

7:00 P.M. Unmold guacamole and arrange on serving plate with crackers, chips, or pita

Mix flour and liquid from stew to make paste and stir into stew

Put salad together

Slice bread

Take cake out of refrigerator

7:45 P.M. Cook noodles

Reheat stew; add mushrooms

8:00 P.M. Serve beef stew with noodles on the side, salad, and bread

Make coffee

Clear plates

Serve cake and coffee

enjoy the compliments

a summer dinner for 6

This would be a nice meal to cook with a friend. The recipe for the summer squash pudding serves four to six, so to make certain there is enough and have a little left over for seconds, double the recipe.

⊟1 Bruschetta with Tomato Topping   54

⊟1 Grilled Salmon and Tabbouleh Salad   65

⊟1 Summer Squash Pudding   163

⊟2 Plum Compote   201

Espresso, coffee, or tea

purchases

Two Weeks Before

Extra-virgin olive oil and virgin olive oil

Garlic

Balsamic vinegar

Salt

Whole black pepper

2 cups coarse bulgur

Reduced-sodium soy sauce

Ground cumin

Sugar

Dry white wine

Whole cloves

Cinnamon stick

Alcoholic and nonalcoholic beverages

Tea

Four Days Before

16 large, firm, ripe red or black plums

Vanilla ice cream or frozen yogurt, or heavy cream, or crème fraîche (for
    plum compote)

1 lemon

Lemongrass

½ dozen eggs

½ pint each regular and light sour cream

2 large shallots

Coffee: espresso, regular, or decaf

Two Days Before

1¼ pounds ripe plum tomatoes

2 large ripe tomatoes

Bunch fresh thyme

Bunch fresh basil

1 baguette

4 pounds yellow or summer squash
1 bunch fresh chives
Bag peeled baby carrots
Bunch celery
½ pound Kirby cucumbers
1 head red leaf lettuce

One Day Before
6 (8-ounce) salmon fillets

Day of Party
Bread
Table decorations (flowers, etc.)

preparations

Two Weeks before the Party
Buy ingredients listed under "two weeks before"

One Week before the Party
Make sure the silver is polished and the table linens are clean

Four Days Before
Buy ingredients listed under "four days before"

Two Days Before
Buy ingredients listed under "two days before"
Make plum compote
Start making ice

Day Before
Make summer squash pudding
Start to make grilled salmon and tabbouleh salad and wash salad greens
Make bruschetta
Make ice cubes
Set the table and take out serving pieces

Day of Party (guests invited for 8 P.M.)
By midday, buy bread and table decorations
In the afternoon *take a nap!*

7:15 P.M. Take squash pudding, tabbouleh, and plum compote from refrigerator;
      set up coffee maker
7:40 P.M. Preheat oven to 350 degrees for pudding
7:45 P.M. Bake squash pudding
7:50 P.M. Whip cream, if serving with plum compote
      Reheat bruschetta, top it, and serve
8:30 P.M. Pour wine
      Remove squash pudding when it is done and set oven to broil for
        salmon (if using broiler)
      Broil or grill salmon; chop tomato and add to tabbouleh
      Slice bread
      Arrange salmon and tabbouleh on lettuce in bowl and serve with squash
        pudding and bread
      After main course is finished, clear plates, make coffee, and serve plum
        compote with vanilla ice cream, yogurt, crème fraîche, or whipped
        cream

take a bow

a vegetarian dinner for 6

Nonvegetarians will be perfectly happy with this meal. The tabbouleh recipe serves 4 to 6, so make 1½ times the recipe if you don't want to skimp. Make only half of the tiropetas recipe unless you would like to have some in the freezer for another occasion. The recipe for spicy eggplant suggests serving it over rice. Do not serve over rice at this meal.

❄Tiropetas   37

⊟1 Spicy Eggplant and Peppers   132

⊟1 Tabbouleh   189

⊟1 Raita   186

❄Original Plum Torte   232

Espresso, coffee, or tea

purchases

Two Weeks Before

½ pound phyllo dough, preferably fresh

1 pound unsalted butter

¼ pound feta cheese

4 ounces large-curd cottage cheese

Small piece Parmigiano-Reggiano

1 dozen eggs

Bunch fresh parsley

Salt

Whole black pepper

Ground nutmeg

Toasted sesame oil

Garlic

Hot chile paste with garlic

Hoisin sauce

Rice vinegar

Small bottle dry sherry

Reduced-sodium soy sauce

Dark brown sugar

Granulated sugar

Cornstarch

2 cups low-sodium vegetable stock

Raisins

Cumin seeds

Ground white pepper

1½ cups fine-grain bulgur

Olive oil

Ground cinnamon

Small bag unbleached flour

Baking powder

12 Italian (purple or prune) plums

Alcoholic and nonalcoholic beverages

Tea

Candles

Two Days Before
3 pounds eggplant
Knob fresh ginger
2 pounds red and yellow peppers
16 to 18 green onions (2 or 3 bunches)
3 large lemons
2 to 3 bunches parsley (3 cups chopped)
3 large ripe tomatoes
1 pound Kirby cucumbers
2 cups nonfat or low-fat plain yogurt
Bunch fresh mint
1 serrano (or jalapeño) chile
Vanilla ice cream for plum torte (optional)
Espresso or regular coffee

Day of Party
Bread
Decorations for table

preparations
Two Weeks before the Party
Buy items in shopping list under "two weeks before" and make the dishes
    that can be frozen: the tiropetas and the plum torte

One Week Before
Make sure the silver is polished and the table linens are clean

Two Days Before
Buy ingredients listed under "two days before"
Start making ice

Day Before
Make the raita, the tabbouleh, and the spicy eggplant and peppers
Defrost the tiropetas and plum torte in the refrigerator
Set the table and take out all the serving dishes
Chill the beverages

Day of Party (guests invited for 7:30 P.M.)

By midday, buy bread and table decorations. If frozen food is not completely thawed, remove from refrigerator and thaw, but watch carefully so that the food does not warm up

Chop green onions for spicy eggplant dish

In the afternoon *take a nap!*

6:30 P.M. Take tiropetas, spicy eggplant, and plum torte from the refrigerator

Preheat oven to 325 degrees for tiropetas

Slice bread and place in basket

Set up coffee maker

7:15 P.M. Reheat tiropetas

7:30 P.M. Chop tomatoes and add to tabbouleh and leave at room temperature

8:00 P.M. Slowly reheat the spicy eggplant and peppers on top of the stove; pour wine

8:15 P.M. Stir green onions into eggplant dish and serve with the raita, tabbouleh, and bread

Reduce oven to 300 degrees. While clearing dishes, reheat plum torte for about 10 minutes

After clearing dishes, make coffee

Serve plum torte, with ice cream if desired, and coffee

accept applause graciously

brunch for 16

To make this Sunday brunch, figure you'll devote the weekend to cooking. Make two seafood quiches (just double recipe); double the recipe for the green bean and potato salad, and cut the recipe for the cookies in half. Make two times the recipe for the Sicilian carrots, four times the recipe for the sesame asparagus, and four times the recipe for the blueberry kir sauce.

⊟1 Seafood Quiche   82

Sesame Asparagus   146

⊟1 Sicilian Carrots   153

⊟1 Green Bean and Potato Salad   187

❋William Greenberg's Sand Tarts   245

⊟2 Blueberry Kir Sauce   192

Coffee, tea, or other beverages

purchases

Two Weeks Before

2 pounds unsalted butter

Sugar

1 dozen eggs

Pure vanilla extract

Unbleached flour

3 ounces pecans

Salt

Dry sherry

Cayenne pepper

Ground nutmeg

Olive oil

Extra-virgin olive oil

Toasted sesame oil

White wine vinegar

Dijon mustard

Whole black pepper

Reduced-sodium soy sauce

Sesame seeds

Nonstick olive oil–flavored pan spray

½ cup dried cranberries

1 small package pine nuts

Cornstarch

Crème de cassis

Dry white wine

Alcoholic and nonalcoholic beverages

Tea

Three Days Before

1 large red onion

6 cups fresh or frozen blueberries

2 large lemons

Vanilla ice cream or frozen yogurt

Coffee
1 pound imported Gruyère cheese
4 pounds tiny new potatoes
2 large lemons
Bunch fresh thyme
4 pounds peeled baby carrots or regular carrots

Two Days Before
2 cups fresh crabmeat
1 cup cooked shelled shrimp
3 cups light cream
2 pounds haricots verts or regular green beans
Bunch fresh basil

Day Before
8 pounds asparagus
Flowers or decorations for table

Day of Party
Bread

preparations
Two Weeks Before the Party
Buy items listed under "two weeks before," and make the sand tarts

One Week Before
Make sure the silver is polished and the table linens clean

Three Days Before
Buy items listed under "three days before"

Two Days Before
Buy items listed under "two days before"
Make crusts for quiches
Make blueberry kir sauce
Start making ice

One Day Before

Buy ingredients listed under "one day before"

Fill and bake quiches

Make Sicilian carrots

Make green bean and potato salad

Defrost sand tarts at room temperature; cover tightly; do not refrigerate

Set table and take out serving pieces

Chill beverages

Buy flowers for centerpiece (or other decorations)

Day of Party (guests invited for noon)

Get up early and buy bread

Prepare asparagus and leave at room temperature

10:00 A.M.   Take blueberry kir sauce, green beans and potatoes, carrots, and quiches out of refrigerator

10:30 A.M.   Preheat oven for quiches

11:00 A.M.   Bake quiches; slice bread

Noon   Serve drinks; mix green beans with potatoes; make coffee

12:30 P.M.   Put food out on buffet

After clearing plates, put out blueberry kir sauce, ice cream or yogurt, and cookies

enjoy congratulations

cocktail party for 24

Half of the cooking can be done way ahead. No cooking is required on the day of the party. One recipe of each of these hors d'oeuvres will provide enough to eat for 20 to 24 people.

❋Phyllo with Goat Cheese and Prosciutto (3 dozen)   36

❋Spicy Sausage Balls (4 dozen)   34

❋Cheese Shorties (4 dozen)   27

▯3 Black Bean Dip   49

▯3 Brandied Cheese Roll   43

▯2 Smoked Trout Mousse   55

purchases

Two Weeks Before

1 pound extra-sharp white Cheddar cheese

1 pound unsalted butter

Flour

Cayenne pepper

1 pound spicy chicken or turkey sausage

1 dozen eggs

Unseasoned bread crumbs

Dried sage

Chili sauce

Catsup

Brown sugar

Reduced-sodium soy sauce

White vinegar

1 pound fresh phyllo

½ pound medium-sharp goat cheese

3 ounces cream cheese

1 container large-curd cottage cheese

Bunch fresh thyme

¼ pound prosciutto

Brandy

2 cups walnuts or pecans

Olive oil

2 (15-ounce) cans black beans or 1½ cups dried black beans

Ground coriander

Ground cumin

Whole black pepper

Ground nutmeg

Ground white pepper

Unflavored gelatin

Alcoholic and nonalcoholic beverages

Cocktail napkins

Four Days Before
1 apple
2 (8-ounce) smoked trout
Bunch green onions
Bunch dill
1 pint regular or light sour cream
1 lemon
1 medium onion
1 head garlic
1 lime
1 serrano or jalapeño chile
¾ pound Roquefort cheese
½ pound cream cheese
Crackers
Tortilla chips
Melba toast

Day Before
Parsley for garnish

Day of Party
Flowers or other decorations
Bread

preparations
Two Weeks Before
Purchase ingredients listed under "two weeks before"
Prepare and freeze dishes that can be frozen: phyllo, sausage balls, Cheese
   Shorties

One Week Before
Make sure all the serving dishes and silver are clean

Four Days Before
Buy ingredients listed under "four days before"

Three Days Before
Prepare black bean dip
Prepare brandied cheese roll
Start making ice

Two Days Before
Prepare smoked trout mousse

One Day Before
Defrost frozen hors d'oeuvres in the refrigerator
Set up bar and table and take out all serving pieces and glasses
Buy and wash parsley for garnishes
Chill white wine and soda

Day of Party (guests invited for 6 to 8 P.M.)
By midday, buy bread and flowers. If frozen food is not completely thawed, remove from refrigerator and thaw, but watch carefully so that food does not warm up. If you cannot make ice, buy it
In the afternoon, *take a nap!*
In the afternoon cut Cheese Shorties into slices, wrap, and refrigerate

5:00 P.M. Brown sausage balls and set aside
5:30 P.M. Preheat oven to 400 degrees for Cheese Shorties
Put out brandied cheese roll with bread or crackers
Put out black bean dip and tortilla chips
5:45 P.M. Unmold smoked trout mousse and surround with melba toast
5:50 P.M. Bake cheese shorties; simmer sausage balls and keep warm in chafing dish (if available) or in kitchen
6:00 P.M. Reduce oven to 325 degrees for phyllo
6:20 P.M. Reheat phyllo; do not reheat all of the phyllo at one time—you want them warm when served

relax and enjoy your guests

special lists

first courses

There is no chapter called "First Courses" in this book, but there are a number of dishes that make excellent starters to a meal: just serve smaller portions.

Gravlax with Mustard Sauce or Horseradish Sauce   *60*
Mozzarella, Salmon, and Basil Pinwheels   *62*
Nova Scotia Mousse   *56*
Smoked Trout Mousse   *55*
Spinach Tarte   *35*
Bruschetta   *53*
Maryland Crab Cakes   *77*
Germaine's Scallop Salad   *88*
Cold Poached Salmon with Green Coriander or Dill Mayonnaise   *67*
Spaghetti alla Puttanesca   *74*
Seafood Quiche   *82*
Basil Pesto (with Pasta)   *135*
Asparagus and Zucchini Pancakes with Cheese   *130*

brunch

Sunday brunch is an easy way to entertain because, if you work, it gives you all day Saturday to prepare.

Hot Hors d'Oeuvres
Cheese Shorties   *27*
Mushroom-Filled Mushroom
    Caps   *31*
Spinach Tarte   *35*

Cold Hors d'Oeuvres
Cheese Crisps   *45*
Gravlax with Mustard Sauce or
    Horseradish Cream   *60*

Fish and Shellfish
Cold Poached Salmon with
    Green Coriander or Dill
    Mayonnaise   *67*
Maryland Crab Cakes   *77*
Chesapeake Crab   *78*
Seafood Stew over Linguine   *81*
Seafood Quiche   *82*

unexpected guests

There are so many quick recipes in the book that are perfect for last-minute company, whether they are coming by for supper, brunch, lunch, or just cocktails.

show-off dishes

Here are some suggestions for when you are looking for a show-off dish for a special occasion. "Show-off" does not mean the dish requires special skill. It means either spending more time than you are usually willing to spend, or a handsome presentation without a lot of extra work. Just the thing to make when you are asked to bring a single dish to a party.

Hot Hors d'Oeuvres
Mushroom-Filled Mushroom
    Caps   *31*
Phyllo with Goat Cheese and
    Prosciutto   *37*
Phyllo with Seafood and Basil   *37*
Tiropetas   *37*
Phyllo with Sausage and Mushroom
    Filling   *39*

Cold Hors d'Oeuvres
Nova Scotia Mousse   *56*
Gravlax with Mustard Sauce or
    Horseradish Cream   *60*
Mozzarella, Salmon, and Basil
    Pinwheels   *62*

Fish and Seafood
Cold Poached Salmon with
    Green Coriander or Dill
    Mayonnaise   *67*
Broiled Sake-Marinated Sea
    Bass   *71*
Germaine's Scallop Salad   *88*

Seafood Stew over Linguine   *81*
Seafood Quiche   *82*

Poultry
Marinated Grilled Chicken with
    Black Bean and Mango Salsa   *95*
Baked Imperial Chicken (with
    Cumberland Sauce)   *101*
Chicken Breasts Stuffed with Goat
    Cheese   *99*
Saltimbocca (using turkey
    fillets)   *119*

Meat
Lasagna   *126*
Beef Stew with Burgundy (Boeuf
    Bourguignonne)   *115*
Veal Parmesan   *118*
Saltimbocca (using veal)   *119*
Rack of Lamb   *120*

Vegetarian
Prepare-Ahead Cheese Soufflé   *141*

index

metric equivalencies

Liquid and Dry Measure Equivalencies

Customary	Metric
¼ teaspoon	1.25 milliliters
½ teaspoon	2.5 milliliters
1 teaspoon	5 milliliters
1 tablespoon	15 milliliters
1 fluid ounce	30 milliliters
¼ cup	60 milliliters
⅓ cup	80 milliliters
½ cup	120 milliliters
1 cup	240 milliliters
1 pint (2 cups)	480 milliliters
1 quart (4 cups)	960 milliliters (.96 liter)
1 gallon (4 quarts)	3.84 liters
1 ounce (by weight)	28 grams
¼ pound (4 ounces)	114 grams
1 pound (16 ounces)	454 grams
2.2 pounds	1 kilogram (1000 grams)

Oven-Temperature Equivalencies

Description	°Fahrenheit	°Celsius
Cool	200	90
Very slow	250	120
Slow	300–325	150–160
Moderately slow	325–350	160–180
Moderate	350–375	180–190
Moderately hot	375–400	190–200
Hot	400–450	200–230
Very hot	450–500	230–260